Untangle Network Security

Secure your network against threats and vulnerabilities using the unparalleled Untangle NGFW

Abd El-Monem A. El-Bawab

BIRMINGHAM - MUMBAI

Untangle Network Security

First published: October 2014

Production reference: 1251014

Published by Packt Publishing Ltd.
Livery Place
35 Livery Street
Birmingham B3 2PB, UK.

ISBN 978-1-84951-772-0

www.packtpub.com

Cover image by Pratik P Prabhu (pratikpprabhu@gmail.com)

Credits

Author

Abd El-Monem A. El-Bawab

Reviewers

Ritwik Ghoshal

Vishrut Mehta

Gilbert Ramirez

Abhinav Singh

Tom Stephens

Acquisition Editor

Vinay Argekar

Content Development Editor

Athira Laji

Technical Editors

Faisal Siddiqui

Ankita Thakur

Copy Editors

Janbal Dharmaraj

Alfida Paiva

Project Coordinator

Harshal Ved

Proofreaders

Simran Bhogal

Maria Gould

Ameesha Green

Paul Hindle

Indexer

Monica Ajmera Mehta

Graphics

Abhinash Sahu

Production Coordinators

Arvindkumar Gupta

Conidon Miranda

Cover Work

Conidon Miranda

About the Author

Abd El-Monem A. El-Bawab is a systems engineer with a passion for security. He has about 3 years of experience in the IT field. He is MCITP 2008 Server Administrator, MCSA 2012, MCSE Server Infrastructure, MCSE Private Cloud, and ITIL certified.

He has considerable experience in Untangle's Firewall, TMG, McAfee Sidewinder, Trend Micro Worry-Free Business Security Services, Symantec Endpoint Protection, Symantec Backup Exec, Hyper-V, System Center Suite, ESXi, Citrix XenServer, VDI, Windows Servers, Active Directory, Exchange Server, Office 365, and SMART Service Desk.

You can follow him on Twitter at `@Eng_Monem` and visit his blog at `amagsmb.wordpress.com`.

I would like to thank my mother, brothers, sisters, and all my family members for their continuous support, encouragement, and understanding. Without their support, I wouldn't be able to produce this work.

Special thanks to Mahmoud Magdy for his encouragement and friendship. I would also like to thank Khaled Eldosuky and Ahmed Abou Zaid for their efforts to increase the technical content in the Arab world.

Also, I would like to thank everyone who has contributed to the publication of this book, including the publisher, technical reviewers, and editors.

About the Reviewers

Ritwik Ghoshal is a senior security analyst at Oracle Corporation. He is responsible for Oracle's software and hardware security assurance. His primary work areas are operating systems and desktop virtualization along with developing vulnerability management and tracking tools. Before joining Oracle in 2010, when the company acquired Sun Microsystems, he had been working with Sun since 2008 as part of Sun's Security Engineering team and Solaris team. At Oracle, he continues to be responsible for all Sun systems' products and Oracle's Linux and virtualization products.

He earned a Bachelor's degree in Computer Science and Engineering in 2008 from Heritage Institute of Technology, Kolkata, India.

> I'm heavily indebted to my parents and Sara E Taverner for their continuous help and support.

Vishrut Mehta is currently in the fourth year at IIIT Hyderabad. He is doing his research in cloud computing and software-defined networks under the guidance of Dr. Vasudeva Varma and Dr. Reddy Raja. He has done a research internship at INRIA, France, in which he had to work on various challenges in multicloud systems. He also loves open source and has participated in Google Summer of Code 2013 while working on a project for Sahana Software Foundation. He was also involved in various start-ups and worked on some of the leading technologies.

He was the technical reviewer of *Python Network Programming Cookbook, Packt Publishing.*

> I would like to thank my advisor Dr. Vasudeva Varma and Dr. Reddy Raja for guiding me and helping me in times of need.

Gilbert Ramirez develops software to help other programmers and developers get their job done. He has been a long-time contributor to Wireshark, the premier open source packet analyzer. At Cisco Systems, Inc., he is responsible for software build systems, workflow automation for engineers, and virtualization tools.

He has reviewed *Network Analysis Using Wireshark Cookbook, Packt Publishing*. He has also written books on Wireshark, including *Wireshark & Ethereal Network Protocol Analyzer Toolkit*; *Nessus, Snort, & Ethereal Power Tools*; and *Ethereal Packet Sniffing*, all published by Syngress Publishing, Inc,.

Abhinav Singh is a young information security specialist from India. He has keen interest in the field of Information Security and has adopted it as his full-time profession. His core work areas include malware analysis, network security, and systems and enterprise security. He is also the author of *Metasploit Penetration Testing Cookbook Second Edition* and *Instant Wireshark*, published by Packt Publishing.

Abhinav's work has been quoted in several InfoSec magazines and portals. He shares his day-to-day security encounters at www.securitycalculus.com.

Currently, he is working as a cybersecurity engineer for J.P. Morgan. You can follow him on Twitter at @abhinavbom. You can also contact him at abhinavbom@gmail.com.

Tom Stephens is passionate about software. He has worked on everything from web design to low-level systems engineering to quality management. His broad experience and adaptability has helped him gain a keen insight into software and technology as a whole.

www.PacktPub.com

Support files, eBooks, discount offers, and more

You might want to visit www.PacktPub.com for support files and downloads related to your book.

Did you know that Packt offers eBook versions of every book published, with PDF and ePub files available? You can upgrade to the eBook version at www.PacktPub.com and as a print book customer, you are entitled to a discount on the eBook copy. Get in touch with us at service@packtpub.com for more details.

At www.PacktPub.com, you can also read a collection of free technical articles, sign up for a range of free newsletters and receive exclusive discounts and offers on Packt books and eBooks.

http://PacktLib.PacktPub.com

Do you need instant solutions to your IT questions? PacktLib is Packt's online digital book library. Here, you can access, read and search across Packt's entire library of books.

Why subscribe?

- Fully searchable across every book published by Packt
- Copy and paste, print and bookmark content
- On demand and accessible via web browser

Free access for Packt account holders

If you have an account with Packt at www.PacktPub.com, you can use this to access PacktLib today and view nine entirely free books. Simply use your login credentials for immediate access.

Table of Contents

Preface

Nowadays, network security has become the trending topic besides cloud computing and virtualization. With the increasing number of cybercrimes, all networks, irrespective of whether they belong to a small or enterprise organization, needs to be protected.

Untangle NGFW provides a comprehensive platform that is built on the best-on-the-market application such as zVelo's web filtering technologies that are used by most UTM manufactures. Untangle provides a complete stack of applications that cover the needs of most users.

Accompanied with ease of use, high reliability, great support, and low prices, Untangle NGFW is considered a great choice for network protection.

This book is based on version 10.2.1; slight differences can be found between the different Untangle NGFW versions. Since you have the basic concepts provided here, you can easily deal with any change you meet. Although you can use the free-to-roam style to read this book, this is not advised for beginners since the advanced chapters have some dependencies on the earlier chapters.

What this book covers

Chapter 1, Introduction to Untangle, introduces you to the world of information security and Untangle. This book starts by giving a brief introduction about Untangle, the company. Then, it provides some information about security concepts. After that, it gives a detailed introduction to Untangle NGFW.

Chapter 2, Installing Untangle, guides you on how to build and install the Untangle NGFW server. This chapter first discusses the hardware requirements of Untangle NGFW. Then, it describes the virtualized environment used for this book's examples. Next, the chapter covers how to obtain Untangle installation media, and then it guides you through a step-by-step installation of Untangle NGFW.

Chapter 3, The Initial Configuration of Untangle, walks you through the initial configuration wizard of Untangle NGFW in which we configure the administrator account, interfaces' IPs, and Untangle mode. In addition, it explains the GUI of Untangle NGFW.

Chapter 4, Untangle Advanced Configuration, covers how to configure network-related settings such as interface IP, VLAN, DHCP, DNS, QoS, Routes, NAT, and port forwarding. Also, it discusses Untangle's high availability options.

Chapter 5, Advanced Administration Settings, covers the settings related to Untangle NGFW administration such as the administrators' accounts, Untangle public address, backup and restore, and the e-mail settings for Untangle NGFW to send e-mails to users.

Chapter 6, Untangle Blockers, covers the Untangle applications that protect your network from direct threats such as viruses, spam, phishing, and malicious traffic.

Chapter 7, Preventing External Attacks, covers how you can protect your network from the Denial of Service (DoS) attacks by using intrusion prevention systems to stop malicious traffic and using firewall to limit the number of opened ports.

Chapter 8, Untangle Filters, covers Untangle applications that improve the user's productivity and network performance by blocking access to least important sites such as social networks, and denying traffic from applications such as BitTorrent. In addition, this chapter covers how Untangle NGFW can scan and filter the HTTPS traffic.

Chapter 9, Optimizing Network Traffic, covers how you can save and optimize your WAN bandwidth by limiting nonbusiness-related applications and prioritizing business-related applications. In addition, this chapter will also cover the use of Web Cache to enhance users' browsing experience.

Chapter 10, Untangle Network Policy, shows how it's possible to set access rules based on the Active Directory user and group membership, and how to force users to accept the acceptable use policy before they start using your network resource.

Chapter 11, Untangle WAN Services, describes the Untangle NGFW modules that allow for using WAN services from multiple ISPs to provide higher throughput and a continuous WAN connection to users even if any of the connection has failed.

Chapter 12, Untangle VPN Services, covers the modules that allow Untangle NGFW to provide a VPN connection to its remote users or between two branches.

Chapter 13, Untangle Administrative Services, shows how administrators can simplify their tasks using reporting, automated backups, and premium support, and how they can customize Untangle logos, interfaces, and pages.

Chapter 14, Untangle in the Real World, provides a brief overview of the regulatory compliance related to the IT field. Then, it lists the Untangle NGFW advantages over its rivals. Finally, it provides some examples on how Untangle is used in the small and medium businesses, education, healthcare, government, and nonprofit sectors.

What you need for this book

The examples presented in this book assume that you have a computer system with enough RAM, hard drive space, and processing power to run a virtualized testing environment. Some examples will require the use of multiple virtual machines that run simultaneously. The complete virtualized environment used for this book is described in *Chapter 2, Installing Untangle*.

Who this book is for

This book is for anyone who wants to learn how to install, deploy, configure, and administrate Untangle NGFW. This book has been written for readers at a beginner's level either on network security or Untangle NGFW, but they should be familiar with networks. For those who have more experience with network security, this book can be their quick guide to learn Untangle NGFW. For those with experience on Untangle NGFW, this book can serve as a refresher and validation of their skills.

Conventions

In this book, you will find a number of styles of text that distinguish between different kinds of information. Here are some examples of these styles, and an explanation of their meaning.

Code words in text, database table names, folder names, filenames, file extensions, pathnames, dummy URLs, user input, and Twitter handles are shown as follows: "Backups will store the current Untangle NGFW server settings to the `.backup` file."

New terms and **important words** are shown in bold. Words that you see on the screen, in menus or dialog boxes for example, appear in the text like this: "If your country is not listed in the preceding list, you can choose **other**."

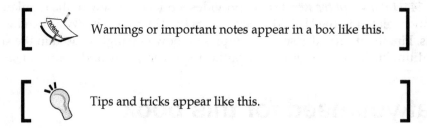

Warnings or important notes appear in a box like this.

Tips and tricks appear like this.

Reader feedback

Feedback from our readers is always welcome. Let us know what you think about this book—what you liked or may have disliked. Reader feedback is important for us to develop titles that you really get the most out of.

To send us general feedback, simply send an e-mail to feedback@packtpub.com, and mention the book title via the subject of your message.

If there is a topic that you have expertise in and you are interested in either writing or contributing to a book, see our author guide on www.packtpub.com/authors.

Customer support

Now that you are the proud owner of a Packt book, we have a number of things to help you to get the most from your purchase.

Errata

Although we have taken every care to ensure the accuracy of our content, mistakes do happen. If you find a mistake in one of our books—maybe a mistake in the text or the code—we would be grateful if you would report this to us. By doing so, you can save other readers from frustration and help us improve subsequent versions of this book. If you find any errata, please report them by visiting http://www.packtpub.com/submit-errata, selecting your book, clicking on the **errata submission form** link, and entering the details of your errata. Once your errata are verified, your submission will be accepted and the errata will be uploaded on our website, or added to any list of existing errata, under the Errata section of that title. Any existing errata can be viewed by selecting your title from http://www.packtpub.com/support.

Piracy

Piracy of copyright material on the Internet is an ongoing problem across all media. At Packt, we take the protection of our copyright and licenses very seriously. If you come across any illegal copies of our works, in any form, on the Internet, please provide us with the location address or website name immediately so that we can pursue a remedy.

Please contact us at `copyright@packtpub.com` with a link to the suspected pirated material.

We appreciate your help in protecting our authors, and our ability to bring you valuable content.

Questions

You can contact us at `questions@packtpub.com` if you are having a problem with any aspect of the book, and we will do our best to address it.

1
Introduction to Untangle

This chapter will introduce you to the Untangle company and its products. Untangle has two product lines: Untangle NGFW and IC Control. In this chapter, we will introduce you to Untangle NGFW and the modules available to be installed on the NGFW.

This chapter will also cover some of the information security basics required to understand the importance of using Untangle NGFW to protect our networks. In addition, the major changes from version 9.4.2 to version 10.2.1 will be covered.

In this chapter, we will cover the following topics:

- Introducing Untangle, Inc.
- An overview of information security
- Introducing Untangle NGFW
- Reviewing the change log

Introducing Untangle, Inc.

Untangle was founded in 2003 as Metavize, Inc. by John Irwin and Dirk Morris with the vision of untangling the complexities of network security and control. In 2006, and after a venture funding round from CMEA Ventures and Rustic Canyon Partners, the company was renamed to Untangle, Inc. and named Bob Walters as the CEO.

Untangle's first product, and its most popular one, is the Untangle gateway platform, which is available under the **GNU General Public License** (**GNU GPL**) v2 license. The Untangle gateway platform is the world's first commercial-grade open source solution for blocking spam, spyware, viruses, adware, and unwanted content on the network. In 2014, after releasing their second product, Untangle, Inc. renamed the Untangle gateway platform to Untangle **Next generation firewall** (**NGFW**). Untangle NGFW is available as an appliance or as software to be installed on a dedicated device. The demo of Untangle NGFW is available at `http://demo.untangle.com/`.

In 2014, Untangle released its second product under the name of **Internet Content** (**IC**) Control. IC Control is an enterprise-grade solution to maximize Internet performance by allowing granular control for every traffic type, scaling to 10 Gbps and offering centralized management for multi-appliance, multi-domain deployments. IC Control is based on Cymphonix Corp. products, which is now part of Untangle, Inc. after Untangle, Inc. acquired it in October 2013. IC Control is now available as appliance only; however, Untangle, Inc. has the intension to convert it to a software-based solution as is the case with Untangle NGFW. The IC Control demo is available at `http://icc-demo.untangle.com/`.

Untangle, Inc. has over 400,000 customers, protecting nearly 5 million people, their computers, and networks. The main sectors that use Untangle products are education, healthcare, nonprofit, and state and local government.

An overview on information security

If you have a public IP, you and your company may be the next victim of the cybercrime business. 75 percent of Internet traffic is malicious (`https://wiki.cac.washington.edu/download/attachments/7479159/White_Paper_6-Feb26-round2-AS-BE+DRAFT.doc`) and the cybercrime business value equals 105 USD billion, which surpasses the value of the illegal drug trade worldwide. In addition, most of the cybercrime attacks are determined, not just opportunistic, and they include the theft of IDs, trade secrets, research and development, and so on. So, you must be ready.

The CIA triad

Your role as a security administrator is to protect the information and information systems from unauthorized access, use, disclosure, disruption, modification, or destruction in order to provide confidentiality, integrity, and availability. The CIA triad is explained as follows:

- **Confidentiality**: Ensuring that the data or an information system is accessed by only an authorized person

- **Integrity**: This means protecting data from modification or deletion by unauthorized parties

- **Availability**: Ensuring that data and information systems are available when required

Types of attacks

The attacker's target is to compromise one or more attributes of the CIA triad, which will allow him to gain access to confidential data and steal it. He may be interested in manipulating data by deleting or modifying some parts of it. Also, his target may be to reduce or interrupt the availability of your services, which could highly impact your reputation. Common methods and attacks that are used by attackers are as follows:

- **Malware**: This is a short name for malicious software. This is used or created to disrupt computer operations, gather sensitive information, or gain access to private computer systems. Some malware types are as follows:

    ° **Virus**: This attaches itself to legitimate applications. Viruses can be used to cause direct damage such as prevent the computer from booting or to open some ports and services, which can be used by the attacker to gain access or steal data. They can replicate themselves and spread from one computer to another.

    ° **Worm**: This is a standalone malware program that has the same damage properties of the viruses. However, unlike viruses, it does not need to attach itself to an existing program.

    ° **Rootkit**: This is a program or a set of programs that usually have kernel level access and effectively can hide from antivirus programs.

- ° **Spyware**: This collects information about what the user is doing and what data is on the user's computer and feeds it to the remote party, which could take advantage of this information. The spyware programs usually change the default search engine and the default home page.

- ° **Keylogger**: This records the key stroke entered by the user. This can be used by the attacker to capture the user's login credentials.

- ° **Backdoor**: This allows the attacker to bypass normal authentication and get remote control of the victim's computer, while attempting to remain undetected.

- ° **Trojan horses**: This type of malware masquerades as a legitimate file or helpful program but the real purpose is to grant unauthorized access to a computer to the hacker. For example, you may download and install a screensaver that will install backdoors to your system.

- ° **Botnet**: This is a collection of Internet-connected computers whose security defenses have been breached and controlled by a malicious party. The set of breached computers could be used to initiate huge attacks.

- ° **Adware**: This is a software installed on the user's computer that will periodically pop up an advertisement that encourage users to buy some products, which is considered to be an annoying and disturbing action.

- **Phishing**: The act of attempting to acquire information such as usernames, passwords, and credit card details (and sometimes, indirectly, money) by masquerading as a trustworthy entity in an e-communication. For example, you may receive a fake e-mail (which looks like it was from your bank) informing you that your password has expired and asking you to change it by logging to the bank using a link that will redirect you to a malicious website (which also looks like as the original bank website). The fake website will capture your login credentials.

- **Spear-phishing**: This is a phishing attempt directed at specific individuals or companies.

- **Whaling**: This is a phishing attempt directed to a company's executives.

- **Spam**: This is an unwanted e-mail that usually includes advertisements, malicious attachments with malware, and phishing links.

- **Denial of Service (DoS) attack**: The attacker tries to make the server unable to respond to customer requests by overloading the server with many requests. The same is also true for applications/services hosted by this server as the attacker may be interested in disabling certain application not the whole server. For example, attacking an Apache HTTP server that's hosting the web service.

- **Distributed Denial of Service (DDoS) attack**: This is the incitation of a DoS attack from multiple computers instead of only one machine. The DDoS attack usually includes the usage of a botnet.

- **Smurf attack**: An example of a smurf attack is when the attacker sends a broadcast ping request to your network. If the attacker did address spoofing, your network devices will send the ping replies to the spoofed address, which will lead to a DDoS attack.

- **Man-in-the-middle attack**: In this attack, traffic between two devices is passed through a rouge device controlled by the attacker. Thus, the attacker can get the original traffic and read the data if the communication is unencrypted, even he may inject malware to the traffic.

- **Privileges escalation**: The attacker will use vulnerability in the operating system or applications to get higher access privileges (for example, root access).

- **Xmas attack**: This is used to get more information from the network scan. So instead of the normal ping and port scans, the xmas attack can analyze the TCP response of the target systems and get more detailed information such as the operating system version and the services running.

- **Typo squatting/URL hijacking**: As a result of typing an error, a user may go to a malicious website. For example, the user may type `http://www.goggle.com` instead of `http://www.google.com`.

Types of controls

The following are three different types of controls we need to implement to keep our network and systems safe:

- **Technical**: This includes the use of technology (that is, software and devices) to reduce vulnerabilities; common technical controls include the usage of security software and devices, access control systems, authentication systems, and encryption.

- **Management**: This is also known as administrative controls. This includes the assessment of risks and vulnerabilities, planning, and writing a security policy.

- **Operational**: This deals with day-to-day procedures and policies that the users should follow. An example of operational controls is change management.

 A list of 20 critical security controls can be found at http://www.sans.org/critical-security-controls/.

Defense in depth

We should use the defense in depth concept in which multiple layers of security controls (defenses) are placed through our network. Some of defense in depth techniques are as follows:

- **Layered defense**: This sets your defense at multiple stages (such as network edge and individual PCs) instead of using only one layer of defense. If that one layer of defense fails, you will be an easy victim for attackers. So, use an antivirus at network edge to protect against downloaded threats and a desktop antivirus to mainly protect against threats coming through the internal network.

- **Multiple tools**: These make the attacker's job harder by using firewalls, antivirus programs, intrusion detection systems, intrusion prevention systems, and so on instead of using only one tool.

- **Update all your systems and programs**: It's important to update all your systems to prevent the exploitation of any discovered vulnerability; only updating your operating system will not block the threat as the attacker may have privileged access from unpatched program such as Java or Flash Player.

- **Don't use the administrator account for daily activities**: As the attacker's goal is to gain privileged access over your network, his job will be easier if you run malware using the administrator account.

- **Read and learn**: Attacker techniques always change and evolve; you need to be always aware of the new techniques and how you can fight these techniques.

- **Think like an attacker**: This will help you to discover your network's weak points.

- **Follow up**: Always review the event logs to be aware of the threat's sources and work on preventing these threats.

Introducing Untangle NGFW

Untangle NGFW is the simplest firewall you will ever use. Untangle Inc. really has done a very good job of simplifying the graphic interface and customizing the firewall settings to suit most companies' needs. Untangle NGFW is a network security device that is placed at the network edge to scan traffic and protect the network from threats. Let's identify the meaning of NGFW, but before identifying NGFW, we will need to explore other terms that may lead to term conflicts:

- **Firewall**: This blocks traffic based on the predefined port and IP-based policies.

- **Stateful firewall**: The firewall sets a stateful table that remembers the user's traffic. The firewall will block all traffic initiated from outside the network and not by an internal user. If the incoming traffic was requested by the internal user (which is determined based on the stateful table), the firewall will allow this traffic.

- **Proxy**: The user sends traffic to the proxy, which will send the traffic to the external world on behalf of the user. The incoming traffic will be ended on the proxy, which will forward it to the appropriate user. As the traffic passes through the proxy, the proxy could scan the traffic and implement policy control based on the IP address, user ID, and so on.

- **Security gateway**: This is also known as application aware firewall or layer 7 firewall. This has the ability to look at the application layer while the traffic passes through it to identify and stop the threats.

- **Unified Threat Management (UTM)**: Instead of buying multiple security devices with different roles and putting them in series (for example, using IPS device and spam filtering device), you can buy an UTM that combines all these roles into one device.

- **NG firewall**: While the UTM is just about collecting services together, NGFW has other specifications, as defined by Gartner:

  - The UTM collocates security services under a single appliance, whereas NGFW integrates them. For example, in UTM, the packet is scanned by the firewall role, then passed to the IPS role and finally to the antivirus role. Whereas in NGFW, the firewall is integrated with the IPS, antivirus, and so on, resulting in a single-pass engine (that is, the packet is scanned by the different rules simultaneously).

  - Include the first generation firewall capabilities, for example, **network address translation (NAT)**, stateful protocol inspection, **virtual private networking (VPN)**, and so on.

  - Integrated signature-based IPS engine.

- ○ Application awareness, full-stack visibility, and granular control.
- ○ The ability to set directory-based policies (for example, policies based on Microsoft Active Directory group membership).
- ○ The ability to decrypt and scan HTTPS traffic.

Based on Gartner's definition, we could say that every NGFW is in necessity a UTM, but not every UTM is a NGFW. So, our Untangle product is a next generation firewall as it perfectly meets the Gartner definition.

 Keep in mind that Untangle scans the traffic while it passes through the device, thus it's not a proxy device.

Untangle NGFW is based on the Debian distro. Untangle NGFW includes the basic networking functionalities such as providing DNS, DHCP, NAT, and static routing. It also provides additional modules to provide antivirus, antispam, and antiphishing solutions. The complete set of Untangle modules will be covered in the next section.

Untangle has two operation modes: it could run as the primary firewall, which is the preferred mode for Untangle NGFW, or it could run behind another firewall, which is useful if you have an in-place firewall and you don't want to risk the headache of removing the other firewall, or if the other firewall provides a functionality that Untangle NGFW is not providing, such as **Data Loss Prevention (DLP)**.

Untangle NGFW modules

In this section, we will see the modules provided by Untangle NGFW to achieve network security and control.

Untangle NGFW can be divided into the kernel, **Untangle VM (UVM)**, and Apps. The UVM controls all the routing and networking functions of Untangle. In addition, any traffic directed to the Untangle NGFW itself is processed by the UVM. The additional functionalities (such as antivirus and antispam) are provided by the modules (Apps), which run inside the UVM.

Untangle NGFW uses the concept of virtual racks, which is a set of modules. Different virtual racks could be assigned to different users. Untangle NGFW has two types of modules, applications and services, based on their functionality on the virtual racks concept.

Applications are unique to each rack. Thus, a rack can include antivirus application while the other doesn't, or one rack can include antivirus application that scans the .exe files and the other rack scans other extensions expect for the .exe files.

Services are shared between racks. So if we configured the Untangle NGFW to integrate with Microsoft Active Directory, all virtual racks can benefit from that.

The Untangle applications are as follows:

- **Web Filter Lite**: This is used to block access to certain websites such as social networking, spyware, and malicious websites. It's open source and free under GPL.

- **Web Filter**: This is a paid application based on zVelo technologies, which have a lot of features over the Lite version.

- **Virus Blocker Lite**: This is used to protect against viruses. It's based on the open source CalmAV and it's provided by Untangle for free.

- **Virus Blocker**: This is a paid version based on the Commtouch, which is an effective antivirus engine for network gateways.

- **Spam Blocker Lite**: This is used to protect against spam. It's based on the open source SpamAssassin project and it's provided by Untangle for free.

- **Spam Blocker**: This is a paid version that uses an additional anti-spam database based on the cloud services from Commtouch, besides the SpamAssassin project.

- **Phish Blocker**: This is used to prevent phishing sites and e-mails. It's open source and free under GPL.

- **Web Cache**: This is used to enhance user experience by storing parts of websites. This will make the websites load faster the next time the user requests them. It's a paid application that is based on the Squid project.

- **Bandwidth Control**: This is a paid application that is used to control bandwidth utilization by allowing higher priority traffic to utilize more traffic than the traffic with lowest priority.

- **HTTPS Inspector**: This is used to allow Untangle to scan encrypted HTTPS traffic. It's a paid application.

- **Application Control Lite**: This is used to block certain applications such as IM and BitTorrent applications from accessing the Internet. It's open source and free under GPL.

- **Application Control**: This provides better application detection and a larger database than the lite version. It's a paid version and is based on Procera Networks' technologies.

- **Captive Portal**: This is used to achieve user authentication before they could use the network resources. It's available for free.

- **Firewall**: This provides the ability to block certain ports, IP addresses, and protocols from accessing the network. It's open source and free under GPL.

- **Intrusion Prevention**: This scans the incoming traffic for malicious traffic and stops it. It's based on the Snort project and is available for free.

- **Ad Blocker**: This is used to prevent sites' advertisements and cookies. It's free and based on the Adblock Plus project.

The Untangle services are as follows:

- **Reports**: This provides summarized details of the Untangle NGFW events. It's open source and free under GPL.

- **Policy Manager**: This allows the creation of different policies for different users, or in other words creating other virtual racks. It's a paid application.

- **Directory Connector**: This is a paid application that provides integration with Microsoft Active Directory and Radius servers, which allow Untangle NGFW to set rules and provide access based on the usernames and group membership.

- **WAN Failover**: This is a paid application that allows an uninterrupted Untangle NGFW WAN service as it moves traffic to/from a failed WAN NIC to other NICs.

- **WAN Balancer**: This allows the use of multiple ISPs to provide a higher bandwidth for your network. It's a paid application.

- **OpenVPN**: This provides free SSL-based VPN services based on OpenVPN.

- **IPsec VPN**: This is a paid application that provides IPsec-based VPN.

- **Configuration Backup**: This is a paid application that automatically backs up Untangle NGFW to the Untangle cloud.

- **Branding Manager**: This allows you to customize how Untangle NGFW looks. It's a paid application.

- **Live Support**: This is a paid application that allows you to profit from the Untangle official support.

In addition to the preceding services, there is the **Shield** module, which runs on the Untangle platform level, which protects against the DoS attacks.

A concept that is worth being discussed here is the false positive and false negative alarms, as the different applications scan the traffic they would generate alarms. The false positive alarm means that the application has classified the traffic to be a malicious traffic while it's a legitimate traffic. This would result in a lot of overhead for the firewall administrator to review all these incorrect alarms.

The false negative alarms means that the application couldn't detect malicious traffic and classified it as legitimate traffic. This is the most dangerous type of alarm as this implies that the traffic has already entered your network and the attack may have been done.

Untangle packages

You can use and buy individual applications or use packages, which are a complete set of applications. Untangle, Inc. provides two packages: the free and the complete one. The free package includes all the free applications and services, while the complete package includes all the paid applications in addition to the free ones. The following table summarizes the applications that can be found in each package:

Package name	Free package	Complete package	Notes
Web Filter	Untangle open source	`zvelo.com`	
Virus Blocker	`clamav.net`	`commtouch.com`	
Spam Blocker	`spamassassin.apache.org`	`spamassassin.apache.org` and `commtouch.com`	
Application Control	`17-filter.clearfoundation.com`	`proceranetworks.com`	
Phish Blocker	√	√	Google's safe browsing API
Captive Portal	√	√	
Firewall	√	√	
Intrusion Prevention	√	√	`snort.org`
Ad Blocker	√	√	`adblockplus.org`
Reports	√	√	
OpenVPN	√	√	`openvpn.net`
Web Cache		√	`www.squid-cache.org`
Bandwidth Control		√	
HTTPS Inspector		√	

Package name	Free package	Complete package	Notes
Policy Manager		√	
Directory Connector		√	
WAN Failover		√	
WAN Balancer		√	
IPsec VPN		√	
Configuration Backup		√	
Branding Manager		√	
Live Support		√	

Licensing Untangle

For free applications and free package, all you have to do is to create an Untangle account and download and install the applications or the package. For the paid applications and package, you will have to buy them. Untangle, Inc. offers monthly or annual subscription for its applications. The charges differ depending on the number of devices that Untangle NGFW will serve.

> Appliances are not licensed by the number of devices behind it; instead they are licensed based on the appliance's capabilities. You could use the appliance for any number of users, but you may notice performance degradation if the number of users exceeded the recommended number as the appliance hardware specifications are related to the number of users.

Untangle, Inc. will charge you based on the total number of unique IPs in your internal network. Untangle uses the classes method for their charging method. The available classes are: 1-10, 11-50, 51-150, 151-500, 500-1500, and 1501+.

Untangle, Inc. says that their customers prefer this method as they get a wide range of user licenses, which allows them to dynamically increase and decrease the number of computers inside the network. The disadvantage of this method is, for example, if you have 51 users, you'll need to purchase the 51-150 class and not the 11-50 class.

Bypassed devices (traffic from these device won't pass through the UVM) will not count. An example of bypassed traffic would be a printer that needs Internet access, and scanning traffic to it won't be necessary.

If you are using Spam Blocker and the number of scanned e-mail addresses is bigger than the number of devices IPs, Untangle will charge you based on the number of e-mail addresses.

The subscriptions are per Untangle NGFW server, so if you have three servers on your network and each server will run the complete package, you'll need to purchase three complete package subscriptions.

If you deployed two Untangle servers in the high availability mode, which is active/passive, you will need to purchase licenses for both servers.

Reviewing the change log

This section will cover the changes Untangle had from version 9.4.2 till version 10.2.1, which will be a good reference for readers with previous experience with Untangle. Untangle Version 10 had many major architectural changes. Thus, there is no upgrade path from version 9.x to version 10.x. A list of important changes is as follows:

- Untangle is now based on Debian 6.0 (squeeze) and 2.6.32 kernel. This should result in slightly better hardware support.

- The networking interface (where the users can configure network related settings) has been improved. If Untangle has more than 2 NICs, any additional interface will be disabled (which was not the default behavior earlier). In older versions, an Untangle user was not able to change any interface name.

- Untangle Interfaces could now be configured with IPv6; however, the applications could not process the IPv6 till now. More information is available at http://wiki.untangle.com/index.php/IPv6.

- HTTPS Inspector is a new application that allows Untangle NGFW to decrypt and scan the HTTPS traffic as HTTP-traffic.

- Attack Blocker has been moved into the Untangle platform and can now be configured under the **Shield** tab located at **Config | System**.

- Spyware Blocker has been merged with Ad Blocker and the remaining obsolete functionality has been removed.

- Add the ability to set routes rules based on the port number and OS type in the WAN Balancer module.

- OpenVPN now has a new simplified implementation (earlier the steps to configure it were too complex).

- POP and IMAP scanning functionality has been removed from the platform due to rare of unencrypted POP and IMAP across WAN links and the delay caused by scanning.

- For versions before 10.1, the application was downloaded from the Internet after installing Untangle. Now, Untangle NGFW comes with the applications preinstalled.

- Beginning from version 10.1, Untangle NGFW could run in high availability mode, where the high availability mode is failover and not load balancing.

- Some enhancements in the memory utilization used by applications (such as Virus and Spam Blocker) while they're not scanning any traffic.

- Beginning from version 10.2, IPsec VPN now supports L2TP for remote access.

- A new application for the Directory Connector that can be installed on domain controllers to monitor the login event logs and report them to Untangle is now available.

- The **DHCP Server** and **DNS Server** tabs moved from **Network | Advanced** to **Network**.

- Version 10.2.1 includes minor hotfixes such as fixing problems caused by HTTPS Inspector to Dropbox clients.

At the time of writing this book, Untangle announced the approach to release version 11.0, which is based on Debian wheezy (7.6) and the 3.2.0 kernel. It also comes with new commercial technologies for the Virus Blocker and Spam Blocker for better performance and efficacy.

This book should be enough for you to deal with the new version. As the book provides the theory behind each module, you'll be able to configure the modules regardless of any changes to the modules' GUI or their underlying technologies.

Summary

In this chapter, we introduced Untangle, Inc. and gave you an overview of its history and products. Untangle NGFW was covered in detail; we talked about how it works and the difference between applications and services and the function delivered by each of them.

We also covered the application packages and had a quick overview of the licensing and change log from version 9.4.2 till version 10.2.1. We saw the difference between a firewall, proxy, security gateway, UTM, and NGFW.

A brief introduction to information security was covered, in which you learned about the danger of cybercrime and the different types of attacks that an attacker could use to compromise the confidentiality, integrity, and availability of the network.

In the next chapter, we will begin our journey with Untangle by showing you how to download and install Untangle NGFW.

2
Installing Untangle

Now, after we have seen an overview of Untangle NGFW in the previous chapter, it's time to get some hands-on experience. However, first, you will need to get a PC with Untangle NGFW installed. This chapter will guide you through building and installing your Untangle NGFW server.

At the beginning, we will define the minimum and the recommended hardware requirements for the Untangle NGFW server. After that, we will see how we can get a copy of Untangle NGFW. Later, we will see how we can write the Untangle NGFW image into a USB or CD to make a bootable installation media. Then, we will go through a step-by-step installation guide. Also, a complete lab environment that can be used to study this book will be included.

In this chapter, we'll cover the following topics:

- Understanding the hardware requirements of Untangle NGFW
- Setting up a lab
- Obtaining the Untangle installation media
- A step-by-step installation guide

Understanding the hardware requirements of Untangle NGFW

Untangle NGFW is a software that can be installed on a standard Intel/AMD-compatible hardware, or can be delivered preinstalled on hardware appliances. Understanding the hardware requirements for Untangle NGFW is necessary to build/select the right server that can perform well without any latency or performance degradation.

In this section, we will cover the different available appliances provided by Untangle, Inc. We will also review the minimum and recommended hardware requirements to build your own Untangle NGFW box. Later, we will discuss the ability to install Untangle NGFW on VM. Finally, we will review the modules' effect on the CPU, RAM, and disk I/O, and how we can tweak them.

Untangle NGFW appliances

Untangle NGFW appliances come in many classes based on the expected number of users and workloads. Buying an Untangle NGFW appliance removes the headache of choosing the right hardware to be used in building your Untangle NGFW server. By using an Untangle NGFW appliance, you also guarantee that your server will perform well under the rated user count.

Untangle, Inc. offers its appliances with the free or the complete package. When you buy an appliance with the complete package, you will pay for the hardware and the subscription in the first year, and for the subscription only in the later years.

Untangle NGFW appliances come with a one year warranty; this could be extended to two or three years for additional money. Also, you can get a cold spare for additional money. The cold spare is another Untangle NGFW appliance that will reside inside your company's *offline* waiting for your primary appliance to fail. When the primary appliance fails, you can get the cold spare online and move the license to it so that it can protect your network instead of the failed appliance.

You can buy appliances from Untangle, Inc. or from the third-party hardware vendors. For more information about the official appliances, visit http://www. Untangle.com/appliances, and for the third-party vendors, visit http://wiki. Untangle.com/index.php/3rd_Party_Hardware_Vendors. The following table shows the specifications of the available Untangle NGFW appliances:

	u10	u50	u150	u500	m1500	m3000
Processor	Intel Atom® single core processor	Intel Atom® dual core processor	Intel Pentium® dual core processor	Intel Xeon® quad core processor	Dual Intel Xeon® quad core processors	Dual Intel Xeon® six core processors
RAM	1 GB RAM	2 GB RAM	4 GB RAM	16 GB RAM	16 GB RAM	16 GB RAM
Hard Drive	160 GB 7200 rpm	160 GB 7200 rpm	500 GB 7200 rpm	500 GB 7200 rpm	1 TB 7200 rpm	1 TB 7200 rpm

	u10	u50	u150	u500	m1500	m3000
Ethernet Ports	4 Gigabit Ethernet ports	4 Gigabit Ethernet ports	6 Gigabit Ethernet ports	8 Gigabit Ethernet ports	8 Gigabit Ethernet ports	8 Gigabit Ethernet ports
Users	1-25	25-75	75-250	250-750	750-1500	1500-5000

Building your Untangle NGFW box

Unlike the case of the hardware appliances, it's your job to determine the hardware specifications when you want to install the software on a dedicated box. Generally, Untangle NGFW requires a dedicated PC with a CD/DVD drive or USB ports and at least two NICs. The following table shows the minimum and recommended hardware specifications for the Untangle server:

Resource	Minimum	Recommended
CPU	1.0 GHz	More than 2.0 GHz
Memory	512 MB	1 to 2 GB
Hard drive	20 GB	More than 40 GB
Network cards	2	More than 3 (for DMZ)

Note that even if you used the recommended specifications mentioned in the preceding table, you may suffer performance degradation with the high workloads and user count. So, as a best practice, follow the same hardware specifications used in the appliances.

 Make sure that you don't have any data that is important or not backed up on the hard disk where you will install Untangle NGFW, as it will format the hard disk.

Virtualizing your Untangle NGFW

You can install Untangle NGFW inside a **virtual machine** (**VM**) with no performance or functionality issues as long as you follow the recommended hardware requirements. However, Untangle will not support you with any issues related to the hypervisor misconfiguration, but it will support you with the Untangle system itself.

To learn how to install VMware tools on your Untangle NGFW VM, visit `http://forums.untangle.com/hacks/34393-updated-way-installing-vmware-tools-untangle-v10-esxi-5-1-5-5-a.html`.

In addition, Untangle, Inc. offers a virtual appliance that can be imported directly to your hypervisor. The virtual appliance can be downloaded from `http://sourceforge.net/projects/untangle/files/`. It's a VM with an OVA extension and can be used with VMware ESXi, Citrix Xen server, VMware Workstation, and Oracle VirtualBox. For more information about the virtual appliance and how you can import it to the ESXi server, visit `http://wiki.Untangle.com/index.php/Untangle_Virtual_Appliance_on_VMware`.

 While the virtual appliance could be used with type 2 hypervisors such as VMware Workstation and Oracle VirtualBox, it's practical to use them only with type 1 hypervisors such as VMware ESXi and Citrix Xen server.

Tweaking your Untangle NGFW

The main factors of server performance are CPU, memory, and disk I/O. This section will discuss the effect of each factor on Untangle NGFW performance. In addition, this section will show you the resource utilization by each Untangle module.

While CPU clock speed and power are important factors, they are the least important factors to consider when dealing with Untangle NGFW. A fairly underpowered CPU could be used to run large sites if you have enough memory and disk I/O. Increasing the CPU speed and number of cores would help to increase Untangle NGFW performance but not to the same point if we increased the memory and disk I/O.

 Intel Atom processors don't have enough power for Virus Blocker, Spam Blocker, and VPN modules.

The running applications and the in-process data are placed in memory. If you are in shortage of memory, Untangle NGFW will keep the current data in process in the RAM and will swap any other data to the hard disk; when it needs something from the swapped data, it will move it to the RAM and swap the other set of data. So, you'll see consistent swapping, or in other words, bad performance and many pauses.

Disk I/O is the most important factor and is the real bottleneck for many implementations. Untangle NGFW does not use flat logfiles; instead, it uses a database to store the logfiles, which dramatically increases the disk I/O especially when generating a report. For example, if you have a 16 core CPU and 16 GB of RAM but a slow hard disk, you'll get bad performance.

> While RAIDs could be used to increase disk I/O and for reliability, it's uncommon to use RAIDs with Untangle NGFW. Untangle NGFW doesn't support software RAIDs. In addition, because it's based on Debian, only reputable hardware RAID controllers can be used; common RAID controllers on motherboards won't be accepted by Untangle NGFW.
>
> In addition, the price of the external RAID controller and the additional hard disks could be used to buy a better hard disk.
>
> Also, the time required to rebuild your server after RAID failure is similar to the time required to rebuild the server from backup after a single disk failure.

In short, use plenty of the three resources while you can, and consider buying an SSD as they have greater disk I/O.

Further tweaking can be done if you understand the utilization of resources by each Untangle NGFW module. Tweaking performance can be done by disabling the application or buy reconfiguring its settings. For example, if you have shortage of memory, disable Web Filter, and if you have shortage of CPU and you have configured Virus Blocker to scan incoming image files, disable this option. The following table shows the resource utilization caused by the Untangle platform and the different applications:

Component/App	Memory	CPU	Disk I/O
Platform	Medium	Medium	Medium
Web Filter	Low	Low	Low
Web Filter Lite	High	Low	Low
Virus Blocker	Medium	Medium	Medium
Virus Blocker Lite	Medium	Medium	Medium
Spyware Blocker	Low	Low	Low
Spam Blocker	Medium	Medium	Medium
Spam Blocker Lite	Medium	Medium	Medium
Phish Blocker	Medium	Medium	Medium
Web Cache	Medium	Low	High
Bandwidth Control	Low	Medium	Low
Application Control	Low	Medium	Low

Component/App	Memory	CPU	Disk I/O
Application Control Lite	Low	Medium	Low
HTTPS Inspector	Medium	High	Low
Firewall	Low	Low	Low
Intrusion Prevention	Low	Medium	Low
Ad Blocker	Low	Low	Low
Reports	Medium	Medium	Very high
Policy Manager	Low	Low	Low
Directory Connector	Low	Low	Low
WAN Failover	Low	Low	Low
WAN Balancer	Low	Low	Low
Captive Portal	Low	Low	Low
IPsec VPN	Low	Low	Low
OpenVPN	Low	Low	Low
Attack Blocker	Low	Low	Low
Configuration Backup	Low	Low	Low
Branding Manager	Low	Low	Low
Live Support	Low	Low	Low

Setting up your lab

I recommend that you build your own lab environment to get comfortable with Untangle NGFW and practice the different scenarios before deploying it to your production environment. You can use virtualization platforms such as VMware Workstation or Oracle VirtualBox to build the lab environment.

In our lab, we have ABC bank and Acme school as fictional organizations. ABC bank uses two Untangle NGFWs in a high availability mode. It has two internal subnets for the servers and users, and it uses a leased line for the Internet connectivity.

Acme school has two locations. The HQ has Untangle NGFW running in the router mode, protecting two subnets (internal and DMZ). The remote branch office has an existing firewall, which Acme school decided to replace with Untangle NGFW. So, Acme school deployed Untangle NGFW in the bridge mode behind the existing firewall till the expiration of the firewall license. After the license expiration, Untangle NGFW will be deployed in the router mode. Acme school use ADSL for the Internet connectivity. It uses two ADSL lines in the HQ and only one ADSL line in the branch office.

The remote laptop is used to test the connection from outside organizations and to implement a remote access VPN.

The following figure shows the lab environment used in this book:

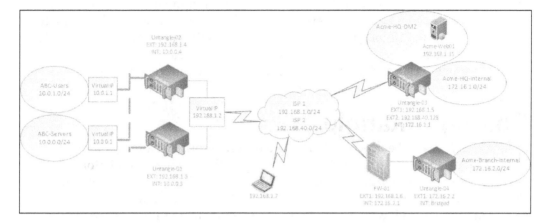

The 192.168.1.0/24 subnet is selected to be used as the external interface for all the Untangle NGFW servers to simplify the process of routing between the devices. The detailed environment components are listed in the following table:

ABC-Servers		
ABC-DC01	10.0.0.5	Domain controller
ABC-EX01	10.0.0.10	Exchange server
ABC-LY01	10.0.0.12	Lync server for VOIP
ABC-Users		
ABC-Client01	10.0.1.15	Normal user PC
ABC-CEO01	10.0.1.60	CEO PC
Printer01	10.0.1.99	Printer that needs Internet connection
Acme-DMZ		
Acme-Web01	192.168.1.15	Web server
Acme-HQ-Internal		
Acme-DC01	172.16.1.5	Domain controller
Acme-FS01	172.16.1.7	File server
Acme-EX01	172.16.1.10	Exchange server
Acme-Client01	172.16.1.105	Normal PC
Acme-Client02	172.16.1.106	Normal PC
Acme-Branch-Internal		
WG-Client01	172.16.2.45	Normal PC

Most of the time, we will deal with the components listed in the preceding table. However, additional components may be used in special scenarios, but they will follow the same environment design.

The lab environment is quite large, but not all the environment components will be used at the same time. You can practice most of this book's scenarios using only two machines, one as the Untangle server and the other as the client that we will apply our policies on. Also, for scenarios that require the use of more than one client VM, you can use one VM and change its IP to simulate using different clients.

Getting Untangle

Untangle NGFW can be downloaded in two different formats: ISO and IMG. The ISO format can be used to create CDs or directly with virtualization platforms, while the IMG format is used to create bootable USB drives. To get your copy of Untangle NGFW, browse to www.Untangle.com/store/get-Untangle and select the version you want to download, whether it's ISO or IMG and whether it's 32- or 64-bit, as shown in the following screenshot:

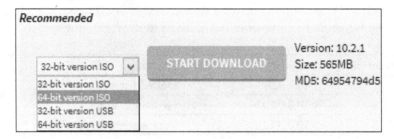

After selecting the desired version, click on the **START DOWNLOAD** button to start downloading your Untangle copy.

 Use the 64-bit version of the Untangle server when you are going to use 4 GB or more of RAM on your PC as this will utilize all available memory and provide performance enhancements.

Writing your image

Now, after you've successfully downloaded the Untangle NGFW image, it's time to write this image to a suitable media drive, which will be used to install Untangle NGFW.

Windows users can burn ISO files directly to a CD using Windows Disk Image Burner, which is available with Microsoft Windows 7 or later versions of Windows, or by using third-party applications such as Nero, Power ISO, and ISO Burner. Different options and tools are also available for Mac and Linux users.

You can make a bootable USB drive from the IMG file by using applications such as Win32DiskImager, RMPrepUSB, or Rufus. Personally, I prefer using Rufus as it's the simplest and fastest application for this purpose; you can get it at `http://rufus.akeo.ie`.

 Mac and Linux users can use UNetbootin, which is available at `http://unetbootin.sourceforge.net/`.

To make your Untangle bootable USB drive, first attach the USB drive into your computer and then start Rufus, as shown in the following screenshot:

Select **DD Image** and click on the CD drive icon next to it. This will open a Windows explorer window from where you can browse to the IMG file location to select it. Then, click on the **Start** button on the program; it will take less than a minute to complete the process.

 The USB drive will be renamed to Debian Installer, and its drive letter will be removed so it will disappear from the **My Computer** window, but you can still find it under **Computer Management** | **Disk Management**.

Untangle NGFW installation guide

Untangle NGFW installation is a very simple and straightforward process. If you have installed a Linux OS before, you will be familiar with the steps in this section and you can skip this section. However, if this is the first time you will be installing a Linux OS, you will need to go through this section.

Step 1 – booting and selecting the installation mode

We'll need to boot a dedicated PC using the Untangle NGFW installation media we have just created.

 You may need to change the boot device order to be able to boot from the installation media. The simplest way to achieve this is by pressing *F12* at the time of starting your computer (this may differ depending on your hardware manufacturer). The boot menu will display and you can select the desired device.

Successfully doing this will introduce you to the menu shown in the following screenshot, where you can select whether you want to use the graphical or text mode installation. Both modes will walk you through the same wizard; the only difference is the interface. Depending on your VGA card, select the right option for you.

The text interface is shown in the *Step 3 – Configuring the system locale* section, while the graphical interface is shown in the upcoming sections.

Step 2 – selecting the installation wizard language

In this section, we will need to select the installation wizard language. The selected language will be used in the installation process and will be the default language for the installed system. Note that you can change the system language later after the installation. Choose the language you want from the menu and then click on **Continue** as shown in the following screenshot:

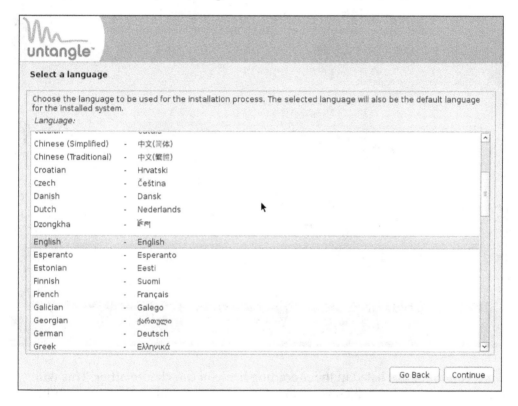

Step 3 – configuring the system locale

In this section, you'll need to select your location as this will help the system to adjust the server time to your time zone and set the system locale. A list of suggested locations will appear based on the language you select in the previous step, as shown in the following screenshot:

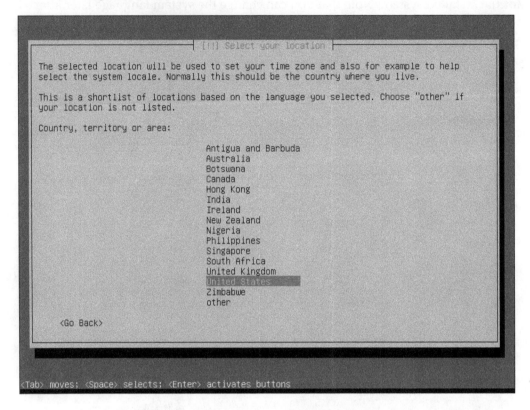

If your country is not listed in the preceding list, you can choose **other**. This will open a new menu from which you can select your continent/region; as a result, another menu with the countries, territories, and areas located in the selected continent/region will appear, where you can select your country. The following screenshot shows the two menus:

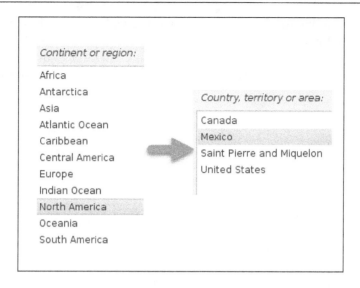

If there is no locale defined for the combination of language and country you have selected, you will be prompted to select a locale from the previously selected language's default locales. For example, if you have selected the English language and selected Algeria (an Arabic locale) as the location, you will be prompted by the installation wizard to select one of the English locales as shown in the following screenshot:

Country to base default locale settings on:		
Antigua and Barbuda	-	en_AG
Australia	-	en_AU.UTF-8
Botswana	-	en_BW.UTF-8
Canada	-	en_CA.UTF-8
Hong Kong	-	en_HK.UTF-8
India	-	en_IN
Ireland	-	en_IE.UTF-8
New Zealand	-	en_NZ.UTF-8
Nigeria	-	en_NG
Philippines	-	en_PH.UTF-8
Singapore	-	en_SG.UTF-8
South Africa	-	en_ZA.UTF-8
United Kingdom	-	en_GB.UTF-8
United States	-	en_US.UTF-8
Zimbabwe	-	en_ZW.UTF-8

You can go back in the installation wizard at any time to change the configurations. Just press the **Go Back** button in any menu. This will display the Debian Installer Main menu, which contains all setup steps. All that you have to do is select the step you want and press **Continue**. The next screenshot shows the **Debian installer main menu** window:

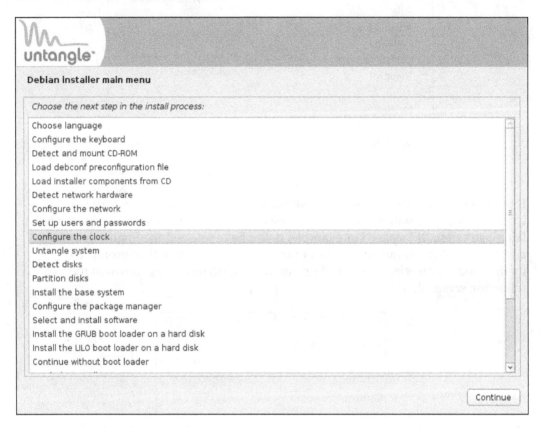

Step 4 – configuring the keymaps

The keymap is the keyboard layout you will use. Different countries have different keyboard layouts. For example, using *Shift + 2* in the US keyboard will give you the @ symbol, while using the same combination in the UK keyboard will give you the " symbol. The following image shows the difference between the UK and US keymaps:

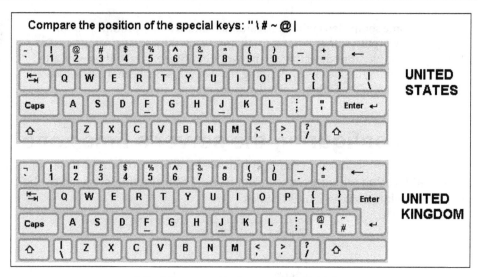

http://www.goodtyping.com/difteclats.htm

In the Untangle NGFW installation wizard, select the desired keymap and press **Continue**.

After that, the installation wizard will try to detect and mount the CD, load the installer components from the CD, detect the network hardware, and configure the network. Those steps will be streamlined and you will not be prompted for anything.

Some setup steps will be streamlined and will not prompt you for any input; neither the steps will appear on the screen as progress. For example, after detecting the network hardware, you will be prompted to configure the clock, skipping the two steps between them, which are shown in the **Debian installer main menu** window.

Step 5 – configuring the server's time zone

Based on the selected location in the previous steps, a list of different time zones related to that location will appear to select from. The following screenshot shows the time zones related to the United States:

Step 6 – reviewing the hardware rating summary

Based on the summary of your hardware rating and whether or not it meets the recommended requirements, a value will be displayed, as shown in the following screenshot. You may have different values based on your hardware specifications, such as great, OK, and insufficient on 64-bit:

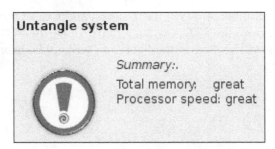

Step 7 – preparing the hard disk

Untangle NGFW will need to format the hard disk as shown in the following screenshot:

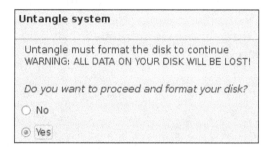

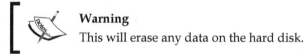

> **Warning**
> This will erase any data on the hard disk.

You must press **Yes** to continue with the installation process.

After that, the Untangle NGFW installation wizard will prompt you to create two hard disk partitions, as shown in the following screenshot. Again, you have to select **Yes** to be able to continue with the installation process:

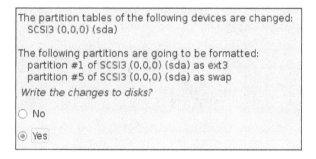

The two partitions are partition #1, which will contain the Untangle server system files and is formatted as ext3 (ext3 is a filesystem used by Linux systems), and the other partition is partition # 5, which will be used as memory swap space (when the RAM is full and the system needs more RAM space, the inactive pages in the memory will be moved to this swap space partition to free some space on the RAM); the partition is formatted as swap, which is similar to to the page file in Microsoft Windows operating systems.

By pressing **Continue** in the previous window, you will start the installation process. It will take about 10 minutes to complete the installation.

Step 8 – completing the installation

Eventually, the **Finish the installation** window will be displayed as shown in the following screenshot. It informs you that the installation process has completed, and asks you to remove the installation media from the PC and then restart the system. Thus, you can boot to the Untangle NGFW system instead of booting into the installation wizard again. Just press **Continue** to exit this wizard and let the Untangle NGFW server restart.

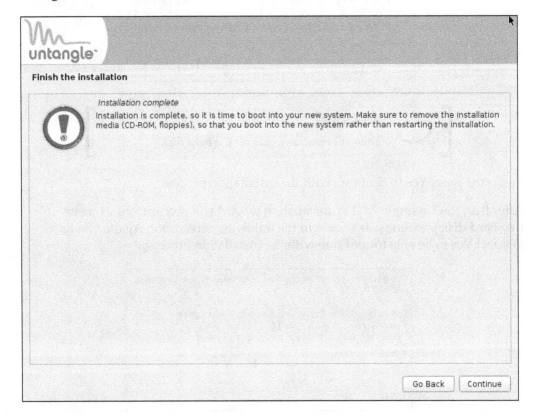

Summary

In this chapter, you saw that Untangle NGFW is available as a downloadable software or as an appliance to be purchased. We defined its hardware requirements. You also learned how to download an Untangle image, how to make a bootable media from this image, the lab environment to be used to practice the scenarios in this book, and finally, had a step-by-step guide through the installation process.

In the next chapter, we'll see the initial configuration of the server.

3
The Initial Configuration of Untangle

Now, after we have successfully completed the installation of Untangle NGFW, it's time to decide how we want to set and run it in our network. This can be achieved through the initial configuration wizard.

First, we will cover the different boot options of Untangle NGFW. After that, we will cover the initial configuration wizard. Essentially, in the initial configuration wizard, we will see how the different NICs will work. Then, we will configure which NIC will face the Internet and which one will face the internal network. We will also configure their IPs. In addition, we will set the admin account password and the automatic upgrade behavior.

After completing the initial configuration, we will need to start downloading and installing the different applications. This requires us to have an Untangle account and to register the Untangle server to this account to be able to install the applications. In this chapter, we will see how we can achieve this. In addition, we will review Untangle NGFW's GUI. Eventually, we will look at the different options available to manage and administer Untangle NGFW.

In this chapter, we are going to cover the following topics:

- Understanding the Untangle boot menu
- The initial configuration wizard
- Creating an Untangle account and registering the server to it
- The Untangle GUI
- The administration console

Understanding the boot options

After the initial restart, a menu with different boot options will be displayed, as shown in the following screenshot:

```
Debian GNU/Linux, kernel 2.6.32-5-untangle-amd64
Debian GNU/Linux, kernel 2.6.32-5-untangle-amd64 (safe video mode)
Debian GNU/Linux, kernel 2.6.32-5-untangle-amd64 (kern video mode)
Debian GNU/Linux, kernel 2.6.32-5-untangle-amd64 (hardware safe mode)
Debian GNU/Linux, kernel 2.6.32-5-untangle-amd64 (recovery mode)
```

If no button is pressed within 5 seconds, the option used on the previous boot is automatically chosen. The different boot options are as follows:

- **default boot**: This is the best option for most servers, and provides you with the best graphical experience.

- **safe video mode**: This is another video configuration that may work if the default option fails. It attempts the most basic video configuration in a low resolution (1024 x 768).

- **kern video mode**: This is another video configuration that may work if the previous options fail.

- **hardware safe mode**: This is another option that might be better for some hardware. It disables APIC and ACPI, and hides the bootsplash screen.

> **Advanced Programmable Interrupt Controller (APIC)** is an architectural design intended to solve interrupted routing efficiency issues in multiprocessor/multicore computer systems.
>
> **Advanced Configuration and Power Interface (ACPI)** is an open standard that allows the operating system to directly configure, power-manage, and thermal-manage the motherboards. Simply, it changes the way your board communicates with CPU, RAM, PCI slots.

- **recovery mode**: This option launches the recovery utility, which will be covered later in *Chapter 5, Advanced Administration Settings*.

To start the initial configuration wizard, select any boot option except the **recovery mode** option.

The initial configuration wizard

The setup wizard will open automatically when Untangle NGFW first boots.

 If you do not have a keyboard, mouse, and monitor connected to the Untangle server, the setup wizard can be reached by plugging a DHCP-configured laptop into the internal interface, and opening a browser at `http://192.168.2.1/`.

Step 1 – selecting the wizard language

The first step of the initial configuration wizard is to choose the language that will be used through the wizard. Select the language you wish and then press **Next** to continue:

After selecting the desired language, a welcome screen that thanks you for choosing Untangle will be displayed; press **Next** to proceed to the next step.

Step 2 – setting the admin password and server's time zone

In this step, you will be asked to set a password for the admin account; the username will be admin, and the password should be three characters at least. Additionally, we will be asked to set the server time zone, which is useful in the preinstalled Untangle NGFW cases (for example, appliances). In our case, we will not have to change these settings as it will reflect the settings that we have configured in *Chapter 2, Installing Untangle*. Put in your password and change the time zone if necessary and then press **Next**:

Step 3 – mapping the network cards

In this step, we will map the physical network cards to the desired logical interfaces (that is, determine which physical NIC will act as the external interface and which one will act as the internal interface). An external interface will be the Internet-facing one while the internal one will face the local network.

Identify Network Cards

Important: This step identifies the external, internal, and other network cards.

Step 1: Plug an active cable into one network card to determine which network card it is.
Step 2: Drag and drop the network card to map it to the desired interface.
Step 3: Repeat steps 1 and 2 for each network card and then click *Next*.

Name		Device		Status	MAC Address
External	⊕	eth0	●	connected 10000 full-duplex VMware	00:0c:29:06:2a:34
Internal	⊕	eth1	●	connected 10000 full-duplex VMware	00:0c:29:06:2a:3e
Interface Gamma	⊕	eth2	●	connected 1000 full-duplex Intel Cor...	00:0c:29:06:2a:48
Interface Delta	⊕	eth3	●	connected 1000 full-duplex Intel Cor...	00:0c:29:06:2a:52
Interface Epsilon	⊕	eth4	●	connected 1000 full-duplex Intel Cor...	00:0c:29:06:2a:5c

If you have more than two interfaces, the third interface and beyond are disabled by default. You can't rename the interfaces at this step. Managing the interfaces is covered in *Chapter 4, Untangle Advanced Configuration*.

To determine whether the physical network cards are mapped to the correct interface, plug in one cable at a time and verify that it is in the correct position. For example, unplug all network cables from Untangle NGFW. Plug in a cable into the desired external physical network card. If the green light on the external interface of the wizard lights up, that physical network card is mapped to the correct interface. If the green light on another interface lights up, you should drag that device to the external interface using the arrow icon next to the device name. Alternatively, you can select the dropdown on the device and choose the desired device.

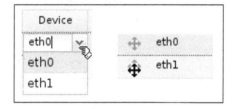

Step 4 – configuring the Internet connection

In this step, we are going to configure the external (WAN) interface settings. So, we will configure the interface IP and its gateway and DNS. These settings can be retrieved automatically through **DHCP** or can be configured manually using static configurations; the third option is **PPPoE**.

Acquiring automatic configurations from DHCP

The default option is **Auto (DHCP)**, in which the current automatically-assigned address will be displayed if an address was successfully acquired. The **Auto (DHCP)** option is typical in home and small networks where ISPs provide no static addresses and DHCP is used to hand out addresses. Also, if Untangle is installed behind another device that serves DHCP, this option can be used.

The following screenshot shows the external interface settings of Untangle-01 used in our lab environment:

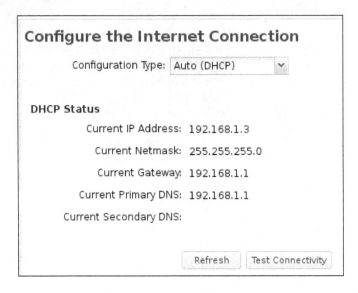

You can ensure the server's ability to connect to the Internet by pressing the **Test Connectivity** button. Also, the connectivity test will be run automatically if you pressed **Next**.

Manually configuring the interface settings

For larger networks, a static configuration is preferred. In a static configuration, you manually add the IP configurations using values provided by your ISP.

If Untangle is being installed behind another firewall doing **network address translation (NAT)**, the ISP's public address should not be used. It is common to use the gateway's IP plus one. For example, if 192.168.1.1 is the gateway for Untangle, you can use 192.168.1.2 for the address for Untangle and 192.168.1.1 as the gateway.

The other option is to let Untangle NGFW do the **point-to-point protocol over Ethernet (PPPoE)** authentication instead of the modem. Also, in this option, you'll need to enter the configuration given to you by your ISP.

If you're in the router mode and have a PPPoE WAN connection, contact your ISP and see whether the modem can do the authentication and pass the IPs to the Untangle server so that you can set the external interface to static. This is a much better situation than having the Untangle server do the PPPoE login as some features (such as multi WAN) will not work with interfaces set to PPPoE.

Step 5 – configuring the Untangle NGFW operation mode

The Untangle NGFW operation mode is determined based on how the internal interface is configured. So, when we say that we are going to configure the Untangle NGFW operation mode, what we are really going to do is configure the internal interfaces.

Untangle is not a proxy; it acts as a transparent filter for traffic. So, you do not point browsers to the Untangle server for traffic filtering as you would with a proxy. Computers on your network will either use Untangle as their gateway, or your network will force their traffic to flow through it. Untangle has two operation modes, router and bridge modes.

Understanding the router operation mode

In the router mode, Untangle will be the edge device on your network and will serve as a router and firewall. You will need to configure the internal interface with a private static IP address (that is, 192.168.2.1). The following diagram shows how Untangle NGFW in the router mode can be deployed in your environment:

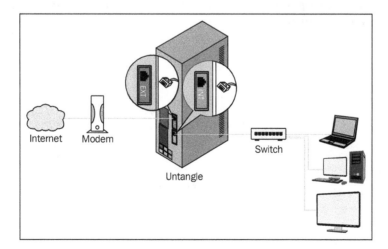

Using the router mode, you can decide whether you want to let Untangle act as a DHCP server or not. In addition, NAT will be enabled so all internal machines will have private addresses and share one public IP (the address of the external interface configured in the previous step).

> If you are using the Untangle server in an Active Directory environment, it's better to disable the DHCP service of the Untangle server and use the Windows server DHCP instead.

The interfaces will be configured as follows:

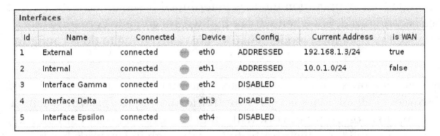

Interfaces						
Id	Name	Connected	Device	Config	Current Address	is WAN
1	External	connected	eth0	ADDRESSED	192.168.1.3/24	true
2	Internal	connected	eth1	ADDRESSED	10.0.1.0/24	false
3	Interface Gamma	connected	eth2	DISABLED		
4	Interface Delta	connected	eth3	DISABLED		
5	Interface Epsilon	connected	eth4	DISABLED		

Understanding the transparent bridge operation mode

In the transparent bridge mode, Untangle is installed behind an existing firewall and sits between your existing firewall and main switch, whereas in the bridge mode, Untangle is transparent. This means that you won't need to change the default gateway of the computers on your network or the routes on your firewall. The following diagram shows how Untangle NGFW in the transparent bridge mode can be deployed in your environment:

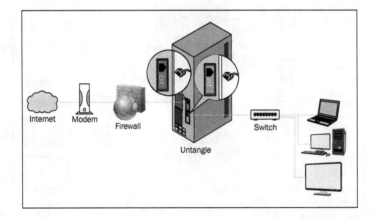

The bridge mode defines the external interface as static and the internal interface as bridged to the external. Thus, the internal interface does not have its own address and simply shares the external's address. It also disables DHCP and NAT by default. An example of Untangle-04 interfaces is shown in the following screenshot:

Id	Name	Connected		Device	Config	Current Address	is WAN
1	External	connected	●	eth0	ADDRESSED	172.16.2.2/24	true
2	Internal	connected	●	eth1	BRIDGED		

You can configure these settings by selecting the operation mode, providing an internal interface IP, and deciding whether to enable the DHCP service or not.

 We can only configure the internal interface (interface number 2); any additional interfaces can be configured later.

The following screenshot shows the operation mode's selection screen. The subnet configured in the following screenshot is the ABC-users subnet on Untangle-01:

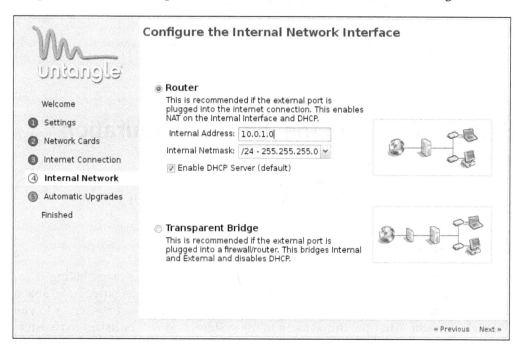

Step 6 – configuring the automatic upgrade settings

Here, we will be asked to configure the automatic upgrade settings. These settings are related to the Untangle system itself and will not affect the update behavior of the Untangle filters, such as the signature updates of the Virus Blocker and Spam Blocker, as these filters will continue to automatically update regardless of which setting is selected here. You can allow automatic upgrades or disable them. If the option of automatic upgrades is enabled, the server will automatically check for new versions and upgrade automatically between 1 a.m. and 2 a.m. every morning. The following screenshot shows different automatic upgrade options:

Configure Automatic Upgrade Settings

◉ Install Upgrades Automatically

Automatically install new versions of Untangle software.
This is the recommended for most sites.

○ Do Not Install Upgrades Automatically

Do not automatically install new versions of Untangle software.
This is the recommended setting for large, complex, or sensitive sites.
Software Upgrades can be applied manually at any time when available.

Note:
Signatures for Virus Blocker, Spam Blocker, Web Filter, etc are still updated automatically.
If desired, a custom upgrade schedule can be configured after installation in the Upgrade Settings.

Step 7 – finishing the initial configuration wizard

Now, we have completed the initial configuration wizard and are ready to download and configure the applications; press **Finish** to load the Untangle system.

Registering your server

You need an Untangle account to manage your subscriptions, invoices, billing information, and so on, even if you are using the free applications only. To be able to start download and use the different apps, you need to assign the new server to your Untangle account. After the initial login to the system, you will be asked to register your server as shown in the following screenshot:

Unleash the power of Untangle applications.

Thank you for installing Untangle. In order to load apps into your rack, please register for a free account..

Registering gets you the following benefits:

- Get access to "My Account" on untangle.com.
- Manage your contact info, licenses, renewals and servers from one dashboard.
- Easily transfer licenses between systems.

Registration only takes a second and is required for application installation. Be assured that we will never spam you or share your contact information with anyone..

LOGIN TO REGISTER

Click on the **LOGIN TO REGISTER** button. This will open a new window in which you can log in with your existing Untangle account or register for a new account. The registration process is very simple. You will be prompted only for your first and last names, e-mail address, and a password for this account, as shown in the following screenshot:

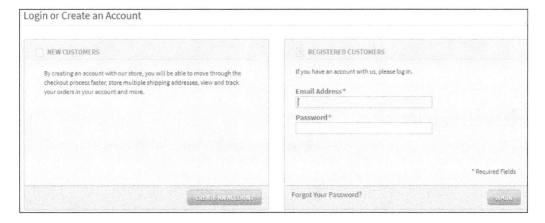

After successfully logging in with your Untangle account, the new server will be added to your account under the **Servers** tab, as shown in the following screenshot:

After setting the Untangle account under which Untangle NGFW will be added, you will be asked whether you want to install the recommended apps (that is, the complete package) or whether you want to install apps manually later. Here, I have selected **No, I will install the apps manually** to show you how to add the apps manually later:

Reviewing the GUI

Untangle NGFW GUI is one of the simplest and richest user interfaces you could ever work with. The following screenshot shows the Untangle interface along with the description of the different components:

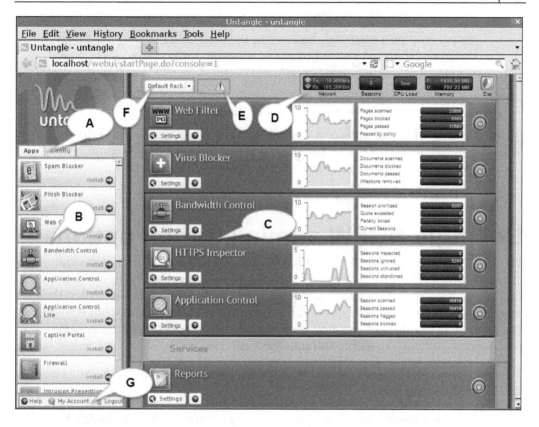

- **A**: These are **Apps** that allow you to manage the different Untangle NGFW modules. **Config** allows you to configure the Untangle NGFW server.

- **B**: If **Apps** is selected, this section will show the applications available to be installed. If **Config** is selected, this section will show the different configuration settings.

- **C**: This section contains the installed modules. Each module has a faceplate that displays the scan traffic status. In addition, managing the applications is done through this faceplate.

- **D**: This section monitors the server resources' utilization, the amount of traffic, and the number of sessions.

Hovering over any of the monitors will show a pop up with detailed information.

- **E**: Administration alerts appear in this area. An example of administration alerts could be a warning about using the Internet Explorer to manage Untangle NGFW. A full list of administration notifications can be found at `http://wiki.untangle.com/index.php/Administrative_Alerts`.

- **F**: This drop-down menu is used to switch between the different virtual racks or to select the session viewer or the host viewer.

- **G**: This gives you an access to the Untangle wiki through the **Help** button. You can also access your Untangle account from the **My Account** button, and finally, you can log out from this administration console by clicking on the **Logout** button.

Untangle NGFW administration options

The initial installation and configuration of Untangle NGFW is often done via the local console (that is, a keyboard, mouse, and monitor directly attached to the server). As the Untangle server will normally be located inside a data center, the local console is not a suitable solution for day-to-day administration, but it is still necessary if any issue is preventing remote administration. Additionally, some functionality are only available through the local console.

When you boot your Untangle NGFW using the local console, the following options will be available for you:

- **Launch Client**: This allows you to manage Untangle NGFW locally through the Iceweasel browser.

- **Reboot** and **Shutdown**: This enables you to reboot or shut down your Untangle NGFW server. The options are also available through the browser administration console.

- **Recovery Utilities**: This allows you to recover Untangle NGFW. This tool is described in *Chapter 5, Advanced Administration Settings*.

- **Terminal**: This allows you to manage Untangle NGFW through the command line.

The preceding options are illustrated in the following screenshot:

Any configurations done via the terminal are not supported by Untangle, Inc. and may lead to the loss of server support, although throughout this book, we will use the GUI to configure our server.

The terminal is useful for troubleshooting. A list of troubleshooting commands can be found at `http://forums.untangle.com/installation/13877-list-good-troubleshooting-commands.html`.

Untangle NGFW can be administered remotely via a web browser or via SSH, as follows:

- **Web browser from LAN**: This uses the IP of the internal interface of Untangle NGFW. Also, the host name of Untangle NGFW could be used if it's resolvable. An example would be `http://10.0.0.1`.

- **Web browser from WAN**: This uses the IP of the external interface of Untangle NGFW. Also, the hostname of Untangle NGFW could be used if it's resolvable. The administration is available only via HTTPS and it's disabled by default. An example would be `https://203.0.113.1`.

- **Using SSH**: SSH is disabled by default, and we suggest you keep it as is. As the case with the terminal, any changes done through SSH are not supported by Untangle, Inc.

Summary

In this chapter, you learned about the different boot options of the Untangle server and the different methods to administer the server locally and remotely. We also walked through a step-by-step guide of the initial configuration wizard and reviewed the router and the bridge operation modes. Additionally, we learned how to create an Untangle account and how to register the server to that account. We also quickly reviewed the Untangle GUI.

In the next chapter, we are going to do a more advanced configuration that is related to the Untangle server.

4
Untangle Advanced Configuration

At this point, Untangle has the basic configuration that will work for most networks. However, some networks require some more configurations. Any additional interfaces that are installed on Untangle NGFW were not available to be configured during the running of the initial configuration wizard. In this chapter, we will learn how to configure additional interfaces.

In addition, this chapter will teach you about the placement options for Untangle NGFW, and how the traffic is passed through the system. Also, this chapter will show you how to configure an Untangle NGFW hostname and the ports that the Untangle NGFW services run at (such as, the Administration Interface) to allow any internal services that use the same port to work. Also, we will cover Untangle functionality such as router, DNS, and DHCP.

After that, we will cover the concept of Untangle NGFW rules and how they work. Next, we will cover some rules such as port forwarding and NAT. Eventually, this chapter will end with a guide on how to troubleshoot any connectivity issues.

In this chapter, we will cover the following topics:

- Untangle NGFW placement options
- Untangle NGFW architecture
- Managing Untangle NGFW interfaces
- Configuring Untangle high availability
- Configuring the Untangle NGFW hostname

- Configuring Untangle NGFW Services ports
- Untangle network services such as router, DNS, and DHCP
- Untangle rules
- Network troubleshooting

Untangle placement options

There are several key rules to how Untangle NGFW operates that should be understood before deploying Untangle NGFW in an advanced/complex network:

- **Untangle must be installed in line**: Untangle NGFW is a gateway product that is designed to be in line with network traffic. Deploying Untangle NGFW without installing it in line is not likely to work. Examples of the Untangle NGFW in-line functionality include Spam Blocker, which will filter SMTP as it passes through Untangle NGFW; it will not store and forward the e-mails to your e-mail server like some products. In addition, Web Filter will filter web traffic as it passes through Untangle NGFW; it does not operate as a proxy that you point your clients' browsers to send web traffic.

- **Untangle MUST have a working Internet connection**: Many Untangle NGFW modules depend on cloud services to get definitions and query them about URLs and so on. Untangle NGFW must have a working and consistent connection to the Internet; this includes unfiltered HTTPS, HTTP, and DNS access to various cloud services.

- **Untangle routes ALL traffic according to its routing table**: When Untangle NGFW receives packets on an interface, it will look up where to send it in the routing table/rules (this also includes bridged interfaces). If you have a subnet that Untangle NGFW doesn't know about or have a route for, then the traffic will be sent back to the default gateway even if those hosts are internal. For Untangle NGFW to operate correctly, you must configure Untangle NGFW with a complete routing table so it knows how to reach all hosts on your network.

After considering the mentioned rules, it is time to decide where to place Untangle NGFW on the network. Since Untangle NGFW must be installed in line with all network traffic, we will have the following placement options:

- **Installing Untangle NGFW as the gateway/firewall for the network (Router Mode)**: This is the simplest and recommended approach. This approach allows Untangle NGFW to leverage its full set of features including WAN Failover and WAN Balancer. This also places it in a suitable place to handle other separate internal networks that may only connect at the gateway (such as wireless segments). In addition, if you have tagged VLANs, it is much simpler to manage them using this approach.

- **Installing Untangle NGFW behind an existing gateway/firewall in flow with traffic (Transparent Bridge Mode)**: Often, organizations don't want to replace an existing gateway/firewall. Installing Untangle NGFW in this mode allows it to scan and process network traffic without providing the routing functions of your firewall.

- **Installing Untangle NGFW in front of an existing firewall or device that performs NATing**: Though this option is technically possible, it's not recommended. Firewalls/gateways use NAT to allow all internal hosts to share external IPs; thus, Untangle NGFW will not be able to differentiate between internal hosts (as the traffic coming from them will appear as if it comes from the other NAT device). So, the Untangle NGFW functionality (such as web filters, reports, shields, and so on) will be severely compromised.

Understanding the architecture of Untangle NGFW

The Untangle NGFW architecture includes a kernel—Untangle VM (UVM)—and apps.

Untangle NGFW itself runs on the UVM; thus, any traffic directed to Untangle NGFW local services (such as the administration console) will be processed on the UVM. In addition, unlike other Linux products, the network processes (such as routing, NATing, and so on) are done on the UVM and not the kernel.

Untangle applications run on the UVM. When traffic comes to the Untangle NGFW server, the packets' stream will be endpointed on the UVM and reconstructed at layer 7 (the application layer). The data then flows through the applications for scanning, and if passed, the data is eventually put back into new packets and sent on its way.

So, the possible actions that can be done on incoming streams are as follows:

- Incoming streams can be *bypassed* at the kernel level (the traffic will be forwarded to its destination without scanning)
- Incoming streams can be *dropped* at the kernel level (based on filter rules, the traffic can be blocked based on its criteria, way before being scanned by the applications, which increases resource utilization)
- Incoming streams can be *forwarded* to Untangle NGFW local services (such as the administration interface)
- Incoming streams can be *forwarded* to be scanned by the applications (different actions can be done based on the scan result, such as passing or blocking the traffic, or modifying the traffic contents)

The following figure shows the architecture of Untangle NGFW:

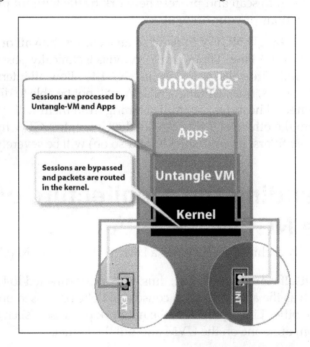

Managing Untangle NGFW interfaces

In the initial configuration wizard, we have configured both the internal and external interfaces. Any additional interfaces are disabled by default and must be configured before we can use them. This section will cover the different use cases of the additional interfaces. In addition, it will cover the different configuration settings of the Untangle NGFW interfaces.

Common uses of additional interfaces

This section concludes the different uses of additional interfaces; detailed configurations will be described later in this chapter. The different uses include:

- **Additional WAN interfaces**: Adding additional WAN interfaces is useful to have a reliable Internet connection by failover / load balancing between the different interfaces. Just configure the new interface as a WAN interface and enter the IP configuration details provided to you by your ISP.

- **Additional internal interfaces**: You may have different subnets inside your network. In the initial configuration wizard, we configured only one internal interface; any other internal interfaces need to be configured. Just configure the new interface as a non-WAN interface and enter IP configurations suitable for the subnet you want to add.

- **Demilitarized Zone (DMZ)**: If you have servers with public IP addresses, you can isolate them from your internal network by putting them inside the DMZ. This is done by bridging the additional interface to the external interface.

- **Additional NICs for existing networks**: For redundancy, you can make two interfaces serve the same subnet. For example, if you want to provide redundancy for the internal subnet, you will need to bridge the additional interface to the internal interface.

Configuring Untangle NGFW interfaces

We can configure the Untangle NGFW interfaces, review their details, remap them, create VLAN interfaces, and perform basic troubleshooting by navigating to **Config | Network | Interfaces**. The different options available under the **Interfaces** screen are as follows:

- **Edit**: This opens the interface configuration menu

- **Remap Interfaces**: This allows you to change the mapping between a physical device and logical interfaces

- **Refresh**: This refreshes the interface's connection status (that is, **connected** or **disconnected**)

- **Add Tagged VLAN Interface**: This allows you to create up to 4094 virtual LAN interfaces that share the same logical interface (that is, a physical NIC)

- **Test Connectivity**: This verifies that the server is connected to the Internet

- **Ping Test**: This launches the **ping test** for configuration troubleshooting

The following figure shows the details of Untangle-01 interfaces:

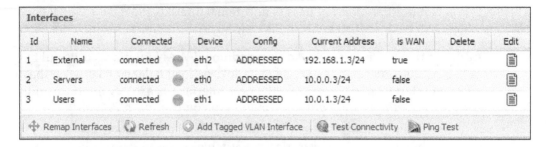

Id	Name	Connected	Device	Config	Current Address	is WAN	Delete	Edit
1	External	connected ●	eth2	ADDRESSED	192.168.1.3/24	true		📄
2	Servers	connected ●	eth0	ADDRESSED	10.0.0.3/24	false		📄
3	Users	connected ●	eth1	ADDRESSED	10.0.1.3/24	false		📄

✛ Remap Interfaces 🔄 Refresh ⊕ Add Tagged VLAN Interface 🌐 Test Connectivity 📡 Ping Test

The different configuration types available for Untangle NGFW interfaces are:

- **Addressed**: The interface will have its own IP address and configuration
- **Bridged**: The interface doesn't have its own address, and all the traffic is directed to another interface
- **Disabled**: The interface will not respond to any traffic
- **VLAN**: VLANs or Virtual LANs are commonly used to create completely separated subnets (including separate broadcast domains) that share the same wire using 802.1q tagging (IEEE 802.1q is a standard that defines a system of tagging for Ethernet frames)

Addressed interfaces

To configure an Untangle NGFW interface in order to make it an addressed interface, select the **Addressed** config type under the **Edit** menu. Under the **Edit** menu, you can provide the **Interface Name** and select whether it will be a **WAN interface** or not.

As addressed interfaces have their own IP and configurations, we will need to configure these settings. Untangle NGFW interfaces can be configured using IPv4 and IPv6. However, IPv6 is disabled by default.

The required IP settings are the **Interface IP**, its default gateway, DNS, and DHCP servers. These configurations can be provided either automatically or manually.

Only WAN interfaces can be assigned dynamic IPs, while non-WAN interfaces can only be assigned static IPs.

It's advisable to configure the interface from the top of the page downward, as the available options vary depending on the selected settings.

The following table covers the available IPv4 configuration settings:

Option	Description
Config Type	**Static**: This interface has a static IPv4 address. **Auto (DHCP)**: This interface will use DHCP to automatically acquire an address. **PPPoE**: This interface will use PPPoE to acquire an address. This option is only available for WAN interfaces because non-WANs can only be statically configured.
Static Config Type	
Address	This is the manually-entered IP address. It is only shown if **Config Type** is **Static**.
Netmask	This is the manually-entered netmask. It is only shown if **Config Type** is **Static**.
Gateway	This is the manually-entered static gateway. It is only shown if **Config Type** is **Static**.
Primary DNS	This is the first manually-entered DNS server for DNS queries' resolution. It is only shown if **Config Type** is **Static**.
Secondary DNS	This is the second manually-entered DNS server for DNS queries' resolution. It is only shown if **Config Type** is **Static**.
Auto (DHCP) Config Type	
Address Override	The address entered here will be used instead of the one acquired by DHCP. It is only shown if **Config Type** is **Auto (DHCP)**.
Netmask Override	The netmask entered here will be used instead of the one acquired by DHCP. It is only shown if **Config Type** is **Auto (DHCP)**.
Gateway Override	The gateway entered here will be used instead of the one acquired by DHCP. It is only shown if **Config Type** is **Auto (DHCP)**.
Primary DNS Override	The primary DNS entered here will be used instead of the one acquired by DHCP. It is only shown if **Config Type** is **Auto (DHCP)**.
Secondary DNS Override	The secondary DNS entered here will be used instead of the one acquired by DHCP. It is only shown if **Config Type** is **Auto (DHCP)**.
Renew DHCP Lease	This sends a new lease request to the DHCP server. It is only shown if **Config Type** is **Auto (DHCP)**.
PPPoE Config type	
Username	This is the PPPoE username as provided by your ISP. It is only shown if **Config Type** is **PPPoE**.
Password	This is the PPPoE password as provided by your ISP. It is only shown if **Config Type** is **PPPoE**.

Option	Description
Use Peer DNS	If checked, the DNS settings provided by the PPPoE server will be used. It is only shown if **Config Type** is **PPPoE**.
Primary DNS	This is available if **Use Peer DNS** is not checked; the entered settings will be used as the primary DNS for DNS queries' resolution. It is only shown if **Config Type** is **PPPoE**.
Secondary DNS	This is available if **Use Peer DNS** is not checked; the entered settings will be used as the secondary DNS for DNS queries' resolution. It is only shown if **Config Type** is **PPPoE**.
Advanced Options	
IPv4 Aliases	These are additional IP addresses that can be concurrently used with the configured IP.
IPv4 Options — NAT traffic exiting this interface (and bridged peers)	This is only available for WAN interfaces and, by default, it is checked. It will NAT all traffic that exits from this interface and any interfaces bridged to — Additional information can be found in the **NAT Rules** part.
IPv4 Options — NAT traffic coming from this interface (and bridged peers)	This is only available for non-WAN interfaces, and by default, is unchecked. It will NAT all traffic that comes from this interface and any interfaces bridged to. Additional information can be found in the **NAT Rules** part.

The following table covers the IPv6 configuration options:

Option	Description
Config Type	**Disabled**: This interface has no IPv6 configuration. **Static**: This interface has a static IPv6 address. **Auto (SLAAC/RA)**: This interface will use SLAAC to automatically acquire an address. This option is only available for WAN interfaces because non-WANs can only be statically configured.
Address	This is the IPv6 static address. This is allowed to be blank, which means no IPv6 address will be given. It is only shown if **Config Type** is **Static**.
Prefix	This is the IPv6 static prefix. It is only shown if **Config Type** is **Static**.
Gateway	This is the IPv6 static gateway. It is only shown if **Config Type** is **Static**.
Primary DNS	This is the primary DNS used for DNS resolution. It is only shown if **Config Type** is **Static**.
Secondary DNS	This is the secondary DNS used for DNS resolution. It is only shown if **Config Type** is **Static**.
IPv6 Aliases	These are additional IP addresses that can be concurrently used with the configured IP. This is only available on non-WAN interfaces.

Option	Description
IPv6 Options—Send Router Advertisements	This is only available for non-WAN interfaces. If checked, route advertisements will be sent to this interface.

 When you create, delete, or modify settings on Untangle NGFW, the new settings will not be immediately applied. The affected option will be highlighted with a color that reflects the changes made on this option. Green highlights reflect a newly created option, orange highlights reflect a modified option, and the red highlights reflect a deleted option. You will need to confirm these modifications by clicking on the **Apply** or **OK** buttons, or you can discard them via the **Cancel** button.

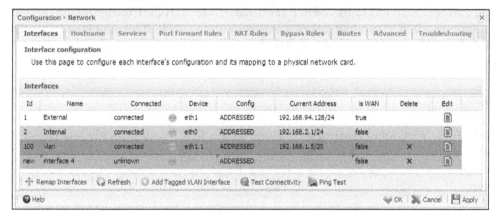

The following figure shows the external interface on Untangle-03 where it's configured statically with an `192.168.1.5` IP. In addition, it has an alias IP of `192.168.1.10`.

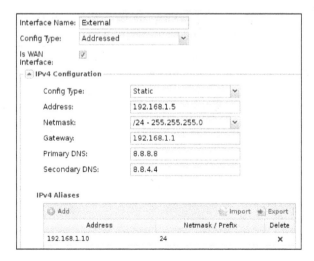

The following figure shows the configuration settings of the server's interface on Untangle-01:

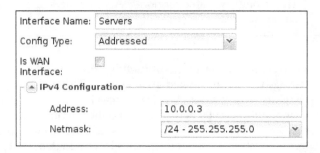

As part of the interface configuration, we will need to configure how internal interfaces will respond to the DHCP requests. Under **DHCP Configuration**, we can configure the DHCP serving settings of this interface. DHCP serving is only available on addressed non-WAN interfaces. The following table shows the different DHCP configuration settings:

Option	Description
Enable DHCP Serving	This allows Untangle NGFW to serve a DHCP request on this interface
Range Start	This is the beginning of the DHCP address pool; if this is blank, Untangle will automatically choose an address based on the interface's static address
Range End	This is the end of the DHCP address pool; if this is blank, Untangle will automatically choose an address based on the interface's static address
Lease Duration	This is the validity duration of the provided DHCP leases in seconds
Gateway Override	This defines the gateway to be provided in the DHCP leases; you can specify a value or leave it blank to use the static gateway of this interface
Netmask Override	This defines the Netmask to be provided in the DHCP leases; you can specify a value or leave it blank to use the static netmask of this interface
DNS Override	This defines the DNS settings to be provided in the DHCP leases; you can specify a value or leave it blank to use the static DNS settings of this interface

Option	Description
DHCP Options	Here, we can configure additional DHCP options such as PXE and NTP servers. You can find a list of the different DHCP options at `http://www.networksorcery.com/enp/protocol/bootp/options.htm`. For example, to specify an NTP server, we will use the following format: `enabled = true, description = "time server", and value = "42,192.168.1.2"` In the preceding code, `42` is the NTP option number, and `192.168.1.2` is the NTP server. The value must be specified in a valid dnsmasq format, as described at `http://www.thekelleys.org.uk/dnsmasq/docs/dnsmasq-man.html`.

The following figure shows the DHCP settings for the server's interface on Untangle-01. The gateway is configured to be overridden by the Virtual IP used for Untangle high availability.

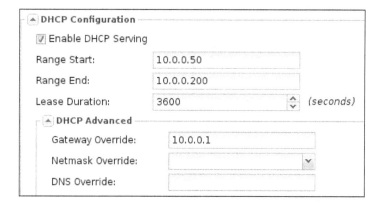

Bridged interfaces

In Untangle NGFW, when two interfaces are bridged, this means they are effectively sharing a configuration (that is, they are in the same zone, or they both connect to the same network space). The different modes to use bridged interfaces include:

- **Standard bridge mode**: The most common scenario is to use the standard bridge mode where the external interface is bridged to the internal interface. This is extremely useful when there is a firewall upstream.

The following figure shows Untangle-04 located on Acme-Branch, which is located behind an existing firewall. The old firewall IP is 172.16.2.1, and you can see that Untangle shares the same subnet.

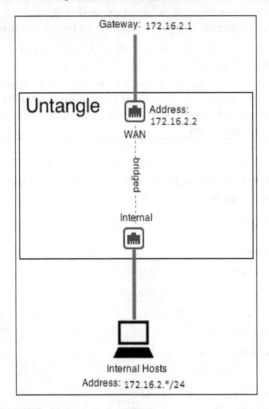

- **DMZ Bridge**: This is useful in scenarios when you have public servers and want to keep them separate from the internal network to avoid NAT/port forwarding issues. The DMZ interface is bridged to the external interface (so that the server would be as it is on the Internet directly and not behind a firewall).

The following figure shows the configuration of a DMZ interface on Untangle-03:

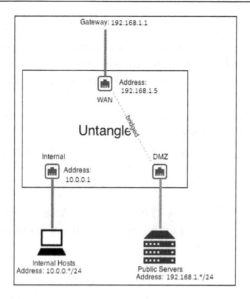

- **Additional Port**: This bridge mode can be used to provide alternate ports to existing interfaces/zones. Be careful, as the traffic between the two interfaces goes through Untangle!

  For example, if **Interface 2** is configured as 10.0.1.4/24 and **Interface 3** is bridged to **Interface 2**, then they are both effectively 10.0.1.4. Basically, **Interface 3** becomes an additional port for the **Interface 2** network.

  The following figure illustrates the Additional port case.

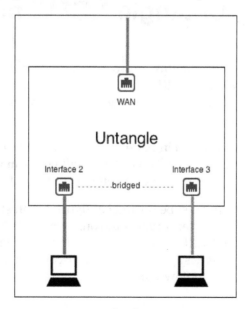

VLANs

VLANs have several uses. The first is to create multiple, completely separate internal subnets on a network without using multiple physical networks; the second use is when you are limited with a number of interfaces on your server.

Using VLANS requires VLAN-enabled switches and products throughout the network.

If you want to use a single network card but you don't care about keeping the two LANs separate, you don't need VLANs and can just use aliases/routes.

You can create a VLAN interface by clicking on the **Add Tagged VLAN Interface** button on the bottom of the interface's screen (**Config | Network | Interfaces**). You will just need to complete the following data:

- **Interface Name**: Give a name for this interface
- **Parent Interface**: This is the logical interface under which the VLAN interface will be created
- **802.1q Tag**: This tag is used to differentiate between the VLANs, and can take a value from 1 to 4094

After providing the preceding data, you can configure the interface as any normal interface.

Configuring Untangle NGFW high availability

The Untangle NGFW high availability approach is based on the **Virtual Router Redundancy Protocol (VRRP)**. VRRP is a network protocol that provides redundancy and high availability when using a *statically* configured router on a **Local Area Network (LAN)**.

Multiple Untangle servers can run in parallel to provide a high availability configuration. Thus, one Untangle NGFW server will be the **master** (that is, the server with the highest priority) and the other servers will be the **slaves**.

All Untangle NGFW servers must be on and configured with static IPs and with a VRRP virtual address. The master server is the only Untangle NGFW to answer/handle traffic routed to the VRRP virtual address. When the master server fails, the slave server with the next highest priority will take over the master role; thus, the network traffic will continue to flow without any interruption.

You will need to configure the clients to connect to Untangle NGFW servers using the VRRP virtual address.

There is zero state sharing between Untangle NGFW servers. The session tables are separate, so sessions will be reset if the slave takes over. Furthermore, application data is not shared or synchronized between servers.

 All Untangle NGFW servers' interfaces must be configured statically, and there must be no bridged interfaces. Parallel Untangles configured as bridges will create a bridge loop.

The high availability options can be configured by navigating to **Config | Network | Interfaces | Redundancy (VRRP) Configuration**. The available options include:

- **Enable VRRP**: This enables/disables the VRRP.
- **VRRP ID**: This is used to define the members of the same VRRP group. The VRRP ID must be unique on the server.
- **VRRP Priority**: This defines the priority of the server; based on this priority, the master server is selected, along with the next server to take over the master role when a failure occurs.
- **VRRP Aliases**: This includes the virtual addresses that will be used in server communication instead of their real IPs; the traffic coming to this virtual address will be forwarded to the master server.

The following screenshots show the configurations done on Untangle-01 and Untangle-02 to make them work on a high availability mode. Untangle-01 is configured to be the master (since it has the highest priority). We will have three VRRP IDs (one for the external interface, another for the server's interface, and the final one for the user's interface).

 You can still configure HA for just the external interface or the internal interface.

The following figure shows the settings done on the external interfaces on both the servers:

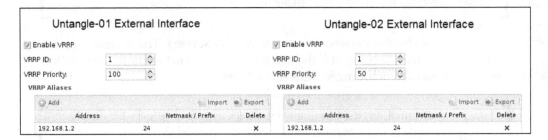

The following figure shows the server interface VRRP settings on both the servers:

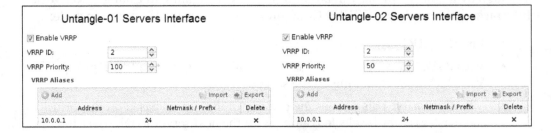

If Untangle NGFW is providing DHCP, configure Untangle-01 as the authoritative one with 10.0.0.1 as the **Gateway Override**, and configure Untangle-02 in the same way as Untangle-01 but as non-authoritative. This way, Untangle-01 will handle all DHCP leases unless it is down, in which case Untangle-02 will handle DHCP.

VRRP acts very quickly in the case of a failure, and usually switches in less than a few seconds. However, TCP sessions will be reset as the state is lost.

To test the VRRP functionality, open CMD on ABC-Client01 and write Ping 8.8.8.8 -t. Then, try to unplug one interface at a time; you'll notice that the failover is done within a few seconds.

Configuring the Untangle NGFW hostname

The hostname settings can be configured by navigating to **Config | Hostname**. In this tab, we can set the **fully qualified domain name (FQDN)** of the Untangle NGFW server (that is, the hostname + domain name). The FQDN can be used in Untangle NGFW's publicly-available services such as the VPN, and in quarantines; you will need to ensure that the Untangle NGFW FQDN is resolvable in DNS to the Untangle NGFW public IP.

Dynamic DNS is helpful in dynamic IP scenarios as instead of configuring your services with an IP that could be changed at any time, you will configure the services with a domain name that will dynamically resolve to the current dynamic-assigned IP.

There are many Dynamic DNS providers that can be used with the Untangle NGFW server; you will need to subscribe with a Dynamic DNS service provider before you can start to use their services.

The following screenshot shows the hostname configuration for Untangle-01:

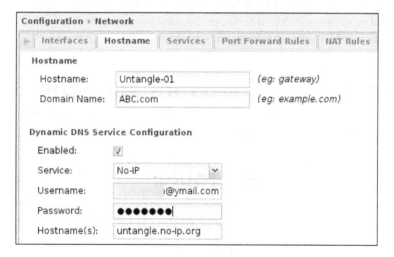

Configuring Untangle NGFW Services ports

The Services settings that are available by navigating to **Config | Network | Services** are used to define the ports that will be used to access the web services hosted on the Apache server located on Untangle NGFW, such as the Administration interface, Spam Quarantine, Reports, and Blockpages.

By default, ports 80 and 443 are used to access these services. TCP traffic directed to the primary address of each interface on the HTTPS port will be forwarded to the local web server to provide services. So, when you have an internal service that needs to run on the default HTTPS port, you'll have to change the Untangle NGFW Services port, or add an alias IP to the interface and port forward the traffic directed to the alias IP to the internal service.

For example, if we set the new HTTPS port to 4343, we will use `https://172.16.1.1:4343/` to access the Untangle-03 administration console instead of the default `https://172.16.1.1/`.

HTTP access to Untangle NGFW services form external interfaces is prohibited and is only available for non-WAN interfaces. So, cases where you will need to change the HTTP services port are rare, but you can do so.

Untangle NGFW network services

In this section, we are going to learn about the Untangle NGFW functionality as a router, DNS server, and DHCP server.

Untangle NGFW as a router

If we have a certain subnet that is not directly attached to an Untangle NGFW interface (that is, behind another local router), we will need to define how Untangle NGFW can reach this subnet (that is, the route to this subnet). If no route was set, all the traffic destined to this subnet will be directed to the default gateway instead.

Untangle NGFW only supports static routes. You can configure the routes by navigating to **Config | Network | Routes**.

To set a route, we will need to define the following settings:

- **The destination network**: This is the remote subnet (for example,
  10.0.5.0/8)

- **The Next Hop**: This defines how we can reach the destination network
  (that is, the local router interface that is seen by the Untangle NGFW);
  there are two options to use as the next hop:
    - **Using IP address**: All traffic to the destination network will be
      routed to the specified IP address
    - **Using Untangle NGFW interface**: All traffic to this network will
      be routed locally on the specified IP address using ARP to resolve
      those hosts

- **Refresh Routes**: This button will show you the current routing table, as
  displayed on the following screenshot:

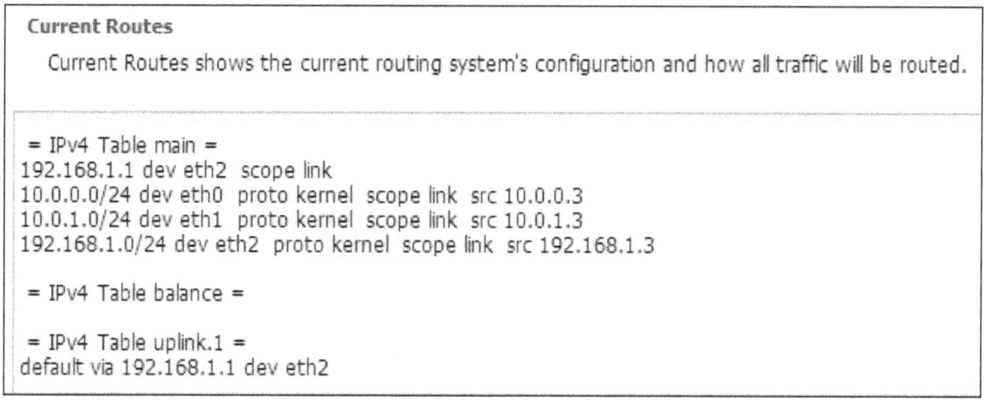

Current Routes

Current Routes shows the current routing system's configuration and how all traffic will be routed.

```
= IPv4 Table main =
192.168.1.1 dev eth2  scope link
10.0.0.0/24 dev eth0  proto kernel  scope link  src 10.0.0.3
10.0.1.0/24 dev eth1  proto kernel  scope link  src 10.0.1.3
192.168.1.0/24 dev eth2  proto kernel  scope link  src 192.168.1.3

= IPv4 Table balance =

= IPv4 Table uplink.1 =
default via 192.168.1.1 dev eth2
```

The Untangle NGFW DNS service

Untangle NGFW DNS Server Options are available at **Config | Network | DNS Server**. A DNS server is used to resolve hostnames to its IP addresses. The external DNS queries are forwarded to the DNS configured in the interface settings. The internal DNS queries can be resolved via preconfigured **static** entries set on Untangle NGFW or by forwarding the query to another internal DNS server.

The static entries can be configured under **Static DNS Entries**, and this is suitable for servers that have a static IP. The following figure shows a DNS record for Acme-EX01 configured on Untangle NGFW:

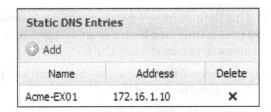

To forward the DNS queries to an internal DNS server, you will need to add the server under **Local DNS Servers.** The following figure shows that `172.16.1.5` is configured to resolve any queries about `Acme.local`; in addition, it's configured to resolve any reverse DNS lookups about the `172.16.1.*` subnet (to configure the reverse DNS lookup settings, add `subnet.in-addr.arpa` as the domain):

It's typical for small environments to use the Untangle DNS server, while for Active Directory environments, it's better to use the Active Directory integrated zone option.

 You can set the DHCP settings under the internal interfaces to distribute the DNS configurations of your internal DNS directly, or you can leave it unchanged, which will distribute Untangle NGFW IP to be used to resolve the internal DNS queries. If the Untangle NGFW is configured to resolve the DNS queries, then we have to configure settings under **Config | Network | DNS Server**.

The Untangle NGFW DHCP service

We can configure DHCP serving for a particular interface by checking **Enable DHCP Serving** under that interface configuration. The DHCP Server tab (**Config | Network | DHCP Server**) gives us the ability to set DHCP reservation by setting **Static DHCP Entries**; thus, a certain MAC address will always get the same IP.

In addition, we are able to review the active DHCP leases and their expiration time, and we can even make them static entries under **Current DHCP Leases**:

Current DHCP Leases				
MAC Address	Address	Hostname	Expiration Time	Add Static
00:0c:29:72:45:e8	172.16.1.105	Acme-Client01	2014-09-16 1:39:48 am	+

DNS and DHCP advanced options

Untangle DNS and DHCP services are based on the DNSMasq server. We can configure the custom dnsmasq options for advanced DHCP and DNS configurations under **Config | Network | Advanced | DNS & DHCP**.

A list of dnsmasq command formats can be found at http://www.thekelleys.org.uk/dnsmasq/docs/dnsmasq-man.html.

Please note that this option is for advanced users, and any misconfiguration will result in halting of the DHCP and DNS services.

Configuring advanced network options

Some advanced network settings can be found by navigating to **Config | Network | Advanced**. The **Options** tab has the following advanced configuration options:

- **Enable SIP NAT Helper**: Most SIP solutions handle NAT on their own, but sometimes, rewriting of an address inside SIP by the NAT device is necessary. Enabling this will enable bypassed SIP sessions to be rewritten in the kernel. By default, this is off.

- **Send ICMP Redirects**: ICMP redirects are used to alert machines if a shorter route to their destination is available. By default, this is on.

- **Enable STP (Spanning Tree) on bridges**: If you want to connect your Untangle server to a switch via two cables for redundancy, you should check this option to ensure a loop-free topology.

- **DHCP Authoritative**: If this is enabled, all DHCP serving is authoritative. By default, this is on.

 If we have two running DHCP servers, one is authoritative and the other is non-authoritative. The client will always accept the DHCP leases provided by the authoritative server. However, the use of the non-authoritative DHCP is still critical as when the authoritative server fails, the non-authoritative server will provide the DHCP leases.

The **Network Cards** tab has the following options:

- **Maximum Transmission Unit (MTU)**: This is used to determine the packet size. The default value is **Auto**, which has a maximum value of `1500`, and you are suggested to not change it.

- **Ethernet Media**: This configures the duplexity of the network card. The default value is **Auto**. If your NIC can't automatically configure the duplex mode, or it performs poorly with the **Auto** option, then you can change this value.

Understanding Untangle NGFW rules

Before we take another step forward in this chapter, it's suitable to review the Untangle rules first. After understanding the anatomy of Untangle rules, we will cover some network-related rules such as port forwarding and NATing rules.

Many Untangle applications use rules such as Firewall, Application Control, and Bandwidth Control. All of these rules are based on the same logic.

Rules are used to categorize the traffic and define the action to be taken based on this categorization. For example, Firewall can decide whether to block or pass traffic depending on the destination port, source address, protocol, and so on.

Rules are evaluated against every session in order, from top to bottom. If a rule match is found, the action defined in that rule will be taken directly, and no additional rules are evaluated. If the traffic doesn't match any rule, the action will be defined by the application, which is usually doing nothing.

The properties of Untangle NGFW rules are as follows:

- **Enable checkbox**: This determines whether the rule is to be checked against the traffic or not. When unchecked, the rule will be simply skipped.

- **Description**: By default, **[no description]** will appear for all rules, so it's advisable to write what each rule does for easier troubleshooting.

- **Conditions**: This defines the traffic properties that should be met before taking an action. The rule will be considered matched if and only if all of the conditions are true.

  Untangle NGFW uses a large set of conditions; there are some generic matchers that are common to the different applications such as Sources Address, Destination IP, and Destination Port. In addition to this, there are some application-specific conditions such as *Application Control: Application*, which is used by Application Control to block a particular application. The full conditions list is available at http://wiki.untangle.com/index.php/Rules#Condition_List. You need to set a value for the condition to match. For example, to know the difference between an **IP Address** of 192.168.1.5 and 192.168.1.*, please visit http://wiki.untangle.com/index.php/Untangle_Rule_Syntax.

- **Action**: This defines the action to be taken if a matched rule is found; the actions are application-dependent. However, common actions include:

  - **Allow/Pass**: This will allow the traffic that matches with this rule
  - **Log**: This will allow the traffic but will log it on the event logs and the reports so that the administrator can review them and take any necessary actions
  - **Block**: This will block and log the traffic

Port forward rules

Port forwarding is used to forward traffic destined to the server's public IP to a specific internal IP based on a specific criterion. For example, if you want to have remote access on an internal computer (such as 172.16.1.100) via a remote desktop from outside (that is, you should use the public IP), you should set a port forward rule that will forward port 3389 from the public address to the internal address of the desired machine. Port forward rules can be managed by navigating to **Config | Network | Port Forward Rules**.

There are two ways to add port forward rules (that is, simple rules and advanced rules). Simple rules are the easiest way to configure port forwarding, and it is suggested to always use simple port forward rules where possible as they cover the most common use cases and prevent misconfiguration errors. You can create simple rules via the **Add Simple Rule** button; you will need to specify the traffic to be forwarded (protocol and port) and the destination computer.

 The destination on the simple rules is *Destined Local*, which means any traffic coming to Untangle NGFW on any external IP address.

The following figure shows a simple rule that will forward any traffic directed to port 443 on Untangle-01 to your internal exchange server (10.0.0.10) in order to provide OWA for the external users. Note that you'll need to change the administration interface port from 443 to something else for port forwarding to work properly. If the admin interface was using port 443, any coming traffic will be ended on the admin interface (that is Untangle NGFW) and will not be forwarded.

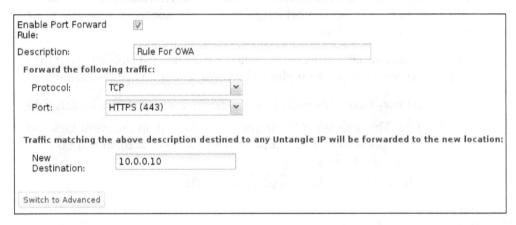

The **Switch to Advanced** button will open the rule for editing on the advanced mode, which allows for additional configurations. In addition, you can add advanced rules directly via the **Add** button.

The advanced mode can be used in the cases when we want to port forward a certain port for two or more devices. For example, to have remote access to computer **A**, we will use the external IP and the default remote desktop port 3389, so we can't use the same port to access computer B; instead, we will use the same external IP address and any unused port (for example 3399); then, we have two options, first is to configure computer B to accept RDP traffic from the new port, or let Untangle NGFW to remap the traffic from the new port to the default port before it is directed to computer B.

Additionally, the advanced mode can be used for protocols, either to TCP and UDP (for example, ICMP); also, it allows for additional conditions to limit when a port forward rule will be matched. For example, we can limit traffic forwarding to traffic from a specific interface, specific IP range, and so on.

The following figure shows an advanced rule on Untangle-03 that will forward any traffic that is directed to `192.168.1.10` (public static IP for exchange) on port 443 to the internal exchange server:

If you are having issues with port forwards, it is suggested to follow the Port Forward Troubleshooting Guide available at `http://wiki.untangle.com/index.php/Port_Forward_Troubleshooting_Guide`.

Additional rules are required for this book's scenario to work properly. You will need to forward traffic destined to port 53 to your domain controller, traffic to port 587 to your SMTP server, and traffic to port 21 to your FTP server, and if you are using the FTP passive mode, you will need to configure the port range on the FTP server and the Untangle NGFW server; an example of a port range to be used by the passive mode is `50000` to `60000`.

NAT rules

Network Access Translation (NAT) is used to allow internal devices to communicate with the external world through the Untangle NGFW public IP. For example, when an internal machine (for example 10.0.1.105) makes a connection to a public server (for example www.google.com), the Untangle NGFW server rewrites the source address to the public IP address of Untangle NGFW (for example 192.168.1.2) on the way out. When the return traffic in that session returns to 192.168.1.2, it is rewritten back to the internal address and then forwarded to the internal server.

There are three different methods of NATing: Static NAT, Dynamic NAT, and NAT PAT. Static NAT is a 1:1 relationship, and thus, if we have four public IP addresses, only four predetermined internal devices can access the Internet; Dynamic NAT is also a 1:1 relationship, but differs in that any four devices can access the Internet instead of the predetermined devices in the case of Static NAT; NAT **PAT** (**Port Address Translation**) is a many-to-one relationship, and thus, any number of devices can share the same public IP address, and the server will differ between the traffic by the different ports.

There are three ways to configure NAT on Untangle NGFW:

- **The NAT traffic exiting this interface (and bridged peers) option on a WAN interface configuration**: Any and all traffic that exits from this WAN interface or bridged peers will be NAT'd to auto, which *is the current primary address of this WAN interface.* In other words, all sessions that leave the external interface will use the external interface's primary IP. This option is enabled by default.

- **The NAT traffic coming from this interface (and bridged peers) on non-WAN interfaces**: All traffic from this interface will get NAT'd to auto, which is the primary address of whichever interface the traffic exits from. This option is not enabled by default.

 The default behavior of NATing is to allow outgoing traffic and block the incoming traffic unless it was a response to a session initiated from the internal devices, or there is a rule that allows the traffic to enter the network. This not only helps to protect against attacks initiated from the Internet, but it also will stop communications between the different internal subnets (if the option is enabled on the non-WAN interfaces).

If you want internal networks to be able to speak with each other (that is, 10.0.0.5 should be able to reach 10.0.1.105 on a different interface), then you do not want to NAT between those networks. This means that you should uncheck **NAT traffic coming from this interface (and bridged peers)** on both the LAN interfaces, and check **NAT traffic exiting this interface (and bridged peers)** on the WAN(s).

If you wish that the internal networks should be completely separate such that they cannot communicate with each other, NAT can be done by checking **NAT traffic coming from this interface (and bridged peers)** on the non-WAN interfaces. This means that the different subnets will be completely separated.

The following figure illustrates the different NAT cases:

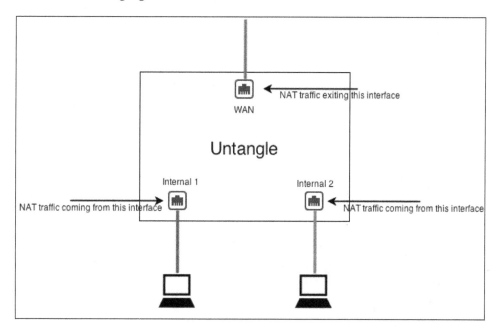

- **NAT rules**: Like all rules, the NAT rules are evaluated in order. The session will be NAT'd according to the first matching rule. If no rule is matched, the session will be NAT'd according to the checkboxes in the **Interfaces** settings. If there is no rule match and all NAT options in **Interfaces** are disabled or do not match the session in question, the session is not NAT'd, and it is sent with the original source address.

There are two actions in NAT rules. The first is auto, which is equivalent to the NAT traffic exiting this interface (and bridged peers) option in WAN, and the second is custom, which allows you to specify the new IP address.

Occasionally, custom rules may be needed. For example, we have two public IPs, 192.168.1.5 and 192.168.1.10. By default, all the traffic will be NAT'd to the primary address 192.168.1.5. However, if we have a mail server (172.16.1.10) that we need to send mails from 192.168.1.10, we will need to add a NAT rule stating that traffic from the mail server should be NAT'd to 192.168.1.10. To do this, we will add a rule with Source Address equal to 172.16.1.10, where NAT Type is Custom and New Source is 192.168.1.10. The rule is shown in the following figure:

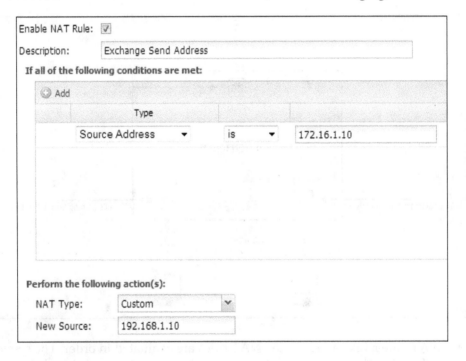

Bypass rules

Bypass rules allow the traffic to pass through the kernel directly to its destination, skipping the layer 7 scanning and processing. This could be used for performance reasons (especially in environments with over 1,000 users) to save server resources and to prevent delays (resultant from scanning) for some sensitive traffic such as VOIP. The bypass rules can be managed by navigating to **Config | Network | Bypass Rules**.

For example, the default VoIP (SIP) session bypass rule is set with the `Destination Port = 5060` and `action = Bypass` conditions. The following figure shows a rule to bypass traffic from ABC Banks Printer as we are not interested in scanning its traffic:

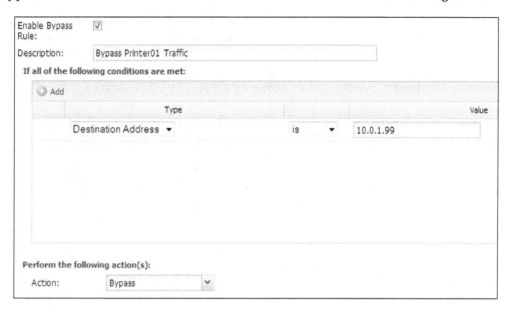

QoS rules

Quality of Service (QoS) is a mechanism to ensure high-quality performance for delay- and bandwidth-sensitive applications such as VoIP. Based on rules, whenever latency-sensitive traffic arrives on the Untangle NGFW server, it will immediately be processed at the cost of less important traffic such as IM. QoS has a great effect on the network performance and important protocols, especially when the bandwidth is saturated. However, when misconfigured, it could have detrimental effects on the network performance. The QoS settings are available under the **Config | Network | Advanced | QoS** menu.

The seven priorities

There are seven QoS priorities that determine how Untangle NGFW will treat its related traffic. Each one of the top four priorities can use all the available bandwidth if no higher priority class has traffic; if there is traffic from a higher priority, the available bandwidth will be split between them with a ratio related to the difference in priorities. The bandwidth will be split equally for traffic from the same priorities.

The bottom three priorities are always limited even if no higher priority class consumes any traffic. The limit ratio differs depending on whether there is traffic from another priority or not.

The following table shows the default values of how the traffic will be divided between the different priorities; these values could be changed, but it's not advisable to do so. The limit value sets the maximum amount of bandwidth available to this priority under any circumstance, while the reservation value sets the minimum amount of bandwidth available to this priority under any circumstance.

Priority	Upload Reservation	Upload Limit	Download Reservation	Download Limit
Very High	50%	100%	50%	100%
High	25%	100%	25%	100%
Medium	12%	100%	12%	100%
Low	6%	100%	6%	100%
Limited	3%	75%	3%	75%
Limited More	2%	50%	2%	50%
Limited Severely	2%	10%	2%	10%

Configuring the QoS settings

By default, QoS is disabled; you can enable it by checking the **Enabled** checkbox. However, **WAN Bandwidth** should be set before enabling QoS. The following screenshot shows the **QoS** tab:

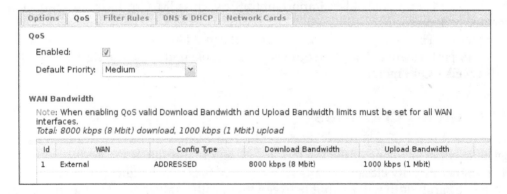

- **Default Priority**: This determines the priority assigned to traffic that doesn't match any QoS rule. It is advisable to leave this as the default setting of **Medium**.

- **WAN Bandwidth**: This should be set to 85-95 percent of your theoretical line speed (in Mbps) because of losses due to noise and distortion. It's critical to correctly configure this part as the different QoS priorities' bandwidth will be calculated dependent on this bandwidth. Misconfiguring this option or inefficient applying of the priorities may lead to very slow traffic for all your clients. You should configure this setting for all of your WAN interfaces.

QoS runs only on WAN interfaces and doesn't run on internal or DMZ interfaces. In addition, QoS can't be used with PPPOE interfaces.

Rules run on all traffic, regardless of which WAN interface the traffic is coming from. However, different WAN interfaces are treated separately. Thus, the bandwidth setting on each WAN interface is separate, and they are treated as separate resources that are divided among traffic independently.

Configuring the QoS rules

Untangle NGFW comes with some predefined rules to optimize some of your critical services. Untangle NGFW provides predefined priorities for Ping, DNS, SSH, and OpenVPN under the **QoS Rules** part. It's advisable to not change these default settings.

In addition, you can create custom rules to prioritize the traffic you wish under **QoS Custom Rules**, which provides an easy way to prioritize or deprioritize certain traffic. Also, Untangle NGFW provides two default rules for VOIP traffic. The QoS custom rules only work with **bypassed** traffic, and they don't have any effect when traffic is not bypassed.

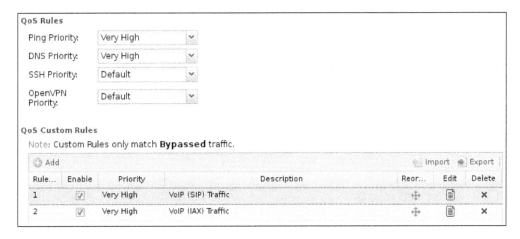

Reviewing the QoS status

QoS Statistics shows the status of the recent activity of the QoS. These statistics are reset at every reboot. **QoS Current Sessions** shows the current active sessions and the assigned priority of each. The following screenshot shows the QoS Statistics:

Interface	Priority ▲	Data
QoS Statistics		
🔄 Refresh		
⊟ Interface: External Inbound		
External Inbound	1 - Very High	108 bytes
External Inbound	2 - High	0 bytes
External Inbound	3 - Medium	2193 bytes
External Inbound	4 - Low	0 bytes
External Inbound	5 - Limited	0 bytes
External Inbound	6 - Limited More	0 bytes
External Inbound	7 - Limited Severely	0 bytes

Filter rules

Filter rules are kernel-level iptables "filter" rules. They can be configured under **Config | Network | Advanced | Filter Rules**.

Forward Filter Rules have a functionality that is similar to the **Firewall** application on Untangle NGFW. Both can be used to block/pass traffic depending on that traffic's criteria. However, the Forward Filter Rules differ from the Firewall app in that they can scan the bypassed traffic; they also apply to all protocols while the Firewall application only can be used with TCP and UDP. Firewall rules have more application-layer conditions available such as **Client has exceeded Quota** and **HTTP: Client User OS**.

Input Filter rules apply to sessions destined to the Untangle NGFW server's local processes. Many preconfigured rules exist and you would not have to create any new rules. It's also advisable to not change any rule settings except **Allow HTTPS on WANs** and **Allow SSH** as any other changes may result in security compromise and server malfunctioning.

Input Filter Rules						
⊙ Add						
Rule...	Enable	Description	Block	Reor...	Edit	Delete
1	☐	Allow SSH	☐	✥	🖹	✕
2	☐	Allow HTTPS on WANs	☐	✥	🖹	✕
3	☑	Allow HTTPS on non-WANs	☐	✥	🖹	✕
4	☑	Allow PING	☐	✥	🖹	✕
5	☑	Allow IPsec	☐	✥	🖹	✕
6	☑	Allow DNS on non-WANs	☐	✥	🖹	✕
7	☑	Allow DHCP on non-WANs	☐	✥	🖹	✕
8	☑	Allow HTTP on non-WANs	☐	✥	🖹	✕

Troubleshooting

Untangle NGFW offers different tools that you can use to troubleshoot your network connectivity; the different tools can be located by navigating to **Config | Network | Troubleshooting**. The following table lists the different troubleshooting tools and their function:

Setting	Description
Connectivity test	This tests the ability of your Untangle NGFW to resolve and connect to http://updates.untangle.com.
Ping test	This tests the ability of Untangle NGFW to reach the remote destination using echo requests. The remote destination can be entered as a hostname or IP.
DNS test	This tests the ability of Untangle NGFW to resolve a domain name and get its IP.
Connection test	This tests the status of a port on a remote machine; just enter the remote machine name or IP and the desired port.
Traceroute test	This is used to see the different hops between you and the remote machine.
Download test	Untangle will try to download the following file: http://cachefly.cachefly.net/5mb.test.
Packet test	This is a simple packet-sniffing tool based on Tcpdump; just specify an interface and a timeout value to view the traffic on this interface.

In the Microsoft world, a reboot may solve your system issues. This is not the case in the Linux world. When you have a connectivity issue, it's important to successfully specify the exact problem. The following checklists could help you with your troubleshooting.

On Untangle NGFW:

- Use the connectivity test, does it succeed?
- Using the ping test, can it ping the gateway of Untangle NGFW?
- Using the ping test, can it ping 8.8.8.8 (Google DNS, which considers highly available destinations to test against)?
- Using the ping test, can it ping www.google.com?
- Using the connection test, can it connect to www.google.com port 80?

On a client behind Untangle NGFW:

- Can the PC ping Untangle NGFW's internal IP? (doesn't apply for the bridge mode)
- Can the PC ping Untangle NGFW's external IP?
- Can the PC ping the gateway of Untangle NGFW?
- Can the PC ping 8.8.8.8?
- Can the PC perform DNS lookups? (open a command window and run nslookup google.com or host google.com)
- Can the PC ping www.google.com?
- Can the PC open a browser to www.google.com?
- Can the PC open a browser to Untangle NGFW's internal administration interface?

On a machine outside the network (if available):

- Can the machine ping the Untangle gateway's IP?
- Can the machine ping Untangle NGFW's external IP?
- Can the machine open a browser to the HTTPS administration on Untangle NGFW?

By answering these questions, it will greatly narrow down where the problem is likely to exist, which will make it far easier to find the problem or make it easier for someone to help you.

Summary

In this chapter, we covered the different placement options for Untangle NGFW; we also took a look at how the traffic is moved between the kernel, the UVM, and the applications. In addition, we covered how to configure Untangle NGFW interfaces, and the high availability options.

After that, we saw how to configure the Untangle NGFW hostname, and change the default ports that the Untangle NGFW services runs at; then, we saw how to manage the Untangle NGFW functionality as a router, DNS, and DHCP server.

Next, we covered Untangle rules; we first learned about the rules concept and how it works, then we discussed multiple Untangle rules such as the port forward and NAT rules.

Eventually, we ended the chapter with a section that can help you diagnose your connectivity problems.

In the next chapter, we will continue the configuration of Untangle NGFW. The chapter will discuss the different administration options such as managing the administrator's accounts, allowing remote administration of the server, and determining the hostname that will be used to refer back to the Untangle NGFW in e-mails sent from it, such as the Quarantine Digest.

After that, the chapter will teach you how to manage Server SSL certificates, which are used to access Untangle services from the outside world, and are used with the HTTPS Inspector application. Next, the chapter will cover how to configure the e-mail settings to allow Untangle to send required e-mails such as daily reports; in addition, we will see how we could use the Spam Quarantine feature.

Furthermore, the chapter will cover how to create local user accounts, upgrade the server, and back up and restore the server while monitoring the server. Eventually, the chapter will cover how to review the system information and license details.

5
Advanced Administration Settings

So far, we have our Untangle NGFW server up and running and its advanced networking settings have been configured. In this chapter, we will learn how to enhance the administration experience of Untangle NGFW.

We will cover how to manage the administrators' accounts, how administrators can remotely administrate Untangle NGFW, how to configure Untangle NGFW to be publicly available on the Internet, and how to configure Untangle NGFW regional settings. Furthermore, the chapter will cover how to make Untangle NGFW only parse certain protocols. Then, we will cover the support options available from Untangle, and how to change the administration console theme.

In addition, this chapter will cover the configuration of the digital certificates used by Untangle NGFW to provide secure access to its services such as the administration console, and to be used with the HTTPS inspector application. We will also learn how to configure Untangle NGFW to send e-mails and how to manage the spam quarantine.

Furthermore, the chapter will cover how to create local users on the Untangle NGFW that can be used to allow users to authenticate and apply different policies on them. The process of upgrading the Untangle NGFW and the backup and restore of the server will also be covered.

Eventually, the chapter will cover how you can monitor your Untangle NGFW and review the system information and the license details.

In this chapter, we will cover the following topics:

- Configuring the administration settings
- Managing Untangle SSL certificates
- Configuring Untangle NGFW e-mail settings
- Managing the Untangle NGFW local directory
- Exploring Untangle NGFW server upgrade
- Backing up and restoring Untangle
- Monitoring the Untangle NGFW server
- Looking at system information and license details

Configuring the administration settings

In this section, we will learn how to manage the administrator accounts, configure the remote administration options, configure the public address that will be used by the Untangle modules to give external users access to the services provided by these modules, configure the regional settings, specify which protocols Untangle will be able to understand and interact with, review the different support options available on Untangle NGFW, and finally, changing Untangle NGFW skins.

Managing the administrator accounts

We can manage Untangle NGFW administrator accounts under **Config | Administration | Admin**. Under this tab, we can create additional administrator accounts, change the accounts' password, and assign e-mail addresses to the accounts.

By default, we have the admin account created during the initial configuration wizard. We can add an additional account that has administrative privileges over the Untangle NGFW server through the **Add** button, as shown in the following screenshot:

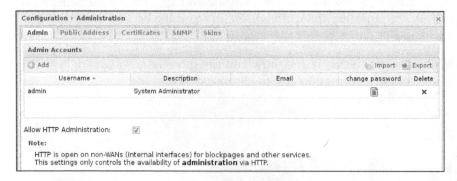

Configuring the remote administration settings

We can manage Untangle NGFW either through HTTP, HTTPS, or SSH. In this section, we will see how we can configure the different options related to the remote administration.

HTTP remote administration is allowed for the internal subnets only. You can't use HTTP to access Untangle NGFW from the external interfaces. You can disable/enable the HTTP remote administration from the **Allow HTTP Administration** checkbox located under **Config | Administration | Admin**.

 Disabling the HTTP administration is only related to the administration console. Any other HTTP-related services such as the captive portal will continue using HTTP as normal.

By default, HTTPS remote administration of Untangle NGFW is allowed for the internal interfaces and disabled for the external interfaces. You can allow the usage of HTTPS on the external interfaces by checking the **Allow HTTPS on WANs** checkbox located under **Config | Network | Advanced | Input Filter Rules**.

In addition, SSH remote administration is disabled by default. You can enable it by checking the **Allow SSH** checkbox located under **Config | Network | Advanced | Input Filter Rules**.

 Enabling SSH is not recommended by Untangle. However, if you want to enable it, ensure that you have a strong password for your administrator account.

Configuring the public address of Untangle NGFW

Some Untangle NGFW services need to be externally accessible. For example, the Quarantine Digest sends e-mails to the users. The e-mails include a link that refers back to the Untangle NGFW server. The address used in this link (that is, the public address) should be externally accessible. These settings could be configured under **Config | Administration | Public Address**.

The different options that can be used as the Untangle NGFW public address are as follows:

- **IP address from External interface**: This uses the IP address of the primary interface. This is recommended if Untangle NGFW has a routable public static IP address.

- **Hostname**: This will use the hostname configured in *Chapter 4, Untangle Advanced Configuration*. This option is recommended if the FQDN of the Untangle NGFW server is resolvable both internally and externally.

- **Manually Specified Address**: This option will use custom configured IP/ hostname and port number. This option is suitable for Untangle NGFW servers installed on a transparent bridge mode behind another firewall. You can configure port forward on the other firewall (using the new custom port) to the Untangle NGFW server.

Configuring the regional settings

Regional settings include the time, time zone, and language settings. The regional settings can be configured under **Config | System | Regional**.

Using the correct time and time zone on your server are very important aspects as the events will use the server time as their timestamp, and the time-based policies will also use the server time.

Untangle NGFW uses **Network Time Protocol** (**NTP**) to automatically sync its time. The current time is shown under the **Current Time** part. If you noticed any time deviation between the server time and the real time, you can force time synchronization via the **Synchronize Time** button. In addition, you can modify your time zone from the **Timezone** drop-down list.

You can change the system language by selecting the desired language from the **Language** drop-down list. If you didn't find your language in the drop-down list, you can press the **Download New Language Packs** hyperlink, which will send you to pootle.Untangle.com where you can download or even create a new language pack. The downloaded language packs can be imported to Untangle NGFW under the **Upload New language Pack** part.

Configuring Untangle NGFW processing of protocols

Many of the Untangle NGFW applications depend on certain protocols such as HTTP, FTP, and SMTP. You can configure whether you want Untangle NGFW to process these protocols under **Config | System | Protocols,** as shown in the following screenshot:

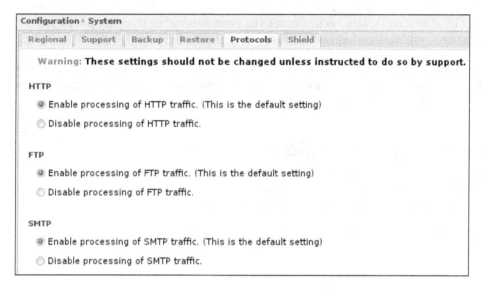

When the processing of a certain protocol is enabled, Untangle NGFW will be able to translate the sessions to the right format and forward them to the dependent applications. If the protocol processing is disabled, the sessions will still be treated as a binary stream but will not be parsed and unparsed and hence the dependent application functionality will be affected.

You should not change these settings unless instructed to do so by support.

The available protocols and the visibility of the **Protocols** tab itself depends on the currently installed applications.

Understating the available support settings

Untangle offers different options for support purposes such as allowing Untangle's support team to access your server, and manually restart or shut down the server from the administration console. Furthermore, you can rerun the initial configuration wizard anytime you wish to reconfigure the Untangle NGFW server. The support settings can be accessed from **Config | System | Support**.

For support purposes, you can allow the Untangle support team to access your server by checking **Allow secure access to your server for support purposes**. No changes will be needed on any firewall in front of Untangle NGFW.

In addition, you can manually reboot or shutdown the server by pressing the **Reboot** or **Shutdown** buttons. Also, you can rerun the initial configuration wizard at any time by pressing the **Setup Wizard** button.

Changing Untangle NGFW skins

Skins control the look and feel of the administration interface. You can select a skin from the existing skins or upload a new custom skin under **Config | Administration | Skins**, as shown in the following screenshot:

Creating custom skins requires extensive work and knowledge of HTML and CSS. You can download *Untangle Skins Cookbook*, which gives you instructions on creating custom skins, from `http://wiki.untangle.com/images/c/c1/Untangle-Skin-Cookbook.zip`.

The following screenshot shows the Dell skin designed by MikeTrike:

Managing Untangle SSL certificates

Untangle uses the digital certificates to provide secure access to the Administrative Console and Email Quarantine via SSL. In addition, digital certificates are also required for the HTTPS Inspector application. The Untangle NGFW certificates settings can be configured from **Config | Administration | Certificates**.

The certificate authority

A default **certificate authority (CA)** is automatically created during the server's initial installation. This CA is used to create and sign the imitation certificates used by the HTTPS Inspector application. It also generates the default server certificate that is used to securely access the administration console.

We can keep using the default CA, or we could create a new CA if we want to customize the information contained in the root certificate. To create a new CA, press the **Generate Certificate Authority** button; this will present a pop up in which we will need to enter the details to be included in the Subject DN of the new root certificate. The **Common Name (CN)** field is the only mandatory field; all other fields are optional. As this is not a server certificate, the CN field could be anything you like (for example, Untangle-CA).

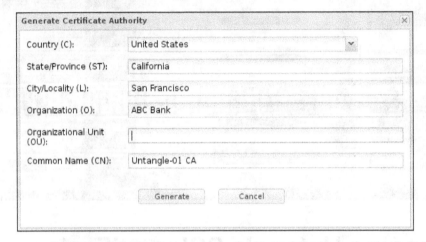

To eliminate the certificate security warnings on the client computers, you will need to add the Untangle CA root certificate to the clients' trusted root CA. We can get the Untangle root certificate by pressing the **Download Root Certificate** button to download the `root_authority.crt` certificate file.

Adding the Untangle CA root certificate to the clients trusted root CA is covered in *Chapter 8, Untangle Filters*.

The server certificate

The Server Certificate is used with the SSL connections to the server such as the Administrative Console and the Email Quarantine pages. We can keep the default certificate or generate a new server certificate for the customization of the included information. The new certificate can be issued either by the server internal CA or by a third-party CA.

The server's internal CA is more suitable in cases where the HTTPS Inspector is enabled. The HTTPS Inspector only uses the internal CA. Thus, the internal CA root certificate will be already imported to the clients for the proper functionality of the HTTPS Inspector, and you will not need to do any additional configuration to the clients.

If you don't plan to use the HTTPS Inspector, it's more suitable to use an external CA that is already trusted by the client computers such as VeriSign, Thawte, or even Active Directory CA. So, you won't have to install the new root certificate on the different clients.

You can generate a new server certificate signed by the local CA by clicking on the **Generate Server Certificate** button. You will be presented with a pop up in which you could enter the server certificate's **Subject DN** details. The only mandatory field is the **Common Name** (**CN**) field, which should be the server name (for example, Untangle-01.ABC.local); all other fields are optional. Once created, the Untangle NGFW server will start to use the new server certificate immediately.

To generate a new server certificate issued by a third-party CA, we first need to have **Certificate Signing Request** (**CSR**). To create the CSR, press the **Create Signature Signing Request** button, which will open a pop up in which you will need to enter the Subject DN details to be included in the CSR. Once you have completed the form, click on **Generate**. A `server_certificate.csr` file will be downloaded to your computer.

The CA will use the CSR file to issue the new server certificate. You'll need to import the new certificate to the server so that it can start using it. This can be done via the **Import Signed Server Certificate** button.

Configuring the e-mail settings of Untangle NGFW

Some Untangle NGFW features such as Reports and Spam Blocker require Untangle NGFW to be able to send e-mails to administrators and end users. In this section, we will cover how to configure Untangle NGFW to send e-mails. In addition, this section will cover how to make Untangle NGFW trust particular senders such that it will not scan any e-mails coming from those senders by the Spam and Phish Blockers.

Furthermore, this section will cover how to manage Untangle NGFW quarantine, which is used to temporarily store spam e-mails instead of delivering them to the intended recipient and give that recipient the option to release or delete the spam messages. The e-mail settings can be configured under **Config | Email**.

Configuring the outgoing e-mail server

Untangle NGFW is able to send daily spam quarantine digest e-mails to the related users and daily server activities summary reports to the administrators. Thus, we will need to configure the way Untangle NGFW will use to send these e-mails. Untangle NGFW can send e-mails directly using the SMTP daemon or through SMTP relay. These settings are available under **Config | Email | Outgoing Server**.

If **Send email directly** is checked, Untangle NGFW will use the SMTP daemon to send the e-mails without relying on another e-mail server. Untangle NGFW will look up for the recipient domain MX record and will send the message to that address.

As many ISPs block port 25 to prevent spam, Untangle NGFW will not be able to send e-mails directly and the usage of SMTP relay will be required. To use SMTP relay, check the **Send email using the specified SMTP Server** option and provide the relay SMTP server IP address or hostname, the server port, and any authentication credentials, if required.

 You may have to configure the SMTP relay server to allow Untangle NGFW to relay e-mail through it.

The **Email from Address** section is the from e-mail addresses that will appear on all e-mails sent by the Untangle NGFW server except to the e-mails released from the quarantine.

The following figure shows the configurations used on Untangle-03 where Acme-EX01 is used as a SMTP relay for Untangle-03:

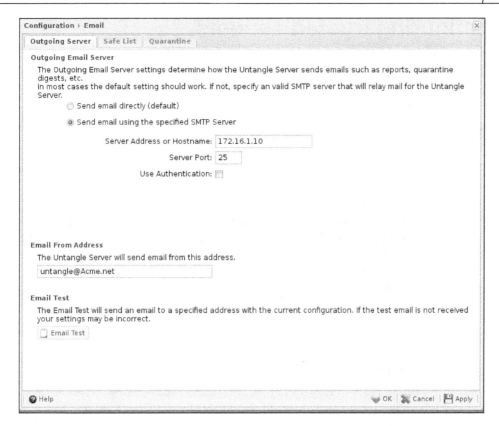

The **Email Test** button sends a test e-mail from the configured **Email from Address** section to validate the server configurations. You will need to define the recipient of that test e-mail. The following screenshot shows a test e-mail sent from Untangle-03 to Acme Administrator:

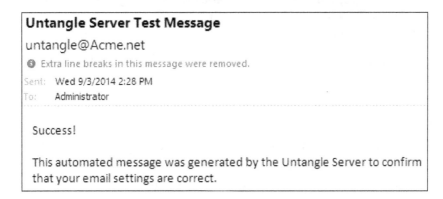

Configuring trusted senders

Safe lists are used by the Spam Blocker and Phish Blocker applications to define trusted sources whose e-mails will not be scanned in order to save resources and/or avoid false positives. These settings can be configured under **Config | Email | Safe List**.

- **Global Safe List**: This is applicable to all users. All e-mails from a listed address will not be scanned by Spam Blocker or Phish Blocker. You can add a single e-mail address or even an entire domain to the list using `*@example.com`.

- **Per-User Safe List**: Each user's e-mail address has its own safe list. Thus, e-mails from a certain address will not be scanned for this certain user, while it will be scanned for the remaining users. A user can add a single e-mail or an entire domain, or even disable the scanning of all the received e-mails by adding `*`. Users can edit their safe lists via the quarantine web application that is accessible via `https://UNTANGLE_IP:HTTPS_PORT/quarantine/`. In addition, administrators can access and control the users' safe lists from the administration console.

Managing the Untangle NGFW quarantine

When the Spam Blocker and Phish Blocker applications determine an e-mail as spam or phish, these applications should drop this e-mail. However, this could be a legitimate e-mail (that is, false positive) and the e-mail is important. So, instead of dropping the e-mails, they will be delivered to the user's quarantine. Then, the user has the option to review and release the e-mails to his or her inbox or completely delete them.

Daily quarantine digest e-mails will automatically be sent to users with new e-mails in their quarantine. In addition, the users can manually generate a Quarantine Digest from `https://UNTANGLE_IP:HTTPS_PORT/quarantine/`.

The quarantine settings can be configured under **Config | Email | Quarantine**. The different settings are as follows:

- **Maximum Holding Time (days)**: This sets the duration an e-mail will be held on the quarantine before it is automatically deleted.

- **Send Daily Quarantine Digest Emails**: This configures whether to send the daily Quarantine Digest to the users or not.

- **Quarantine Digest Sending Time**: This configures when to send the daily digests.

- **User Quarantines**: This shows a list of the currently existing user quarantines. User quarantines are automatically created when an e-mail is quarantined for this user and will automatically be deleted when no more messages remain. We can release entire user quarantine via the **Release Selected** button or delete the entire user quarantine via the **Purge Selected** button. Additionally, we can view the individual messages in a user quarantine via the **Show Detail** button. We also have the option to release or purge single messages.

- **Quarantineable Addresses**: The e-mail addresses on this list will have quarantines automatically created. All other e-mails will be marked and not quarantined. By default, an entry of * could be found, and it's advisable to not change any settings in this part.

- **Quarantine Forwards**: This is a list of e-mail addresses whose quarantine digest gets forwarded to another account. This is common for distribution lists where the whole list should not receive the digest; instead, the digest would be sent to an administrator who can manage the spam on the distribution list quarantine.

Accessing Untangle's quarantine web application

The users can manage their quarantines through the quarantine web app, which is accessible via `https://UNTANGLE_IP:HTTPS_PORT/quarantine/` or through a link provided in the digest e-mails. The quarantine contains the following tabs:

- **Quarantine Messages**: This shows the currently quarantined messages. You can release and add the sender to the user's safe list or delete the messages

- **Safe List**: This configures the user's safe list

- **Forward or Receive Quarantines**: As discussed earlier, it's better to forward the digest e-mails to the distribution list admin instead of sending this e-mail to all users

    - **Forward Quarantined Messages To**: This defines an e-mail address to forward the quarantined message to it

    - **Received Quarantined Messages From**: This shows the other addresses that have forwarded quarantined messages to this quarantine

 Additional details on Untangle quarantine can be found in *Chapter 6, Untangle Blockers*.

Managing the local directory of Untangle NGFW

We can connect the Untangle NGFW server to different directories of users. Thus, we can apply different policies on different users. For example, we can define which users have access to the social network websites and which users don't have that right.

The directories of users could be the Active Directory, a local directory on the Untangle NGFW server, or a local directory on Radius servers. In this section, we will learn how to manage the Untangle NGFW local directory.

The Untangle NGFW local directory can be managed under **Config | Local Directory**. The created users are used for authentication and applying different policies. They don't have administrative privileges or have access to the admin console.

To add new users to the local directory, click on the **Add** button. This will open the **Edit** window in which you will need to supply a username, first name, last name, e-mail address, password, and expiration time, as shown in the following screenshot:

Only the **User/Login ID**, **Email Address**, and **Password** fields are required.

A login ID can only have alphanumeric values. So, a login ID such as J.Doe is an invalid ID.

The password field can't be left empty. You have to enter at least one character password. Only the administrators have the right to set the user password.

In addition, an expiration date could be set for a specific user. Thus, that user would not authenticate after that date. The **Cleanup expired users** button removes the expired users from the local directory.

Upgrading Untangle

In this section, we will see how to configure Untangle NGFW to look for and install new updates. Upgrade settings are available under **Config | Upgrade**.

We have to perform all the possible upgrades before being able to download and install the different Untangle modules. We have two tabs under **Upgrade**: **Upgrades** and **Upgrade Settings**, as shown in the following screenshot:

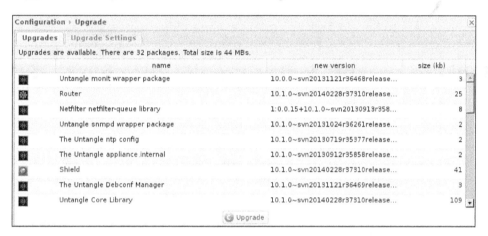

The **Upgrades** tab will only be shown if any upgrades are available to be downloaded. The upgrades will be listed as shown in the preceding screenshot. The upgrade process will download and install all the available upgrades and you cannot select to apply or reject individual updates. To start the upgrade process, press the **Upgrade** button at the bottom. The upgrade process will download the new packages and install them. During the process, do not reboot or power off the server. While the packages are being upgraded, the administration interface will lose connection to the server. The following screenshot shows the upgrade process of Untangle NGFW:

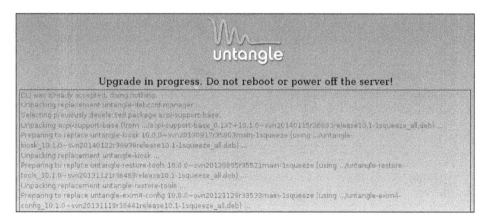

The **Upgrade Settings** tab configures when Untangle NGFW looks for and installs the new upgrades. If **Automatically Install Upgrades** is checked, Untangle will automatically look for new versions and upgrades as defined by **Automatic Upgrade Schedule**. In addition, you have the option to manually look for updates.

Backing up and restoring

In this section, we will cover how to back up and restore all Untangle NGFW configurations, and how to back up and restore individual settings.

Backing up and restoring all Untangle NGFW configurations

You can back up your Untangle NGFW configurations to be restored later in case of server failure or misconfiguration. In addition, the server backup can be restored to another server to simplify the configuration process of the other server by importing the already configured settings. Backup and restore settings are located under **Config | System**.

Backups will store the current Untangle NGFW server settings in the .backup file. The file will include the settings in **Config** and the **Applications**. It will not include the reporting data, the quarantine data, or any unique configuration such as the **unique ID (UID)** of the server.

After clicking on the **Backup to File** button located under **Config | System | Backup**, a backup will be created based on the current configuration. The .backup file can be saved to your local server or to the administration PC.

The **Restore** tab allows you to restore the Untangle configuration settings from the backup files, as shown in the following screenshot:

To restore from .backup file, we'll need to specify the desired restore options, which are as follows:

- **Restore all settings**: This is typically used to restore from failure cases as it will restore all the server configurations including the network settings

- **Restore all except keep current network settings**: This option is useful to maintain a standard configuration across the servers while each server has its unique network settings

After that, you will need to navigate to the desired `.backup` file location and select it. Then, you will need to press the **Restore from File** button to start uploading the restore file to the server and begin the restore process.

> The restore process will reset the server to same state when the backup was done. This means that if any programs have been removed after to the backup, it will be automatically installed again, and any newly installed programs will be removed.
>
> Typically, the only supported versions of the restore process will be the current version of Untangle NGFW and the immediately prior major version. For example, 10.2 will restore 10.2 backups and 10.1 backups, but not 10.0.
>
> After the beginning of the restore process, the Untangle NGFW processes will reboot and you will lose connection to the server. After reconnecting to the server, you will see the settings and configuration restored from the backup file.

Backing up and restoring individual settings

Different Untangle modules and configurations tabs include the **Import** and **Export** buttons, which allows you to back up and restore individual settings.

The following screenshot shows the **Block File Types** list of the Web Filter application. You can back up the configured list as a baseline and restore it to the same server when you need or you can restore it to another server to keep consistent configurations between your servers, as shown in the following screenshot:

File Types							
Add					Import	Export	
File Typ...⬆	Block	Flag	Category	De...	Edit	Delete	
avi	☐	☐	a video file format	.avi...	📄	✕	
bin	☐	☑	an executable file format	.bin...	📄	✕	
cab	☐	☐	an ActiveX executable file format	.ca...	📄	✕	
class	☐	☐	a Java file format	.cla...	📄	✕	
com	☑	☑	an executable file format	.co...	📄	✕	

To back up the list, click on the **Export** button that allows you to export the settings as a **JavaScript Object Notation (JSON)** file. The **Import** button is used to restore the configurations. There are three different restore options:

- Replace current settings
- Prepend to current settings
- Append to current settings

The recovery utility is used to reset the Untangle NGFW server to the factory defaults, rest the administrator credentials, perform/resume upgrades, and configure the remote support settings. The utility can be accessed from the (**Recovery Utilities**) button on the local administration console or by selecting the (**recover mode**) boot option. The following screenshot shows the recovery utility:

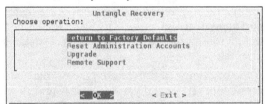

Monitoring your Untangle NGFW

Untangle provides you with many methods to monitor your server. The different methods include using **Simple Network Management Protocol (SNMP)**, syslog, and summary reports.

Using SNMP

SNMP can be used to remotely query and monitor the current state of the Untangle NGFW server. SNMP has two modes: **Get** and **Trap**. Get is when the SNMP server queries the client (that is, the Untangle server) for its state, while Trap is when the client sends an alert to the SNMP server because of a high priority event (for example, high CPU usage for 5 minutes). The SNMP settings are located under **Config | Administration | SNMP**.

To start the SNMP service, check the **Enable SNMP Monitoring** checkbox. The following table shows the different options related to SNMP:

Description	Options
Community	An SNMP community is the group to which devices and management stations running SNMP belong. The SNMP community defines where information is sent. The SNMP community acts as a password. The Untangle server will not respond to requests from a management system that does not belong to its community.
System Contact	The e-mail addresses of the system administrator that should receive SNMP messages.
System Location	This provides a description of the system's location. Simply use the default location if you don't want to specify a location.
Enable Traps	If checked, SNMP traps (events) will be sent to the configured host/port.
Host	This shows the hostname or IP address of the management system that is authorized to receive statistics from the Untangle server.
Port	The default port for SNMP traps is 162.

Syslog and summary reports

Syslog is a method that allows network devices and *nix servers to send event messages to a logging server, usually known as a syslog server. Syslog is useful to keep the events in a centralized place. In addition, Untangle NGFW provides summary reports presented as charts and graphs, which simplify the process of reviewing the server usage. Syslog and reports are covered in *Chapter 13, Untangle Administrative Services*.

Reviewing system information and license details

This section will show you how to access the system information, get the license details, and review the license agreement. These details are available under **Config | About**.

Server information

The **Server** tab shows the current information about the Untangle NGFW server. First, you will find your Untangle server's UID, which is automatically generated during the installation. The UID is a 16 alphanumeric characters code that uniquely identifies your server for licensing and tracking purposes. You should never share the UID of your server.

 Cloning your server after the installation will create two servers with identical UIDs, which will result in problems and licensing issues.

In the second field, you can find the Untangle NGFW server build and the kernel versions. The history and the number of reboots fields are used by Untangle support:

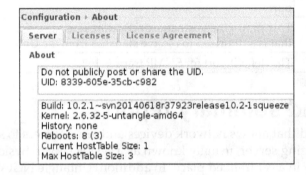

The Licenses tab

The **Licenses** tab shows the licensing state of your apps. The following information is listed for each app: the UID of the server that the app license is assigned to, the license validity period (start and end dates), and the current status of the license that is it valid or not:

Name	App	UID	Start Date	End Date	Valid	Status
HTTPS Inspector	untangle-casi...	8339-605e-35cb-c982	Thu Sep 04 2014 10...	Sun Sep 21 2014 10:...	true	Valid
Application Control	untangle-nod...	8339-605e-35cb-c982	Thu Sep 04 2014 10...	Sun Sep 21 2014 10:...	true	Valid
Spam Blocker (CT)	untangle-nod...	8339-605e-35cb-c982	Mon Sep 01 2014 10...	Thu Sep 18 2014 10:...	true	Valid
Virus Blocker (CT)	untangle-nod...	8339-605e-35cb-c982	Sun Aug 31 2014 13...	Wed Sep 17 2014 13:...	true	Valid
Web Filter	untangle-nod...	8339-605e-35cb-c982	Thu Sep 04 2014 10...	Sun Sep 21 2014 10:...	true	Valid
Web Cache	untangle-nod...	8339-605e-35cb-c982	Wed Sep 10 2014 17...	Sat Sep 27 2014 17:...	true	Valid
Configuration Ba...	untangle-nod...	8339-605e-35cb-c982	Wed Sep 10 2014 20...	Sat Sep 27 2014 20:...	true	Valid
Support	untangle-nod...	8339-605e-35cb-c982	Wed Sep 10 2014 20...	Sat Sep 27 2014 20:...	true	Valid

License agreement

Under the **License Agreement** tab, you can find the **View License** button that opens the licensing and legal information of the Untangle NGFW server and its various applications and packages.

Summary

In this chapter, we learned how to configure the different settings related to the Untangle NGFW administration and its e-mail configurations. We also learned how to create local Untangle users and how to upgrade a server. In addition, we learned how to configure system-related settings. Finally, we reviewed the system information and license details.

In the next chapter, we will begin to deal with the Untangle NGFW apps. The next chapter will cover how we can utilize Untangle NGFW apps to protect our network against different threats such as malware, spam, phishing e-mails, adware, and tracking cookies.

6

Untangle Blockers

After completing the configuration of Untangle networking and administration settings in the previous chapters, we will now start to deal with Untangle modules (also known as apps) and learn how we can utilize them to protect our network. The chapter starts by giving an overview of how to install the different apps, and explaining the applications interface (also known as the faceplate).

Thanks to its position on the network edge, Untangle NGFW can protect your network against a lot of threats before they reach the end user workstations. Among the different threats that Untangle NGFW protects against, this chapter will cover viruses, spam, phishing, tracking cookies, and invasive advertisements.

This chapter will explain how each threat works, and how the anti-threat applications work; also, the chapter will cover the anti-threat technical details, how to configure the anti-threat application, review the scan history, and common issues with the anti-threats and how to avoid them. Finally, the chapter will provide lab-based training for each anti-threat application if possible.

The list of topics that will be covered in this chapter is as follows:

- Dealing with Untangle apps
- Untangle Virus Blocker
- Untangle Spam Blocker
- Untangle Phish Blocker
- Untangle Ad Blocker

Dealing with Untangle NGFW modules

In this section, we will learn how to deal with the different Untangle NGFW modules.

You can add Untangle NGFW modules to your Rack (in other words, install the Untangle NGFW module) by clicking on the module symbol located under the **Apps** menu.

 Some applications will disappear from the **Apps** menu and won't be available for installation if the Rack contains an app that can conflict with the other app functionality. For example, when you install Spam Blocker, Spam Blocker Lite will disappear and won't be available for installation till you uninstall Spam Blocker.

The following figure shows the symbol for Virus Blocker Lite under the **Apps** menu:

Since Untangle NGFW V10.1, Untangle NGFW modules come preinstalled on the system, so that the installation time would be minimized since no download is needed. Untangle will check your license before adding the modules (only required for the paid apps), then it will enable and add the module to the default Rack, as shown in the following screenshot:

After the installation, the app will appear inside the default rack. The following figure shows the Virus Blocker app installed:

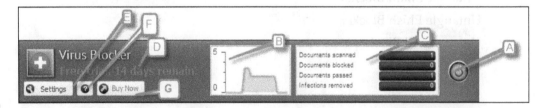

The explanation of the different components of the app faceplate is as follows:

- **A**: This button allows you to start/stop the app. The green color means that the app is running, yellow means that the app is initializing or transiting between the start and stop states, grey means that the app is turned off, while red means that the app is on but an abnormal condition has occurred (for example, the app license has expired).

- **B**: The graph provides a quick view into the activity of the app, and changes in real time as the app processes network traffic. Clicking on the graph will open the session viewer for that app (shown in the following figure):

- **C**: These are the traffic statistics. They show the traffic history since the last system boot. Clicking on the statistics will open a menu from which you can select which statistics are displayed (you can select up to four options) from a list of options:

- **D**: This is the license information. This part shows you notifications related to your license.

- **E**: This button allows you to access the app settings.

- **F**: This button provides you with help about the app by opening the app wiki page. The **Help** button is also available under the app settings.

- **G**: This button allows you to purchase the app.

You can remove the app from the Rack by clicking on the **Remove** button located under the app settings:

Protect your network from viruses

Thanks to its position at the network edge, Untangle Virus Blocker scans the incoming HTTP, FTP, and SMTP traffic to protect your network against viruses, worms, and Trojan horses before they reach the end users' PCs. Untangle offers two versions of Virus Blocker: a paid version based on the **Commtouch** engine and a free version based on Clam AV.

This section will cover how antivirus programs work, the technical details of the Untangle Virus Blocker, how to configure the Virus Blocker, how to review the Scan history, and finally, the common issues with Virus Blocker.

How the antivirus programs work

Antivirus programs have many methods to detect viruses; the most common method is signature-based detection, which is used by Untangle NGFW Virus Blocker.

Each virus has its unique signature (that is, programming code), the antivirus programs maintain a database of these signatures. The antivirus programs scan each file against this database and if any match is found between the file and the database, the file will be considered an infected file.

The following is the code of the EICAR test file developed by the **European Institute for Computer Antivirus Research (EICAR)** and **Computer Antivirus Research Organization (CARO)**, to test the response of computer antivirus programs instead of using real malware:

```
X5O!P%@AP[4\PZX54(P^)7CC)7}$EICAR-STANDARD-ANTIVIRUS-TEST-FILE!$H+H*
```

Understanding the technical details of Untangle Virus Blocker

Virus Blocker is based on the Commtouch (now CYREN) command antivirus engine, the industry-leading antivirus for Gateways, and one of the top 10 zero-hour threat detectors. Virus Blocker Lite is based on the well-respected open source Clam AV. However, some customizations were done on both the programs by the Untangle team to improve their performance and efficiency on Untangle NGFW.

Virus Blocker scans the Web, e-mails, and file transfer protocols in real time at the network edge before they reach the end user machines, which dramatically decreases the threat of being infected by malware, as most malware infections come from the Internet.

In addition, Virus Blocker can scan archives and compressed files (supporting multiple layers of compression within the compressed file) using on-the-fly decompression of these files. Virus Blocker supports many formats such as ZIP, RAR, TAR, GZIP, BZIP2, MS OLE2, MS Cabinet Files, MS CHM, and MS SZDD.

You can run both Virus Blocker and Virus Blocker Lite at the same time with no problem; the file is first scanned by virus blocker and if no infection is detected, it passes to the Virus Blocker lite for scanning. If a virus was detected by the virus blocker, then the file will not pass to Virus Blocker Lite.

Virus Blocker is automatically updated with new signatures to keep your network protected against any new threats. You can track Virus Blocker events (such as scanning, blocking, and cleaning) via the **Event logs** tabs; this requires the Reports app to be installed.

Virus Blocker only scans the attachments of the e-mail messages. If a message has no attachment, then it will not be scanned by the virus blocker. In addition, SMTP scanning works for incoming and outgoing traffic.

Virus Blocker only protects from the threats coming from the Internet, and doesn't protect against internal threat sources such as USB thumb drives, and internal network traffic between internal machines. Thus, it's necessary to use desktop antivirus programs simultaneously with Untangle Virus Blocker.

Virus Blocker settings

In this section, we will cover the different Virus Blocker settings available for the Web, e-mail, and FTP protocols.

Configuring the scanning of the web traffic

Here we can configure the scanning of files coming through HTTP traffic. Any infection founded in the HTTP traffic will be automatically removed. The following screenshot shows the web traffic scanning settings for the Virus Blocker Lite:

The different available settings are:

- **Scan HTTP**: This checkbox enables/disables the scanning of HTTP traffic.
- **Advanced Settings**: Clicking on this option shows/hides the **Edit File Extensions** and **Edit MIME Types** buttons.
- **Edit File Extensions**: This defines the file extensions to be scanned by the Virus Blocker. The list (shown in the following screenshot) includes the commonly used file extensions, and by default, the file extensions with higher probability of being infected by a threat are selected for scanning (for example, the .bin extension is selected for scanning while .avi is not selected).

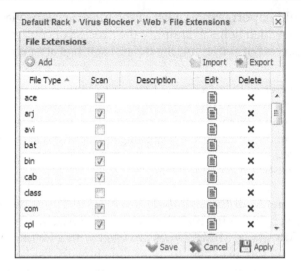

You can change the scan settings from the **Scan** checkbox located next to each file extension, or under the **Edit** menu.

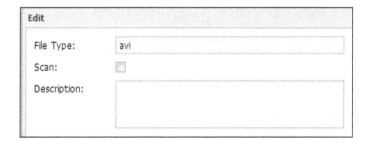

Also, you could add new file extensions via the **Add** button. For example, if you want to scan .txt files, you will need to add it as shown in the following figure:

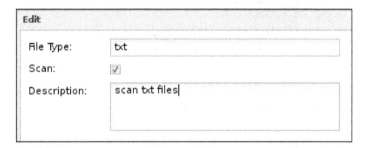

In addition, we could import/export a list of the file extensions via the **Import** and **Export** buttons, which helps to simplify the process of configuring additional Untangle NGFW servers or retrieving the default settings after changing them.

> It's preferred to use a remote browser to perform the import/export process, so that the exported json file could be saved on the administration PC.
>
> The process of importing/exporting the files list is similar to the backup and restore process covered in *Chapter 5, Advanced Administration Settings*.

Multipurpose Internet Mail Extensions Types (**MIME Types**) were originally created for e-mails sent using the SMTP protocol to allow e-mail clients to identify attachment files. Nowadays, MIME Types are used with a lot of other protocols; for example, web browsers use them to determine how to display or output files that are not in HTML format by using the proper extension/plugin (for example, flash player).

> A complete list of MIME Types can be found at http://www.freeformatter.com/mime-types-list.html.

By default, only the message/* MIME Type is listed and scanning is enabled for it. Thus, e-mail messages (.eml) encapsulated in other e-mail messages will be scanned:

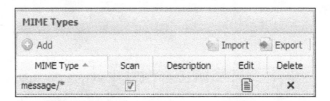

We can add additional MIME types to the list via the **Add** button, and import/export the list of MIME Types via the **Import** and **Export** buttons.

> Adding new MIME Types to be scanned will highly increase the server processing and it's not recommended to do so.

For example, if we want to scan Java scripts, we will add the application/javascript type as shown in the following figure:

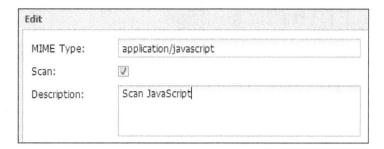

Configuring the scanning of the SMTP traffic

Here we will see how to configure the scanning of SMTP Traffic. Virus Blocker will scan the e-mail attachments for viruses and if a virus is detected, Virus Blocker can remove the infected file, or pass the whole message, or delete the whole message. The following screenshot shows the e-mail scanning settings for Virus Blocker Lite:

The available settings are:

- **Scan SMTP**: This checkbox enables/disables the scanning of SMTP traffic (message attachments).

- **Action**: This is the action that will be taken when a virus is found on a message.

    - **Pass Message**: The original message and its attachments will be delivered to the user untouched; only the subject line will have the [VIRUS] prefix.

    - **Remove Infection** (the default option): The infected files will be removed and the original massage will be delivered to the intended user. Also, the subject line will have the [VIRUS] prefix.

    - **Block**: This drops the whole message and nothing will be delivered to the intended user.

Scanning FTP traffic settings

Here we will look at how to configure the scanning of FTP traffic, as shown in the following screenshot:

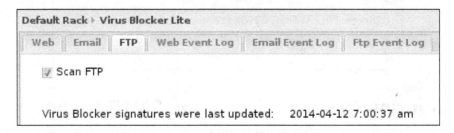

The only available setting is:

- **Scan FTP**: This checkbox enables/disables the scanning of FTP traffic.

Reviewing the scan history

Here we will cover how we can track Virus Blocker scan events. First, we could review the summary of the current sessions (since the last server boot) through the app faceplate as shown in the following figure:

The second way is through the event logs; there are three different types of event logs based on the different traffic type (that is, Web, e-mail, and FTP). The event log functionality requires the **Reports** app. The different event logs are:

- **Web Event Log**: Here we can review the scan history of the HTTP traffic. The following figure shows that Virus Blocker protected ABC-Client01 (10.0.1.15) from downloading different viruses:

The Event Log terms are described in the following table:

Name	Description
Timestamp	Time when the scan occurred
Client	The IP address of the internal machine that requested the traffic
Username	The username who initiated the traffic request, available when using the captive portal
Host	The site from where the traffic was downloaded
URI	The remaining portion of the full URL of the requested traffic
Virus Name	The name of the discovered virus, if any
Server	The IP address of the server from which the traffic was downloaded

- **Email Event Log**: Here we can review the scan history of the SMTP traffic; the following table describes the different SMTP event log terms:

Name	Description
Timestamp	Time when the scan occurred
Client	The IP address of the internal machine that the e-mail was directed to
Receiver	The recipient e-mail address
Sender	The sender e-mail address
Subject	The e-mail subject
Virus Name	The name of the discovered virus, if any
Server	The IP address of the server that sent the e-mail

- **FTP Event Log**: Here we can review the scan history of the FTP traffic; the following table describes the different FTP event log terms:

Name	Description
Timestamp	Time when the scan occurred
Client	The IP address of the internal machine that requested the traffic
Username	The username that initiated the traffic request, available when using captive portal
Filename	The FTP filename
Virus Name	The name of the discovered virus, if any
Server	The IP address of the server from which the traffic was downloaded

The third way is to review the scan history through **Reports**. By default, a daily report would be send to the administrator. In addition to that, the administrator can generate a report by navigating to **Reports | View Reports | Generate Today's Reports** and then access the report by clicking on the **View Reports** button.

The available Virus Blocker reports include:

- **Viruses Blocked**: This gives the average and the maximum viruses' blocks per hour
- **Top Viruses Detected**: This shows the top detected viruses irrespective they were blocked from e-mail, Web, or FTP traffic
- **Top Email Viruses Detected**: This shows the top detected viruses coming via e-mail
- **Top Web Viruses Detected**: This shows the top detected viruses coming through the Web
- **Top FTP Viruses Detected**: This shows the top detected viruses coming through FTP

The following figure shows the **Top Viruses Detected** chart for the Virus Blocker Lite daily report:

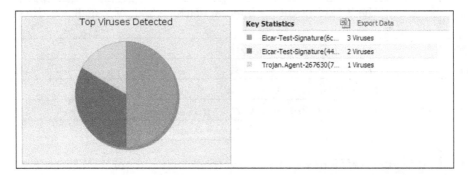

Identifying the common issues with Untangle Virus Blocker

There are some common issues that occur with Virus Blocker that you may face:

- **Windows update traffic is detected as a malware**: This is because the Windows update includes virus definition for the Windows defender. In Untangle NGFW Version 10.2, Untangle added **pass list** (shown in the following screenshot) from which you can specify destinations that you don't want scan traffic from. Microsoft Update is added to the list by default.

Pass Sites				
⊙ Add				
Site ▲	Pass	Description	Edit	Delete
*update.microsoft.com	☑		📄	✕
*windowsupdate.com	☑		📄	✕
*windowsupdate.microsoft.com	☑		📄	✕

For previous versions, you can create a **bypass rule** from the Microsoft update website to your WSUS server, or create another Untangle rack from the **policy manager** that doesn't include the virus blocker and set the traffic from Microsoft update to pass through that rack.

- **Some e-mails with large attachments may not be delivered to the SMTP server**: A timeout may occur at the SMTP server because of the delay caused by the virus blocker due to the message scan.

- **Large infected files don't display the block page, instead they would be downloaded to the destination machine but have a blocked event log status**: Large files are delivered to the client at a slower rate than the rate at which they are actually downloaded to prevent client timeout. After Untangle finishes the scanning of the complete file, it will send the rest of the file to the client immediately if the file was not infected, or it will drop the rest of the file if infection was found. Just checking the file size on the client will show that you don't have the complete file.

Lab-based training

It's the time to test the virus blocker functionality. In this lab, we will use the following machines: **Untangle-01**, **ABC-DC01**, **ABC-EX01**, **ABC-Client01**, **Untangle-03**, **Acme-DC01**, **Acme-EX01**, and **Acme-FS01**.

This part assumes that the different machines are up and running, and configured as instructed in *Chapter 2, Installing Untangle*, and *Chapter 4, Untangle Advanced Configuration*, and no modifications were done on Virus Blocker.

Testing web scanning

For the testing to be done, have a look at the following procedure:

1. On the **ABC-Client01**, browse to `http://www.eicar.org/85-0-download.html`, from where you can download the EICAR test file in many formats:

Download area using the standard protocol http			
eicar.com	eicar.com.txt	eicar_com.zip	eicarcom2.zip
68 Bytes	68 Bytes	184 Bytes	308 Bytes
Download area using the secure, SSL enabled protocol https			
eicar.com	eicar.com.txt	eicar_com.zip	eicarcom2.zip
68 Bytes	68 Bytes	184 Bytes	308 Bytes

2. Try to download the different file formats under the **HTTP part**. The block page will appear for the COM and ZIP formats, as shown in the following figure, while the TXT format can be downloaded:

3. To allow the scanning of the TXT format files, we will need to add the TXT extension by navigating to **Virus Blocker | Web | Edit File Extension | Add**. Now, when you try to download the TXT file format, it will be scanned and blocked by the Virus Blocker.

    Also, if you tried to download the files using HTTPS Connection, Untangle will not be able to recognize the files until you install the **HTTPS Inspector** application.

Testing e-mail scanning

In this test, we will try to send e-mails between `ABC.com` and `Acme.net`, attaching virus files to the messages.

> You can get virus samples from `http://virussign.com/downloads.html`.
>
> The downloadable package is password protected so Virus Blocker will not be able to scan it. However, you can extract it and use the included virus samples on the remaining portion of the lab.

1. In the first step, we will send the e-mail with the attached virus from `ABC.com` to `Acme.net`; the virus blocker on **Untangle-01** is enabled.

    The virus blocker will scan the outgoing SMTP traffic and will take the action defined in the settings part (here, we will remove the infected files and send the message to the original receiver).

    The received message subject will be a warning from Virus Blocker that an infection was found and removed, and the original message will be attached as shown in the following figure:

> The `[VIRUS]` prefix will not appear on the quick view section on OWA, you will need to open the message by double-clicking on it to see the prefix.

2. Now, we will try sending from `Acme.net` to `ABC.com`, and the virus blocker on **Untangle-03** is disabled.

    In this the case, the outgoing SMTP Traffic would not be scanned. However, the incoming traffic would be scanned by the virus blocker on **Untangle-01**.

Again, the infection would be removed and the virus blocker will send an
e-mail with the original message attached to the original recipient just like
what happened in the previous case.

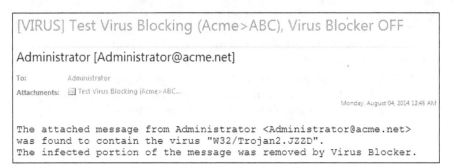

[VIRUS] Test Virus Blocking (Acme>ABC), Virus Blocker OFF

Administrator [Administrator@acme.net]

To: Administrator

Attachments: Test Virus Blocking (Acme>ABC...

Monday, August 04, 2014 12:45 AM

```
The attached message from Administrator <Administrator@acme.net>
was found to contain the virus "W32/Trojan2.JZZD".
The infected portion of the message was removed by Virus Blocker.
```

The event log would appear, as in the following figure:

Timestamp	Client	Server	Virus Name (Commtoucha...	Receiver	Sender	Subject
2014-09-...	10.0.0.10	192.168.1.10	W32/Malware!9219	administrator@acme.net	Administrator@ABC.com	Test Virus Blocking (ABC>Acme)
2014-09-...	192.168.1.5	192.168.1.2	W32/A-d7709921!Eldorado	administrator@ABC.com	Administrator@acme....	Test Virus Blocking (Acme>ABC...

Testing FTP scanning

On the **Acme-FS01**, ensure that the FTP server is running, then import the different
Eicar file formats to the FTP folder (you can also use the virus samples here). On
the **ABC-Client01**, connect to the FTP server and try to download the different
file formats.

> Through the lab scenario provided in *Chapter 2, Installing
> Untangle*, we state that WG-Client01 needs to access the FTP files
> on Acme-FS01. We used ABC-client01 here for lab simplicity.

The files will appear to be successfully downloaded, but only parts of the files are
received on **ABC-Client01**, thus the files would be corrupted and wouldn't run,
and if you tried to open the `Eicar.txt` file, you would find the following code:

```
X5O!P%@AP[4\PZX54(P^)7CC)7}$EICAR-STANDARD-ANTIVIRUS-T
```

This is instead of the original code, as follows:

```
X5O!P%@AP[4\PZX54(P^)7CC)7}$EICAR-STANDARD-ANTIVIRUS-TEST-FILE!$H+H*
```

The event log would be as shown in the following figure:

Timesta...	Client	Userna...	File Name	Virus Name	Server
2014-09...	10.0.0.10		virussign.com_0...	W32/Sality.AD	192.168.1.5
2014-09...	10.0.0.10		virussign.com_0...	W32/Alman.C	192.168.1.5
2014-09...	10.0.0.10		virussign.com_0...	W32/Alman.C	192.168.1.5
2014-09...	10.0.0.10		virussign.com_0...	W32/Malware!9219	192.168.1.5
2014-09...	10.0.0.10		virussign.com_0...	W32/HupigonP.GE	192.168.1.5
2014-09...	10.0.0.10		/Eicar/eicar.com	EICAR_Test_File	192.168.1.5
2014-09...	10.0.0.10		virussign.com_0...	W32/Xorer.S	192.168.1.5

Spam!!...It's something from the past

Spam consists of identical messages that are sent to numerous recipients by e-mail (that is unsolicited bulk e-mail). Spam e-mails may contain commercial advertisements or links to dangerous sites (that is phishing sites, or sites that include malware).

How anti-spam programs work

Anti-spam programs run many tests against the message, and each test will have a score based on the message criteria. The overall score determines if the message is a spam message or not. The different tests include:

- **DNS Black Listing (DNSBL)**: This contains bad-behavior IPs that were automatically collected using spam detection tools or manually reported. A famous example of a blacklist provider is **Spamhaus**.

- **Heuristic/Signature-based content filtering**: This checks for certain known phrases, patterns, and so on; for example, if the message contains **dear client**, instead of the user's real name, or if the message was sent with a high priority.

- **Reputation control**: This is the same as heuristic control filtering but based on analysis algorithms not signature databases.

- **Collaborative content filtering**: This is based on user feedback; for example, when many Hotmail users define a message from the same sender as spam, Hotmail will automatically consider all messages from this sender as spam.

- **Sender Policy Framework (SPF)**: To accept messages from the sender, they must have a valid SPF record to prevent sender address forgery.

- **MX callbacks**: This verifies the message senders with their MX sever.

- **White listing**: This is a local list; all e-mails listed here will automatically be accepted and no other filter can stop it.

Understanding the technical details of Untangle Spam Blocker

Untangle Spam Blocker is based on the **Apache SpamAssassin** project. However, the paid version integrates the Commtouch Anti-spam to improve detection accuracy. Spam Blocker doesn't require you to change your MX record, it will transparently scan the SMTP traffic on its way to the e-mail server.

Unlike Virus Blocker, Spam Blocker, and Spam Blocker Lite can't run simultaneously. In addition, it's a bad practice to use Untangle Spam Blocker after third-party anti-spam solutions (for example, a cloud-based anti-spam solution), as all the e-mails (legitimate, and spam) will be coming from one source, which will make Untangle NGFW consider that source as a specious sender.

From time to time, your inbox may get flooded with spam e-mails, as spammers always change their techniques, and it takes anti-spam solutions some time to understand those techniques and start to release measures against them.

Though the spam blocker pre-configured settings are sufficient for most organizations, you can change these settings at any time if the spam blocker performance isn't enough for you.

Spam Blocker settings

In this section, we will cover the different Spam Blocker settings. The following settings apply on both Spam Blocker and Spam Blocker Lite:

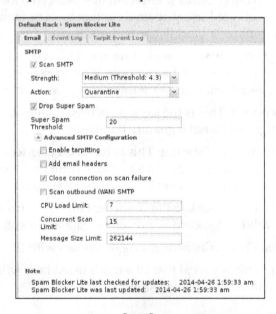

- **Scan SMTP**: This checkbox enables/disables the scanning of the SMTP traffic.
- **Strength**: As discussed earlier, each message will have an overall spam score. Here, we could set the score threshold that when met (message score is equal to or higher than this threshold), the message will be considered as spam and the action listed in the **Action** field will be taken. There are six possible values:
  - **Extreme (Threshold 3.0)**: Any message with at least a score of 3.0 will be considered as spam
  - **Very High (Threshold 3.3)**: Any message with at least a score of 3.3 will be considered as spam
  - **High (Threshold 3.5)**: Any message with at least a score of 3.5 will be considered as spam
  - **Medium (Threshold 4.3)**: This is the default value; any message with at least a score of 4.3 will be considered as spam
  - **Low (Threshold 5.0)**: Any message with at least a score of 5.0 will be considered as spam
  - **Custom**: Here you can enter a custom score

  The lower the selected score, the more chance that legitimate e-mails could be considered spam (known as false positive), and the higher the score, the more chance that true spam e-mails with lower scores could pass (known as false negative).

- **Action**: This covers the action taken on a message if its spam score was high enough; there are four different actions:
  - **Mark**: The message will be delivered to the intended user, but its subject line will have the [Spam] prefix
  - **Pass**: The message will be delivered to the intended user with no modifications
  - **Drop**: Untangle will inform the sending server that the message has been delivered, but it will not deliver the message to the intended user
  - **Quarantine**: Untangle will send the message to the users' e-mail quarantine, thus they can release or delete it

- **Drop Super Spam**: If checked, any e-mails with a spam score higher than the **super spam score** will be dropped; this could be useful if you set the previous action to not drop e-mails. With super spam, you can be sure that the dropped message is definitely spam.

- **Super Spam Score**: This is the score that e-mails must reach to be considered as super spam; the default value is 20.

- **Advanced SMTP Configuration**: Clicking on this option shows/hides the advanced spam blocker configurations.

- **Enable tarpitting**: This option enables Tarpit. When enabled, Spam Blocker will check the sender IP against the DNSBL at every SMTP session initiation. If the IP is found on the DNSBL, the session will be rejected before the remote server can send the message. This helps to reduce the Untangle utilization and save the bandwidth, but could increase the false positives as the sender IP could be temporarily listed on the DNSBL. Note that you had taken your decision based on only one test. It's better to leave it unchecked.

- **Add email headers**: When enabled, Untangle will add the (message spam score and the tests used to get that score) information to the message header.

- **Close connection on scan failure**: If enabled, when the spam test fails, the connection will be closed, thus the sending message will be retested and the scan will be reapplied on it. If disabled, when the spam test fails, the connection will remain active, thus the message will be delivered to the user without proper scanning.

- **Scan outbound (WAN) SMTP**: If enabled, the outgoing SMTP traffic will be scanned. This is an unnecessary option, and it's better to close port 25 for all clients on your network expect to the e-mail server.

- **CPU Load Limit**: The default value is 7. If your CPU utilization exceeded this value, all incoming connections will be rejected by Untangle to prevent more resource utilization, which may led to a server outage.

- **Concurrent Scan Limit**: This limits the maximum number of e-mails that can be scanned at the same time; the default value is 15. If you are receiving a large number of e-mails, you should consider increasing this number, which will increase the CPU utilization. So, it's better to increase it in small amounts until you get the best value that compromises on performance and message volume.

- **Message Size Limit**: This is the maximum size of the messages to be scanned by spam blocker. Messages larger than this size will not be scanned by the spam blocker, as most of the spam messages are small in size, and most of the legitimate messages are larger than the default value listed (256 KB). This option is only related to the spam blocker and does not affect the size of the message delivered to your e-mail server.

 This skip behavior because the message size is only related to Spam Blocker, Virus Blocker will still scan the messages for any viruses.

Reviewing the scan history

As is the case with the other apps, you can review the scanning history from the app faceplate, through the event log, or from the Reports app. There are two different event log types: the spam blocker event log and trapit event log.

The spam blocker event log

The following table describes the spam blocker event log terms:

Name	Description
Timestamp	Time when the scan occurred
Receiver	The recipient e-mail address
Sender	The sender e-mail address
Subject	The e-mail subject
Action	The action taken on the e-mail
Spam Score	The spam score given to the message
Client	The IP address of the internal machine that e-mail was directed to
Server	The IP address of the server that sent the e-mail

The tarpit event log

The following table describes the spam blocker trapit event log terms:

Name	Description
Timestamp	The time when the trapit event took place
Action	The action taken on the e-mail
Sender	The sender e-mail address — for spam, this is often blank
DNSBL server	The DNSBL server that identified the sender server as a spammer

Reports

There are different reports available for Spam Blocker:

- **Total Email**: This shows the total number of messages that were received on a single day and how many are spam and how many are clean

- **Spam Rate**: This gives the maximum and average number of e-mail messages (total/clean/spam) per hour

- **Top Ten Spammed**: This gives the top ten e-mails that received spam emails

The following figure shows the **Total Email** report:

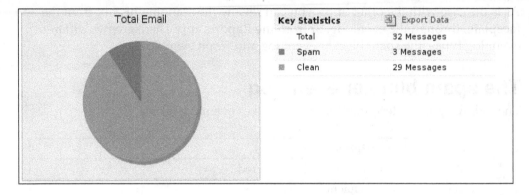

Common issues with Spam Blocker

Spam blocker does not block definite spam—this may be due to a DNS problem, you are probably using public DNS service providers such as Open DNS and Google DNS, or it may be that your ISP DNS service doesn't support DNSBL. The free service of DNSBL websites supports limited spam queries per day (100,000 queries per day for all the queries coming from certain the DNS server), which would be reached very quickly with public DNS service providers.

Lab-based training

Again, we are here to prove Untangle NGFW functionality, this time, we will cover Spam Blocker. In this lab, we will use the following machines:

- **Untangle-01**
- **ABC-DC01**
- **ABC-EX01**
- **Untangle-03**
- Acme-DC01
- Acme-EX01

This part assumes that the different machines are up and running, and configured as instructed in *Chapter 2, Installing Untangle,* and *Chapter 4, Untangle Advanced Configuration,* and no modifications were done on Spam Blocker.

Testing the blocking of incoming spam

In this test, we will send an e-mail from `Acme.net` to `ABC.com` and will include the following code in the message subject:

```
XJS*C4JDBQADN1.NSBN3*2IDNEN*GTUBE-STANDARD-ANTI-UBE-TEST-
EMAIL*C.34X
```

The preceding code is known as **Generic Test for Unsolicited Bulk Email (GTUBE)**, which could be used to test anti-spam programs, as the case of the Eicar file for antivirus programs. The preceding code will make the message score a spam score of 1000 on SpamAssassin.

In addition to the GTUBE test, you could use spam messages coming to your real e-mail for the testing. Also, you could create a new message with the following subjects, which will score 5.3 on the spam score:

- `http://www.gewgul.com/index.html`
- `http://yah0o.com/login.shtml`
- `http://payments.g00gle.com/`
- `https://chaseonline.chase.com/`
- `http://www.xn--paypl-7ve.com/`
- `http://www.itisatrap.org/firefox/its-a-trap.html`

The following figure shows the event log for the Untangle-01 Spam Blocker, which protected ABC Bank from spam messages. The e-mails are coming from Untangle-03 (192.168.1.5) and are destined to ABC-EX01 (10.0.0.10).

Timestamp ▾	Client	Server	Receiver	Sender	Subject	Action (Commtouchas)	Spam sco.
2014-09-04 ...	192.168.1.5	10.0.0.10	administrator @abc.com	Administrator @acme.net	GTUBE Test	drop message	1010
2014-09-04 ...	192.168.1.5	10.0.0.10	lesley.smith@abc.com	Administrator @acme.net	BUSINESS OPPORTU...	quarantine message	6.8
2014-09-04 ...	192.168.1.5	10.0.0.10	chris.white@abc.com	Administrator @acme.net	One million Dollar Don...	quarantine message	6.4
2014-09-04 ...	192.168.1.5	10.0.0.10	Alan.Reid@abc.com	Administrator @acme.net	STOP DEALING WITH...	quarantine message	17.9
2014-09-03 ...	192.168.1.5	10.0.0.10	administrator @ABC.com	Administrator @acme.net	Test Virus Blocking (A...	pass oversize message	0
2014-09-03 ...	10.0.0.10	192.168....	administrator @acme.net	Administrator @ABC.com	Test Virus Blocking (A...	pass outbound messa...	0

As shown in the preceding figure, the GTUBE message scored 1010, which is way higher than the super spam score, so the message will automatically be dropped on **Untangle-01**. Other messages were quarantined depending on their score, not scanned because outgoing e-mails are not configured to be scanned, and other messages were not scanned because of their size.

This skip behavior because the message size is only related to Spam Blocker, Virus Blocker will still scan the messages for any viruses.

Testing the blocking of outgoing spam

The spam message wasn't blocked by the spam blocker on Untangle-03 because by default, Untangle Spam Blocker doesn't scan the outgoing SMTP traffic. We can modify this by selecting the **Scan outbound (WAN) SMTP** option located under the Spam Blocker settings. Thus, the messages would be blocked on Untangle-03, and the event log will be as shown in the following figure:

Timestamp	Client	Server	Receiver	Sender	Subject	Action (Spamassassin)	Spam sco...
2014-09...	172.16.1.10	192.168.1.2	administrator@abc.com	Administrator@acme.net	GTUBE Test AFTE...	drop message	1000
2014-09...	172.16.1.10	192.168.1.2	administrator@abc.com	Administrator@acme.net	GTUBE Test	pass outbound messa...	0

Testing the marking of spam message functionality

Now, we will uncheck the **Drop Super Spam** checkbox on Untangle-03, change the action to **Mark**, and then try to send the message again. The message will be delivered to the original recipient with **[Spam]** added to the message header, as shown in the following figure:

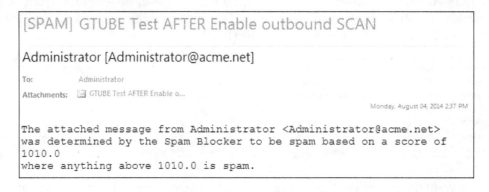

The event log will be as shown in the following figure:

Timestamp	Client	Server	Receiver	Sender	Subject	Action (Commtouchas)	Spam sco...
2014-09...	172.16.1.10	192.168.1.2	administrator@abc.com	Administrator@acme.net	GTUBE Test AFTER E...	mark message	1010
2014-09...	172.16.1.10	192.168.1.2	administrator@abc.com	Administrator@acme.net	GTUBE Test AFTER E...	pass outbound messa...	0

Testing the quarantine functionality

The quarantined messages are not delivered to the intended mailbox, and are instead stored on the user quarantine. This is done so that the user can review them and release or delete what they want.

Accessing the quarantine

By default, a daily quarantine digest would be sent to the user when their quarantine has specious messages as shown in the following figure:

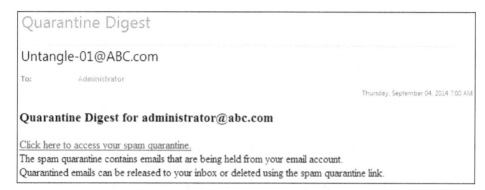

In addition, the user can manually request the quarantine digest anytime by visiting `https://UntangleIP:administration_port/quarantine`.

For Untangle-01, the URL would be `https://192.168.1.3:444/quarantine/`, as we changed the administration port before to 444. If the default port (port 433) is used, you don't need to add the port number to the URL.

The following figure shows that the ABC bank administrator requires Quarantine Digest for their e-mail. By clicking on the **Request** button, the Quarantine Digest message would be sent to the user's mailbox:

By clicking on the link provided in the Quarantine Digest message, the user would access their quarantine, where they can manage the quarantined messages as shown in the following figure:

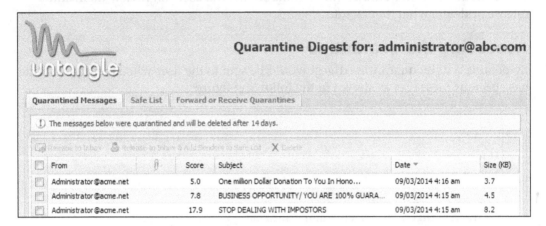

Administrative management of users' quarantines

In addition, the Untangle administrator can manage the user quarantines under **Config | Email | Quarantine | User Quarantines**, where the user can release or purge the whole user quarantine. The following figure shows four users' quarantines:

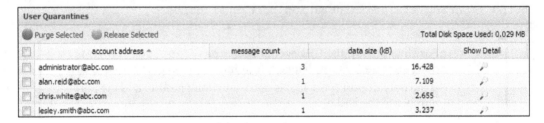

By clicking on **Show Detail**, the Untangle administrator can view the user quarantine details, and can control individual messages:

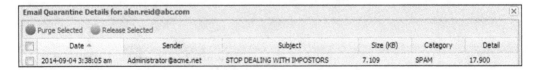

No more phishing

Phishing is the act of attempting to acquire sensitive information such as usernames, passwords, and credit card details by pretending to be a trustworthy entity in electronic communication. For example, you could receive an e-mail (apparently from PayPal) that asks you for your password, or asks you to log in to your account to modify some settings through a malicious URL provided in the e-mail, which redirects to a hacker website (looking like the original site) so that they can steal your credentials. Phish Blocker protects against these fraud e-mails.

Technical details of Untangle Phish Blocker

Untangle Phish Blocker leverages Google's Safe Browsing API, which helps you to protect yourself from dangerous websites. Google maintains a list of dangerous websites; in addition to that, Google analyzes website content and initiates warnings if the website seems dangerous. If the e-mail message contains a URL of one of these dangerous websites, it will be considered a phishing e-mail.

Phish Blocker settings

Here we can enable or disable the scanning of SMTP traffic by the phish blocker. We can also set the action that the phish blocker will take if phishing is found, as illustrated in the following screenshot:

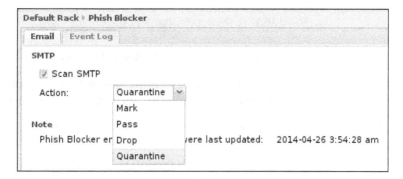

- **Scan SMTP**: This checkbox enables/disables the scanning of SMTP traffic.
- **Action**: The action that will be taken when a message defined as a phishing e-mail. This action can be one of the following possibilities:
  - **Mark**: The message will be delivered to the intended user, but its subject line will have the [Phish] prefix

    °   **Pass**: The message will be delivered to the intended user with no modifications

    °   **Drop**: Untangle will inform the sending server that the message has been delivered, but it will not deliver the message to the intended user

    °   **Quarantine**: Untangle will send the message to the user's e-mail quarantine and thus they can release or delete it

Reviewing the scan history

As is the case in the other apps, you can review the scanning history from the app faceplate, or through the event log, or from the Reports app. The following table describes the event log terms:

Name	Description
Timestamp	Time when the scan occurred
Receiver	The recipient e-mail address
Sender	The sender e-mail address; for spam, it will often be blank
Subject	The e-mail subject
Action	The action taken on the e-mail
Client	The IP address of the internal machine that the e-mail was directed to
Server	The IP address of the server that sent the e-mail

The different available reports available for Phish Blocker include:

- **Total Email**: This shows the total number of messages that were received on a single day and how many are phishing threats and how many are clean
- **Daily Phish Rate**: This gives the maximum and average number of e-mail messages (total/clean/phish) per hour
- **Top Ten Phishing Victims**: These give the top ten e-mails that received phishing e-mails

Utilizing Untangle Ad Blocker

How many times have you been working on important things and been interrupted by a pop-up advertisement? How many times have you been searching for information and got lost because of the number of advertisements that the web page contains?

Have you heard about the possibility of advertisement to download malwares to your computer without even running it? (More info at `http://www.tomsguide.com/us/malware-infested-ads,news-19408.html`.)

How many times you have searched for something, and found that every website you visit after that search will contain advertisements related to that search? Privacy issues, right?

What if I told you that your input into website order forms, registration pages, payment pages, and other online forms are stored on your device on cookies and there is malware specialized in stealing those cookies? (A good read for you to start with is available at `http://www.pcworld.com/article/2046968/attackers-use-ramnit-malware-to-target-steam-users.html`.)

Worried?! No need to worry with Untangle Ad Blocker, which is used to prohibit the invasive advertisements, prevent tracking cookies, and to prevent malware and scam links that come through ads.

 Interested in cookies, advertisements, and privacy? Additional reads for you are available at `http://www.allaboutcookies.org/privacy-concerns` and `http://computer.howstuffworks.com/cookie.htm`.

How it works

Ad Blocker is based on AdBlocker Plus. It simply downloads lists of known ad websites and ad extensions and blocks them whenever a user requests them.

Unlike browser plugins, Untangle Ad Blocker works on the network gateway level so it's not possible for individual users to know that a certain ad has been blocked nor can they choose to unblock a specific ad. This can interfere with the proper functionality of some webpages. Unblocking these functionalities could be high administrative overhead, especially in large companies. So, the default of the Untangle Ad Blocker is to be off.

Understanding the settings of Untangle Ad Blocker

This section covers the different settings of the Untangle Ad Blocker.

Status

The **Status** shows the total available ad filters, and how many filters are enabled. It also shows the total available cookies stopping rules and how many are enabled. In addition, here you can enable/disable the blocking of ads and tracking through the relevant checkboxes:

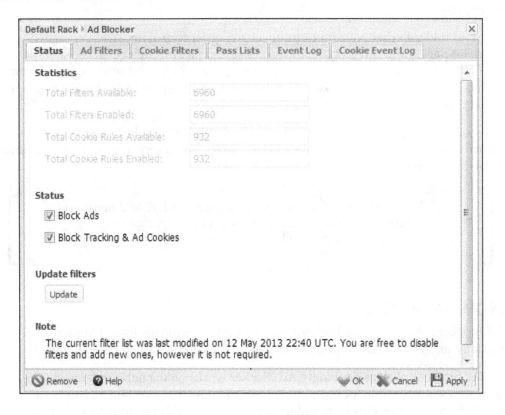

The last update to the filters is shown at the bottom of the page. You can manually update the filters using the **Update** button. After the update, the total number of available ad filters will be changed as shown in the following figure:

Ad Filters

Ad Filters prevent advertisements from appearing in browsers. We have two lists: **Standard Filters** and **User Defined Filters**.

Standard Filters are provided by Untangle NGFW. This list cannot be modified; however, you can enable or disable a certain filter.

In **User Defined Filters**, the user can add custom rules to block ads. The custom rules should be compatible with the AdBlocker Plus rules (the quick start guide is available at https://adblockplus.org/en/filters):

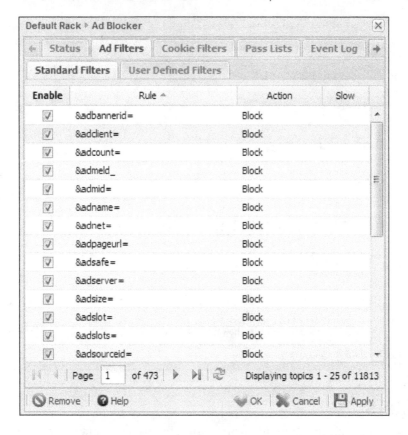

An example of the rules is the first one listed in the preceding figure: **&adbannerid=**. Banners are a form of advertisement located on web pages. Each banner (advertisement) has a different ID; websites can include that definer (**&adbannerid=**) to request the banner. Whenever Ad Blocker sees that definer on the URL, it will block that definer.

Cookie filters

Cookie filters stop certain websites from storing cookies on your computer to prevent these sites from tracking you. As is the case with the ad filter, we have two lists under the **Cookie Filters**: one is the default provided by Untangle, and the other is the user-defined list.

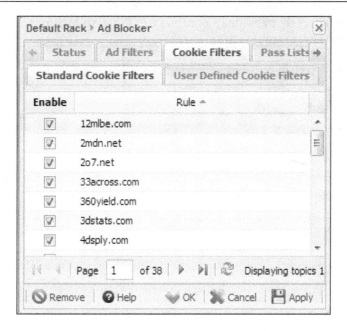

Pass Lists

Here, we can configure the Ad Blocker bypassing settings; **Edit Passed Sites** can be used to allow ads and cookies from certain domains, even if they were blocked by other rules. The **Edit Passed Client IPs** option (shown in the following figure) could be used to prevent Ad Blocker from blocking ads and cookies directed to a certain client.

Reviewing the scan history

As is the case with each application, we could review the scan history from the application faceplate or from the event logs, or from the Reports app.

The application faceplate provides a summary of the scan history since the last restart, and provide a graph for the current traffic:

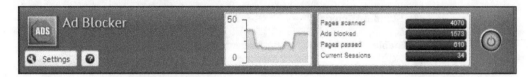

The event logs provide more detailed information about the scanning. Untangle Ad Blocker has two event logs; one is related to the ads and the other is related to the cookies. The following figure shows the ad filters event logs:

Timestamp	Client	Host	Uri	Server	Action (Ad Blocker)
2014-05-25 ...	10.0.1.15	adserver.adtech.de	/addyn/3.0/974/3952683...	195.93.85.9	block
2014-05-25 ...	10.0.1.15	microsoft-office.en....	/ad/df37639bd7f06c9285...	46.28.209.13	block
2014-05-25 ...	10.0.1.15	pagead2.googlesyn...	/pagead/show_ads.js	173.194.35.122	block
2014-05-25 ...	10.0.1.15	googleads.g.double...	/pagead/viewthroughcon...	173.194.35.109	block
2014-05-25 ...	10.0.1.15	googleads.g.double...	/pagead/viewthroughcon...	173.194.35.109	block
2014-05-25 ...	10.0.1.15	pubads.g.doubleclic...	/gampad/ads?gdfp_req=...	173.194.35.109	block
2014-05-25 ...	10.0.1.15	pagead2.googlesyn...	/pagead/show_ads.js	173.194.35.121	block

The following figure shows the cookies filter event log:

Timestamp	Client	Username	Host	Uri	Server	Cookie
2014-05-2...	10.0.1.15		www9.effectivemeas...	/v4/em_js?flag=0&v=&vt=6e0611cef7...	98.124.156.54	.effectivemeasu...
2014-05-2...	10.0.1.15		148927072.log.optimi...	/event?a=148927072&d=148927072&...	50.19.90.2	.148927072.log...
2014-05-2...	10.0.1.15		b.scorecardresearch....	/b?c1=2&c2=30000018rn=0.34447357...	213.158.175.112	.scorecardresea...
2014-05-2...	10.0.1.15		s4.histats.com	/stats/e.php?2057496&@Ab&@R53756...	208.43.241.179	.histats.com
2014-05-2...	10.0.1.15		s4.histats.com	/stats/2057496.php?2057496&@f16&...	208.43.241.179	.histats.com
2014-05-2...	10.0.1.15		b.scorecardresearch....	/b?c1=2&c2=15548145&ns__t=140101...	213.158.175.112	.scorecardresea...
2014-05-2...	10.0.1.15		148927072.log.optimi...	/event?a=148927072&d=148927072&...	54.225.114.159	.148927072.log...

Also, the reports provide a daily summary of the scan history. The available Ad Blocker summary reports are:

- **Blocked Ads**: This gives the maximum and the average ad blocks/logs per hour
- **Blocked Cookies**: This gives the maximum and the average number of cookie blocks per hour
- **Top Blocked Ad Sites**: This shows the top blocked ad sites
- **Top ten blocked cookies**: This shows the top ten blocked cookies

The following figure shows the blocked ads report:

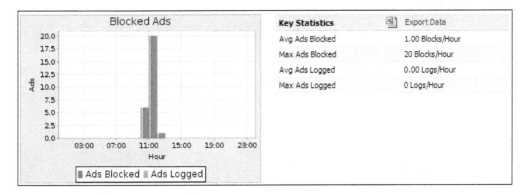

Lab-based training

In this lab, you are free to surf any website from any machine behind Untangle NGFW. We will only compare the resultant page before enabling the ad blocker and after enabling it.

A simple example is shown here for a page that contains ads from `doubleclick.net`; the page before enabling the ad blocker is as follows:

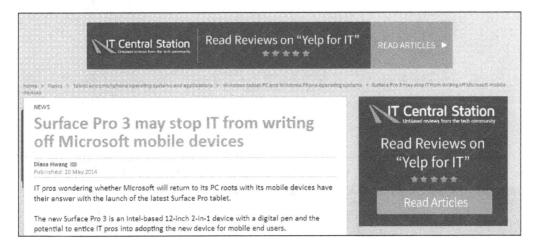

The same page after enabling the ad blocker will look as shown in the following figure:

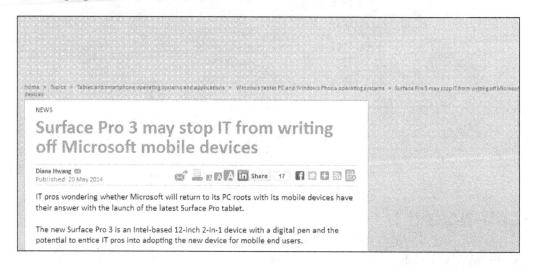

We can allow ads from the previous website by adding it to the **Passed Sites** list as shown in the following figure:

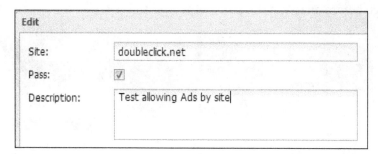

In addition, we could prevent scanning traffic directed to certain IPs via Ad Blocker by setting the **Passes Clients IPs** rule. For example, the following figure shows a pass rule for the IP of one of the ABC Bank IT team PCs:

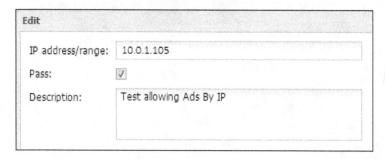

Summary

In this chapter, we have covered how to configure and use the different Untangle Blockers (Virus Blocker, Spam Blocker, Phish Blocker, and Ad Blocker) to protect your network. Each application was covered in full detail starting from how it works, how to configure it and review the scan history, and if it has any common issues and how to solve them.

In the next chapter, we will cover how to protect against Denial of Service attacks using the Untangle shield, protecting our network from malicious traffic using Untangle Intrusion prevention, and limiting access from the Internet to your internal resources using the Untangle Firewall application.

7
Preventing External Attacks

DoS attacks are increasing at an alarming rate. They are really dangerous and can affect your **Service Level Agreement** (**SLA**) and your reputation. In this chapter, we will learn how to be protected from DoS attacks using the Untangle Shield. Attackers can gain access to your network and steal critical data by exploiting known applications or operating system vulnerabilities. Intrusion Detection and Prevention Systems are used to protect against these attacks. In this chapter, we'll learn how to manage Untangle's Intrusion Prevention module. We'll also learn how to limit access from the Internet to your internal resources using Untangle's Firewall application.

In this chapter, we'll cover the following topics:

- The Shield
- Untangle's Intrusion Prevention application
- Untangle's Firewall application

Protecting against DoS attacks

DoS attacks are done by initiating as many sessions as possible on the victim server as an attempt to make this server unresponsive or unavailable. Untangle Shield (previously known as Attack Blocker) is used to protect Untangle NGFW and the network against DoS attacks.

Managing the shield

The Shield (located under **Config | System | Shield**) monitors the clients' session creation rate. Every time a client initiates a session, the Shield will calculate the session creation rate of that client. If this rate is considered to be too high, the Shield will refuse any additional sessions from that client.

The Shield is enabled by default and should not be disabled unless for troubleshooting.

The Shield runs during session initialization, and it only monitors the session creation rate. The Shield is not able to see or scan the session traffic.

The default session creation rate limit is one user (which is a reasonable number of sessions that can be created by a single network device). We can override this default limit via **Shield Rules**.

For example, if clients are connected to Untangle via a router that performs NATing, all the traffic directed from these clients to Untangle will appear to come from the router. So, we will have to create a Shield rule that allows a much higher session creation rate for the router IP. We can select a higher number of users (5, 25, 50, 100, or unlimited).

So, for our case, if we have 100 devices behind that router, we will create a rule that will make Untangle NGFW increase the session creation rate from the router IP by 100 times the normal rate.

To add a rule, press the **Add** button; then, set the rule condition by setting the source address to our router's IP address and the user count to 100 users, as shown in the following screenshot:

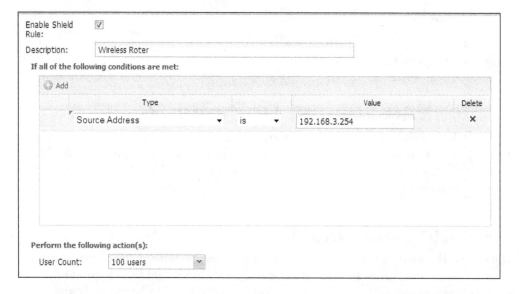

Reviewing the shield events

You can review the scanned/blocked sessions via **Event Log**. This requires the Reports app to be installed:

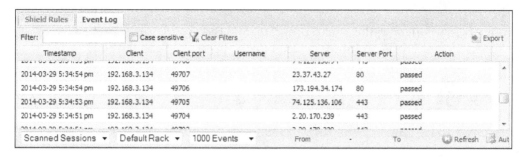

In addition, the Reports app provides a summary of the Shield events, as follows:

- **Sessions**: This gives the average and the maximum number of sessions scanned by the Shield in an hour of a certain day

- **Top ten shield-blocked hosts (by hits)**: This shows the top ten hosts that the Shield dropped sessions from

- **Top ten shield-blocked users (by hits)**: This shows the top ten users that the Shield dropped sessions from

The following figure shows the sessions report:

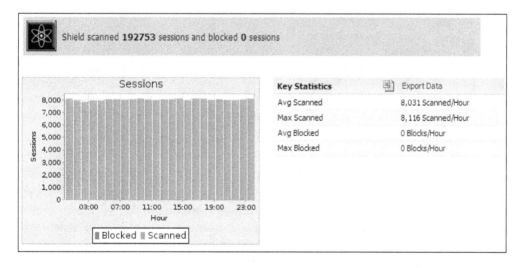

Lab-based training

In this lab, we will initiate a port scan against ABC-Web01 from the external laptop using Nmap (the port scan in itself is not a DoS attack, but it's a simple way to explain the Shield functionality).

From ABC-Web01, start the Nmap program, and then configure **Target** to **192.168.1.15** and **Profile** to **Intense scan**. Finally, press the **Scan** button:

Nmap will start to scan the open ports on ABC-Web01 by initiating a session to every port on ABC-Web01. The Shield will recognize the high session-creation rate and will block them, as shown in the following screenshot:

Timestamp	Client	Client port	Username	Server	Server Port	Action
2014-09-05 12:08:24 pm	192.168.1.7	34237		192.168.1.15	3814	blocked
2014-09-05 12:08:24 pm	192.168.1.7	34236		192.168.1.15	3851	blocked
2014-09-05 12:08:24 pm	192.168.1.7	34236		192.168.1.15	1755	passed
2014-09-05 12:08:24 pm	192.168.1.7	34236		192.168.1.15	2323	blocked
2014-09-05 12:08:24 pm	192.168.1.7	34236		192.168.1.15	5907	blocked
2014-09-05 12:08:24 pm	192.168.1.7	34236		192.168.1.15	2191	blocked
2014-09-05 12:08:24 pm	192.168.1.7	34236		192.168.1.15	3871	blocked
2014-09-05 12:08:24 pm	192.168.1.7	34236		192.168.1.15	5432	blocked
2014-09-05 12:08:24 pm	192.168.1.7	34236		192.168.1.15	1065	blocked
2014-09-05 12:08:24 pm	192.168.1.7	34236		192.168.1.15	49154	blocked
2014-09-05 12:08:24 pm	192.168.1.7	34236		192.168.1.15	3546	blocked
2014-09-05 12:08:24 pm	192.168.1.7	34236		192.168.1.15	1108	blocked
2014-09-05 12:08:24 pm	192.168.1.7	34236		192.168.1.15	1137	blocked
2014-09-05 12:08:24 pm	192.168.1.7	34236		192.168.1.15	49176	blocked
2014-09-05 12:08:24 pm	192.168.1.7	34236		192.168.1.15	41511	blocked
2014-09-05 12:08:24 pm	192.168.1.7	34236		192.168.1.15	9502	blocked
2014-09-05 12:08:24 pm	192.168.1.7	34236		192.168.1.15	3300	blocked
2014-09-05 12:08:24 pm	192.168.1.7	34236		192.168.1.15	1106	passed
2014-09-05 12:08:24 pm	192.168.1.7	34236		192.168.1.15	1972	passed

The Nmap log will show a similar result, which says that the delay between each created session will increase because from the 66 sessions initiated previously, 27 sessions were dropped, as shown in the following screenshot:

```
Increasing send delay for 192.168.1.15 from 0 to 5
due to 27 out of 66 dropped probes since last
increase.
```

Intrusion prevention using Untangle NGFW

Now, you have either opened ports on your firewall for your servers (for example, a web server and/or an e-mail server) to be accessed from outside, or you have internal users who access external sites and have returned traffic.

The traffic coming back to your network can be legitimate or malicious. An **Intrusion Prevention System** (**IPS**) scans the incoming traffic to detect, log, and block any malicious activities.

How intrusion prevention systems work

When we talk about IPS, it is unquestionable that we will also talk about the **Intrusion Detection System** (**IDS**). IPS and IDS are connected technologies. In fact, IPS has the IDS functionalities in addition to the ability to block malicious traffic. In the next section, we will cover the difference between IPS and IDS, how IPS/IDS can identify malicious traffic, and some countermeasures to take when an attack is detected.

IDS versus IPS

The IPS is an inline sensor (traffic must go through it) that lies between the router and your network devices. It scans the traffic before reaching the intended destination and can block it if any malicious traffic is detected. However, because the traffic is scanned by the IPS before it is delivered to the intended device, a small latency will be added, and if only one IPS device is used, it can be a single point of failure if it goes down.

The IDS is not an inline sensor as is the case with the IPS. Instead, we configure switches to forward packets to the IDS for scanning (the promiscuous mode). Thus, it will not be able to directly stop any attack. However, it can be configured to send commands to the router and the firewall to block the traffic's source address.

The following table summarizes the differences between IPS and IDS:

	IPS	IDS
Position in the network	In line with the traffic. The IPS sees it first hand.	Off to the side. The IDS gets a copy of packets.
Latency/delay	Yes, a small delay.	No latency for the traffic.
Can cause DoS attacks	Yes, it is in line.	No, not in line.
Can prevent an attack	Yes, can drop offending traffic.	Not directly.

Identification methods

There are many different methods that can be used to detect malicious activities. These methods are as follows:

- **Signature based**: This is the most used method. The IPS has a signature database that includes thousands of known attack patterns. A signature describes how an attack looks like; for example, a ping sweep attack is when one single IP address is sending multiple ICMP echo requests to a range of other devices. Another signature example is the port scan, which is done when one device sends a TCP SYN request to multiple ports on other devices in a period of 30 seconds.

- **Policy based**: Let's say we want to prevent the usage of Telnet inside our network because it uses clear text. We will create a rule that blocks any TCP traffic directed to port 23.

- **Anomaly based**: This method compares the current network traffic's state to the normal network traffic's state (baseline). For example, if the normal half-formed sessions (when a device sends a TCP SYN request to another device but doesn't receive SYN ACK) in your network are 20 sessions/min, the IPS will consider an attack is happening when the number of these sessions increases to 100 sessions/min.

- **Reputation based**: Some countries are known to launch large cyber-attacks on certain other countries and companies. The IPS is connected to global databases that track these attacks. If any attack is initiated against your country, the IPS will start to protect you against the potential attack by dropping any traffic coming from the attacker countries.

Counter measures

After detecting the malicious traffic, we should start to take actions. These actions include denying that traffic from reaching your network or just logging that traffic for additional study. Additional actions include sending alerts to a specific device or the management machine, sending an SNMP trap to the administrator, and sending a TCP reset to the attacker to close the session.

Information on what to do when an intrusion is detected can be found here:

- In the article *Intrusion Detection FAQ: What Do You Do After You Deploy the IDS?* by *Chris Morris* at `http://www.sans.org/security-resources/idfaq/deploy.php`
- In the book *Intrusion Prevention and Active Response: Deploying Network and Host IPS* by *Michael Rash*

Technical details

Untangle's Intrusion Prevention application is based on the well-known, open source, and widely deployed intrusion prevention and detection system software Snort. Snort uses many detection methods including signature and anomaly-based inspection.

As is the case with all Untangle apps, Untangle's Intrusion Prevention app comes ready for deployment and running with its preconfigured settings. The signature database and the default settings are kept current with the Untangle updates.

The Untangle Intrusion Prevention app defines the signatures as rules. You are free to modify the existing rules to fit your network or create additional rules, which is probably not required.

Untangle's Intrusion Prevention app is signature-based with 2,464 rules, while the number of Snort rules exceeds 11,000. Snort rules cover the OSI 7 layers, while Untangle only scans the traffic passed through the appliance and reconstructed on layer 7. So, the other layers' rules are not needed, and will never be triggered if implemented by Untangle. In addition, any traffic terminated on the Untangle server itself will not be scanned by Untangle's Intrusion Prevention app . However, you can implement a Snort box to work concurrently with Untangle.

Intrusion Prevention settings

This section will cover Untangle's Intrusion Prevention application's **Status** and **Rules**.

Status

The **Status** tab shows information about the Intrusion Prevention app's signature database such as the total number of available signatures and the number of signatures that causes the traffic to be logged or blocked, as shown in the following screenshot:

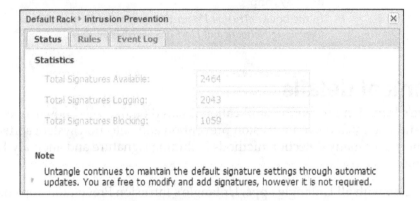

Not all of Untangle's Intrusion Prevention rules are blocked by default, as many of these rules may block unmalicious traffic. Untangle evaluated the rules and set the action to be taken based on the following criteria:

Criteria	Action
If the rule is known to always block malicious traffic	IPS will block and log traffic that matches this rule
If the rule is known to sometimes block malicious traffic (it may also block legitimate traffic if enabled)	IPS will log traffic that matches this rule and will not block any traffic to reduce the false positive
If the rule is known to never block malicious traffic	IPS will neither block nor log the traffic that matches this rule

Reports

Let's first learn how Snort defines the different rules. Each Snort rule has two basic parts: the rule header and the rule options. The rule header contains the following:

- **Action**
- **Protocol**

- **Source_IP**
- **Source_Port**
- **Direction**
- **Destination_IP**
- **Destination_Port**

The options part allows you to create a descriptive message to associate with the rule. In addition, it allows the checking of many packet attributes. For example, if we want to log and block all TCP packets from 192.168.1.50 irrespective of the port when the packet includes 0x70 and associate a message that the packet is a possible exploit, we'll use the following rule:

Drop TCP 192.168.1.50 any > any any (msg:"possible exploit"; content:" | 70 | ";)

The rule states that traffic from 192.168.1.50 from any port going to any address on any port and including 0x70 will be dropped (logged and blocked) and a message of *possible exploit* will be associated with the rule log.

For additional information about Snort rules, visit `http://manual.snort.org/node29.html` and `http://oreilly.com/pub/h/1393`.

The **Rules** part shows all rules defined by Untangle along with the associated action(s) (that is, whether they will block, log, or pass on the traffic) as well as information such as descriptions and signature IDs:

category ▲	block	log	description	id	info	Edit	Delete
attack-responses	✓	✓	(successful kadmind buffer overflow attempt)	1900	no info	📄	✕
attack-responses		✓	(file copied ok)	497	no info	📄	✕
attack-responses	✓	✓	(Microsoft cmd.exe banner)	2123	no info	📄	✕
attack-responses		✓	(command completed)	494	no info	📄	✕
attack-responses	✓	✓	(successful cross site scripting forced download attempt)	2412	no info	📄	✕
attack-responses		✓	(Invalid URL)	1200	no info	📄	✕
attack-responses	✓	✓	(successful gobbles ssh exploit GOBBLE)	1810	no info	📄	✕
attack-responses		✓	(command error)	495	no info	📄	✕
attack-responses		✓	(403 Forbidden)	1201	no info	📄	✕
attack-responses		✓	(successful gobbles ssh exploit uname)	1811	no info	📄	✕

You can modify the block/log settings on any rule by modifying the checkboxes next to it or by clicking on the **Edit** button next to it:

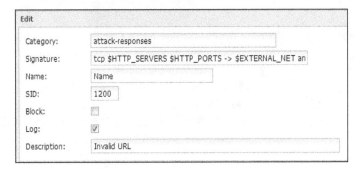

The **Variables** part is used to define variables that can be used in the rules. For example, the previous screenshot shows that the rule uses the **$HTTP_PORTS** variable, which is defined in the following screenshot as port 80 (you can add additional ports such as 443). You can add additional variables and modify the existing ones, but it's advisable to not change the **$HOME_NET** variable, which defines the network to be protected:

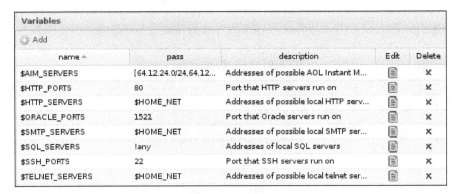

Reviewing the scan history

We are able to review the total number of scanned, logged, and blocked sessions since the last system restart through the application's faceplate. The number of current sessions and the real-time scan graph are also shown:

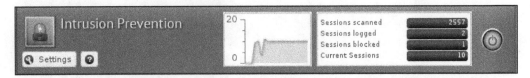

In addition to the application's faceplate, we have the event log and Reports methods. The following table describes the different event log terms:

Name	Description
Timestamp	Time when the scan occurred.
Client	The IP address of the attacker.
Username	The user who initiated the traffic request; this is available when using captive portal.
Blocked	True if the traffic is blocked, and false if not.
Rule ID	The rule that caused this event.
Rule description	The description associated with the rule options.
Server	The IP address of the internal machine the traffic was directed to.

The Reports app provides a daily chart summary of the intrusion application activities. The available reports are as follows:

- **Attacks**: This gives the maximum and the average attacks blocked per hour during a day
- **Top attacks (by hits)**: This shows the rules that matched the attack pattern and how many times

The following screenshot shows the Attacks report:

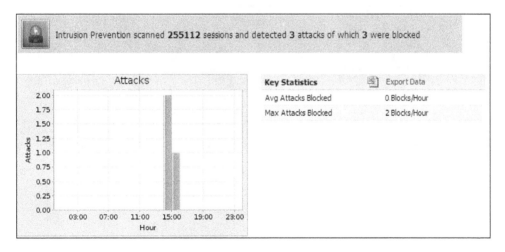

Lab-based training

In this lab, we will use two Windows client machines (one is the attacker and the other is the victim), in addition to the Untangle box that runs in the bridge mode. The bridge mode is selected here to avoid the blocking caused by the NAT to simplify the test process.

In addition, we will need to disable the Untangle Shield before starting this lab to avoid any traffic block caused by it.

In this lab, we will use the external laptop (192.168.1.7), ABC-Web01, and Untangle-03. The lab assumes that Untangle's Intrusion Prevention application is installed and running, the Shield is disabled, the attacker's machine has the Metasploit application installed, and the victim machine firewall is turned off.

> Metasploit is an exploit development framework that includes
> known exploits to help pen testers scan the system defense by
> executing these exploits against the system. For more information,
> visit http://www.metasploit.com/.

Perform the following steps to set up a lab:

1. On the attacker's machine, select **Services** from Metasploit, as shown in the following screenshot:

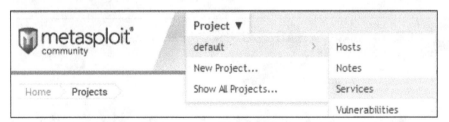

2. A new window will appear. Now, click on the **Scan** button to specify the victim machine to be scanned:

3. A new window will appear; from there, you can enter the IP address of the victim's machine or the entire network address range. Then, press the **Launch Scan** button.

4. The scan will take about two minutes to complete; after that, you can review Untangle's Intrusion Prevention application events. You will find a single logged event with ID **1616**:

Timestamp	Client	User...	Server	Blocked (IPS)	Rule Id ...	Rule Description (IPS)
2014-05-17 3:59:43 pm	192.168.1.7		192.168.1.15	false	1616	named version attempt

5. You can modify the settings of this rule to block the traffic instead of just logging it, as shown in the following screenshot:

web-misc	✓	✓	(htgrep attempt)	1615	no info	📄	✕
dns	✓	✓	(named version attempt)	1616	no info	📄	✕
web-cgi	☐	✓	(Bugzilla doeditvotes.cgi access)	1617	no info	📄	✕

6. Now, retrying the previous steps will result in the following event log:

Timestamp	Client	Us...	Server	Blocked (IPS)	Rule Id (IPS)	Rule Description (IPS)
2014-05-17 3:45:36...	192.168.1.7		192.168.1.15	true	1616	named version attempt
2014-05-17 2:59:43...	192.168.1.7		192.168.1.15	false	1616	named version attempt

7. The result of blocking the traffic can be noticed from the test log as the following line will not appear in the test with the blocked traffic:

```
Nmap Output: Parallel DNS resolution of 1 host. Timing: About 0.00% done
```

Understanding Untangle's Firewall application

Firewalls are used to separate your internal networks from the Internet and to limit access from outside the network to your internal resources. Untangle's Firewall application is a layer 7 firewall, which means it can block traffic based on the protocol, IP, port, and even the Active Directory users and groups.

Technical details

Untangle's Firewall application works in OSI layer 7 (application layer), which allows it to completely understand the traffic and hence filter that traffic based on various application layer conditions such as *Client has Exceeded Quota* and *HTTP: Client User OS*.

Untangle's Firewall application rules define the criteria of the traffic. When this criteria is matched with the rule, the action described on that rule will be taken. The different criteria (matchers) are as follows:

- Source IP address
- Source port
- Source interface
- Destination IP address
- Destination port
- Destination interface
- Protocol
- Active Directory user
- Active Directory group

The actions can be to block and/or flag the traffic. The blocked traffic will always be flagged.

Untangle Firewall rules are similar to the Forward Filter rules located under **Config**, as they can both block/pass traffic based on thier criteria. The differences are as follows:

- Forward Filter rules run on the kernel level, so they can filter the bypassed traffic while Untangle's Firewall application cannot, as it only sees traffic passed through the **Untangle VM (UVM)**
- As the traffic is end-pointed and passed to Untangle's Firewall application for scanning, it could apply layer 7 matchers, while the Forward Filter rules can only apply the lower layers rules

 Always remember that the Filter rules are done on the kernel before passing to the UVM, while Firewall rules are done on the UVM. Thus, the Filter rules are done before NAT, while the Firewall rules are done after NAT for the incoming traffic and would be vice versa for the outgoing traffic.

The default rule of Untangle's Firewall app is **ALLOW ALL**. This is not considered a threat as most Untangle deployments are in the router mode, which is doing NAT, or in the bridge mode behind another firewall or router that is also doing NAT. The NAT rules allow all outgoing traffic and any incoming traffic as a reply for that outgoing traffic, and blocks any outside initiated incoming traffic unless a port forward rule is in place for that traffic.

This achieves the common policy for most organizations. The main use for Untangle's Firewall app is the blocking of unwanted outgoing traffic such as the blocking of port 25 for the entire network except for the e-mail server, and the blocking of all ports except port 80 and 433 for VPN users. However, additional incoming rules can be added if needed.

Firewall settings

Untangle's Firewall application has three preconfigured disabled rules, which can be used as templates or can be edited to suit your network configuration. The different rules can be configured under the **Edit** button and some rule settings can be configured through the **Block**, **Flag**, and **Enable** checkboxes:

Rules							
⊙ Add							
Rule Id	Enable	Description	Block	Flag	Reorder	Edit	Delete
1	☐	Block and flag all traffic destined to port 21	☑	☑	✛	📄	✕
2	☐	Block and flag all TCP traffic from 1.2.3.0 netmask 255.255.255.0	☑	☑	✛	📄	✕
3	☐	Accept and flag all traffic to the range 1.2.3.1 - 1.2.3.10 to ports 1000-5000	☑	☑	✛	📄	✕

Reviewing the events of the Firewall application

We can review the scan activity via the Firewall application faceplate, which shows the number of current sessions and the total number of sessions passed, flagged, and blocked since the last system restart.

The faceplate doesn't have the real-time traffic graph because Firewall doesn't really have sessions; the initial connection is either passed or blocked. The session itself is not moderated once the session is passed.

The second option is to review the Firewall application's event logs, which show when the scan takes place and the source IP address (10.0.1.7), the source port (1219), the destination server IP address (192.168.1.5), the destination port (25), whether the traffic matches a rule (Rule ID), and the action taken (block and/or flag).

Timestamp	Client	Client port	Username	Blocked...	Flagged...	Rule Id...	Server	Server Port
2014-09-05 4:14:00 am	10.0.1.15	49553		false	false	none	10.0.0.5	445
2014-09-05 4:13:43 am	10.0.1.7	1219		true	true	100002	192.168.1.5	25
2014-09-05 4:13:37 am	10.0.1.7	1219		true	true	100002	192.168.1.5	25
2014-09-05 4:13:34 am	10.0.1.7	1219		true	true	100002	192.168.1.5	25
2014-09-05 4:12:49 am	10.0.1.15	49551		false	false	none	173.194.116.3	80
2014-09-05 4:12:49 am	10.0.1.15	49550		false	false	none	173.194.39.37	80
2014-09-05 4:11:56 am	10.0.0.5	63187		false	false	none	213.199.180.53	53

The final option is to use the Reports application. The available reports for the Firewall application are as follows:

- **Sessions**: This shows the maximum and the average number of sessions scanned per hour and how many are blocked and flagged

- **Top ten Firewall flagging rules (by hits)**: This shows the rules that are set to flag matching traffic and how many times the rules are matched

- **Top ten Firewall flagged hosts (by hits)**: This shows the hosts that matched a rule that is set to flag matching traffic and how many times the host matched the rule

- **Top ten Firewall flagged users (by hits)**: This shows the users that matched a rule that is set to flag matching traffic and how many times those users matched the rule

- **Top ten Firewall blocking rules (by hits)**: This shows the rules that are set to block matching traffic and how many times the rules are matched

- **Top ten Firewall blocked hosts (by hits)**: This shows the hosts that matched a rule that is set to block matching traffic and how many times the host matched the rule

- **Top ten Firewall blocked users (by hits)**: This shows the users that matched a rule that is set to block matching traffic and how many times those users matched the rule

The following screenshot shows the sessions report:

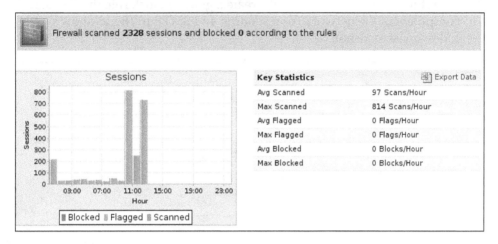

Lab-based training

Let's learn how we can block SMTP traffic for unintended computers. In this lab, we will use Untangle-01, ABC-DC01, ABC-EX01, ABC-Client01, Untangle-03, Acme-DC01, and Acme-EX01.

By default, any device behind Untangle-01 can send SMTP traffic to the Internet. If any of these devices gets infected by a worm that sends spam e-mails to the external world, your IP will get blacklisted. So, we want to only allow our e-mail server to send SMTP traffic to the external world and block any other device:

1. If you tried to initiate a Telnet connection from ABC-Client01 to Acme-EX01, the connection will be accepted. **Telnet 192.168.1.5 25** will give the following message:

2. If we want to block all internal computers from sending SMTP traffic except the e-mail server, we will create a general block rule that denies all computers in the network from sending any SMTP traffic, as shown in the following screenshot:

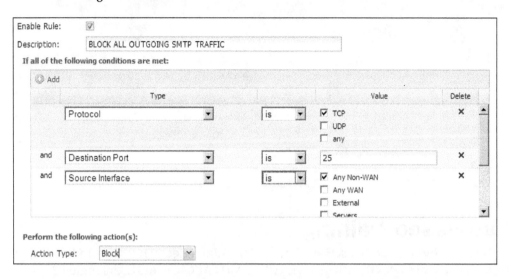

3. Then, we will need to create a rule that will permit the e-mail server to send SMTP traffic, as shown in the following screenshot:

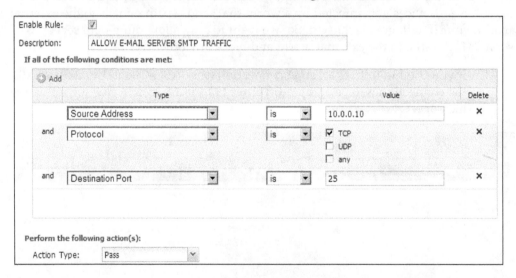

4. We will need to order the rules; thus, the permit rule is the first and then the deny rule comes later:

Rule Id	Enable	Description	Block	Flag	Reorder	Edit	Delete
0	☑	ALLOW EMAIL SEVER SMTP TRAFFIC			✛	🗎	✕
0	☑	Block All Outgoing SMTP Traffic	☑		✛	🗎	✕

5. After applying the changes, the Rule ID will be changed as shown in the following screenshot. Remember that **Flag** will allow the traffic but will create an event log about the session, while **Block** will block the traffic and create the event:

Rule Id	Enable	Description	Block	Flag	Reorder	Edit	Delete
1	☑	ALLOW EMAIL SEVER SMTP TRAFFIC			✛	🗎	✕
2	☑	Block All Outgoing SMTP Traffic	☑	☑	✛	🗎	✕

6. Now, let's initiate a Telnet connection to port 25 again from the ABC-Client01 computer; the connection will be refused with the following message:

```
C:\Documents and Settings\          >telnet 192.168.1.5 25
Connecting To 192.168.1.5...Could not open connection to the host, on port 25: C
onnect failed
```

7. Now, if we try the Telnet connection from the ABC-EX01 computer to the Acme-EX01 computer, the connection will be accepted.

Summary

In this chapter, we covered how to protect against DoS attacks using the Shield, protect against intrusions using Untangle's Intrusion Prevention application, and prohibit access to specific ports using Untangle's Firewall application. The concepts behind each technology were covered. We also saw how to configure, manage, and monitor the applications' activities.

In the next chapter, we will continue covering Untangle applications. This time, we will cover how to block users' access to certain sites based on their category such as pornography and social media.

Most of today's websites are HTTPS, so the regular filtering methods may fail to work properly; thus, there is a need to have an application that can decrypt HTTPS traffic and pass it to the other modules for scanning as a normal HTTP stream. In the next chapter, we will cover the Untangle application for this purpose (HTTPS Inspector). Eventually, we will learn how we can block certain applications (Facebook, Skype, and so on) and protocols' (BitTorrent) traffic using Untangle's Application Control.

8
Untangle Filters

This chapter will cover three other Untangle applications that are related to filtering users' traffic and the applications they use. The first application is the web filter that is used to block users' access to certain websites based on their category (social networking, games, and so on). The second application is the HTTPS Inspector, which is used to fully decrypt HTTPS traffic and pass it to applications as HTTP traffic for processing. The third application is Application Control, which is used to block users from using certain applications and protocols (BitTorrent and Facebook games, for example).

The same method that was used to explain the applications in the previous chapters will be used here; we will first introduce the application, cover how it works and any related technical details, discuss how we can review the event logs, and finally provide lab-based training. The topics that will be covered in this chapter are:

- Untangle Web Filter
- Untangle HTTPS Inspector
- Untangle Application Control

Untangle Web Filter

Web filtering is about blocking access to certain websites based on their category (Pornography, Social Media, Proxy Sites, News, and so on). Untangle provides two versions of the web filter application: the free Web Filter Lite and the paid Web Filter.

Working of Web Filter

When a user requests a website, the web filter application will send the URL of this website to a categorization database, which includes many websites and their category. The database will return the website category to the application, which will take an action (permit/deny access to this website) based on its settings.

Technical details

Untangle Web Filter Lite is based on a community-maintained database that has about 1 million websites in 15 categories and receives few updates per year, while the paid Untangle Web Filter is based on the zVeloDB URL database, which has over 500 million categorized URLs and about 5,000 categories. zVeloDB considers the de facto of web filtering and it's the first choice of many UTM vendors.

In addition, the paid version of the Untangle Web Filter surpasses the free version in the following ways:

- **HTTPS Filtering**: The paid version can filter the HTTPS traffic details without using the HTTPS Inspector, while the free version can't do this.

- **Dynamic categorization of new websites**: The paid version can block new and unknown websites, thanks to Zvelo's dynamic filtering and **Distributed Intelligence Architecture (DIA)**, which can automatically categorize websites based on their content.

- **YouTube for Schools support**: The paid version allows you to access the education videos on YouTube EDU while blocking the remaining YouTube videos.

- **Safe Search enforcement**: The paid version can enforce safe searching on supported search engines such as Google, Yahoo!, ASK, and Bing. Safe Search is a feature on search engines that acts as an automated filter of pornography and potentially offensive content.

- **The password option for the unblock feature**: While the free version has the option to temporarily unblock websites for whoever requests it, the paid version can limit this unblocking to people with a certain password.

Block lists

In this section, we will review the blocking options; we can block whole categories or individual websites, and we can even block specific types of files and MIME types. The following screenshot shows the different block lists avilable on the paid Web Filter:

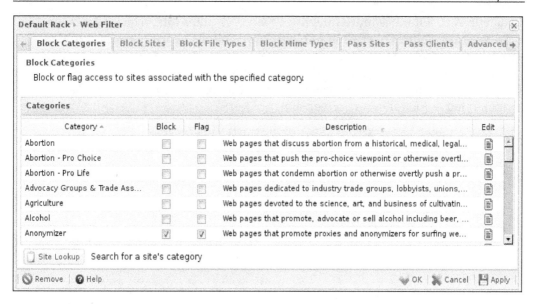

Category-based website blocking

Here, we can configure website blocking based on their category; simply check the **Block** and **Flag** checkboxes next to the desired category to block and/or flag any traffic directed to this category. By default, pornography, sex, anonymizer, and malicious websites are blocked, as shown in the following screenshot:

Untangle Web Filter has more categories than Web Filter Lite, which allows for more granular control over what to block. For example, sports is covered under one category in Web Filter Lite, which widely includes any related websites. It is covered under three categories in the paid Web Filter, which allows us to easily block animal-hunting sports websites while allowing any other sports websites, as illustrated in the following screenshot:

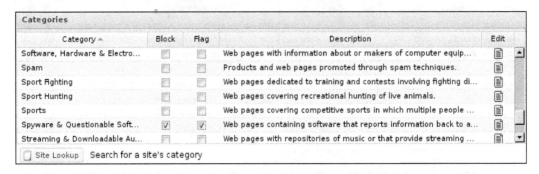

The **Site Lookup** button can be used to search for a certain website category; in addition, we can suggest the changing of the current website category. The following screenshot shows an example of www.espn.com.

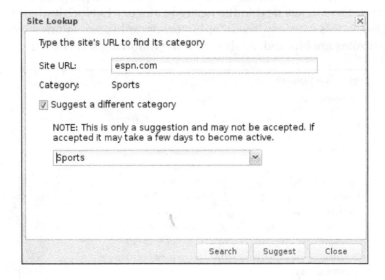

Blocking individual websites

Here, we can block individual websites instead of the complete categories. For example, if we want to block only Facebook while allowing the remaining social networking websites, we can add it to the following list as shown in the next screenshot:

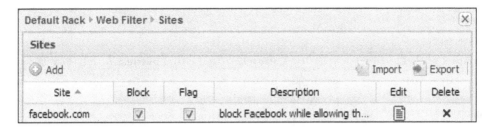

To add Facebook, simply press the **Add** button and complete the form, as shown in the following screenshot:

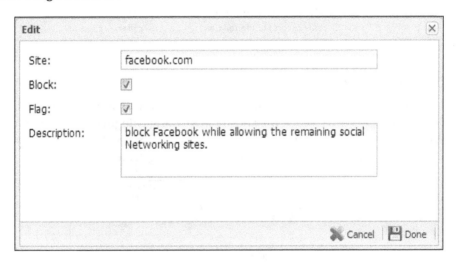

Blocking certain files and MIME types

In addition to blocking whole websites, we can block certain file types (for example, MP3, EXE, and so on). By default, Untangle NGFW will not block any file extension; you will be able to change this whenever you need. You can also add custom file/ MIME types. The following screenshot shows the file types block list:

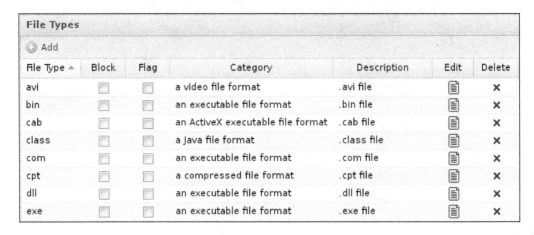

Allowing lists

If we want to block a whole category except for a certain website, we can use the Pass Sites list. For example, if we block the social networking category but want to allow LinkedIn, which is considered a business social networking website, we will need to add LinkedIn to the Pass List, as shown in the following screenshot:

Also, we can allow specific internal IPs to bypass the blocking list. For example, we can allow the CEO's PC to bypass any blocking rules by adding their PC's IP under the Pass Clients list as shown in the following screenshot:

This requires the CEO's PC to have a static IP. If the number of computers you want to bypass is too high, it is preferred to use the policy manager instead of the Pass Clients list.

HTTPS' advanced options

The problem with encrypted traffic is that Untangle NGFW will not have detailed information about this traffic and the destination website. Untangle Web Filter has different methods to deal with encrypted traffic in order to try to figure out what the destination website is. The following screenshot shows the advanced HTTPS options available for Untangle web Filter premium:

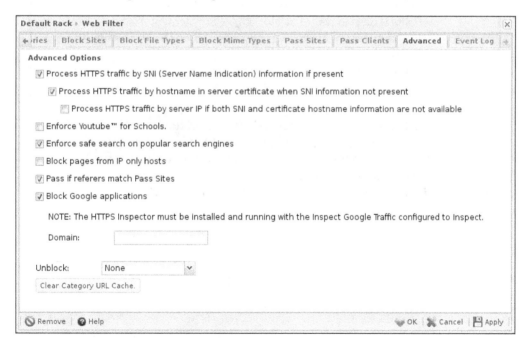

The first method is by using the **Server Name Indication (SNI)**. SNI is an extension to the TLS protocol that indicates in clear text what hostname the client is attempting to connect to at the start of the TCP handshake process. SNI is supported by most of the modern web browsers and operating systems.

> The main purpose of SNI is to allow a single web server to host multiple secure websites. By analyzing the SNI hostname in the client request, the server can decide which SSL certificate to use to encrypt the session. This extension is necessary because the encryption must be established long before the server can ever see the HTTP request, or, it will be too late to use a different certificate.

Untangle will use the hostname listed in the SNI as the URL for the request, and all processes in this request will be done as if it were a normal HTTP traffic. So, if you requested `https://www.Untangle.com/applications`, Untangle Web Filter will see `Untangle.com` as the SNI information and will treat the request as if it was directed to `http://Untangle.com`. To use this method, just check the checkbox next to **Process HTTPS traffic by SNI (Server Name Indication) if present**.

> As Untangle Web Filter cannot decrypt HTTPS traffic. When a website is determined to be blocked, Web Filter will reset the connection instead of showing the block page as it can't modify the encrypting traffic.
>
> In addition, features such as enforcing Safe Search cannot be applied because Untangle NGFW is not able to see the passed traffic.

The second method is by fetching the server name from the HTTPS server if the SNI information is not present. Web Filter will try to get the hostname from the server certificate and will complete the categorization based on this hostname. You can only use this method if the previous one doesn't work; to use it, check the checkbox next to **Process HTTPS traffic by hostname in server certificate when SNI information not present**.

The third method is by using the website's IP address. Sometimes, when the SNI categorization determines that the website should be blocked, this will reset the session. The web browser will retry the request; however, this time, it will not send the SNI information. Hence, Untangle NGFW will determine whether to block or allow the request based on the destination IP. However, as many websites currently use **Content Delivery Networks (CDN)**, many undesired results may appear, such as blocking the complete CDN IP range, which has the desired block site in addition to other websites that you don't want to block, or the categorization database may have a CDN IP that is different than the CDN IP used in your area, which will result in the website being unblocked. Again, you can only use this option if the previous options don't work; just check the checkbox next to **Process HTTPS traffic by server IP if both SNI and certificate hostname information are not available**.

The final method is by using the HTTPS Inspector application, which will fully decrypt traffic and pass it to the web filter for processing. HTTPS Inspector gives more accurate results than the other methods and allows you to utilize the full features of Untangle Web Filter, so it's preferable to use the HTTPS inspector whenever possible as it comes free with the paid version of Untangle Web Filter.

Untangle recommends that you disable the SNI detection methods when you use the HTTPS inspector.

Other advanced options

In this section, we will learn how to configure other Web Filter advanced options. The available options differ based on the version of Web Filter. The Lite version only has the **Block pages from IP only hosts, Pass if referrers match Pass Sites, Block Google applications**, and **Unblock** action menus but does not have the password for the unblock action. The full list of the available options include the following:

- **Enforce YouTube for schools**: YouTube for Schools allows you to limit your students' access to certain educational videos predefined by your teachers, and prohibits their access to non-educational content on Youtube. When you register for YouTube for schools, you will get a unique identifier, which defines your school to YouTube and allows YouTube to enforce your policy. You'll need to enter this identifier on Untangle NGFW for Web Filter to be able to rewrite all URLs with this identifier.

When you are not using the HTTPS inspector, it may be necessary to block all YouTube HTTPS traffic that uses the application control to block encrypted access to YouTube in which Untangle NGFW will not be able to rewrite the URL.

- **Enforce safe search on popular search engines**: Safe Search makes search engines eliminate pornography and potentially offensive entries in the search result. This is supported by Google, Yahoo!, Bing, and Ask search engines.

- **Block pages from IP only hosts**: Usually, malicious websites use IP addresses instead of domain names. When this option is enabled, pages for which users enter an IP address rather than the domain name will be blocked.

- **Pass if referrers match Pass Sites**: An HTTP referer is an HTTP header field that identifies the address of the web page (that is the URI or IRI) that is linked to the resource being requested. By checking the referer, the new web page can see where the request originated. For example, if we have www.free4arab.com on our pass list and have www.facebook.com on the block list, when we click on a link that directs us to www.facebook.com from www.free4arab.com, the requested link will open if this option was selected.

- **Block Google applications**: When this option is enabled, only domains listed in domain are allowed to access Google applications such as Gmail. All other domains are blocked by Google. Multiple domains can be specified, and are separated by commas, for example, Untangle.com, domain.com.

 The HTTPS Inspector must be installed and running with **Inspect Google Traffic** configured to **Inspect**.

- **Unblock**: We can add a button to the block page to allow users to bypass it and continue their browsing. The unblocking will be on-website base and not global unblocking. The different available options are as follows:

    ° **None**: No one will be able to bypass the block page.

    ° **Temporary**: The user will get one hour access to this website.

    ° **Permanent and Global**: The website will be added to the Pass Sites list. Thus, it will be allowed for now and anytime in the future.

    In addition, we can limit the unblocking to certain users who have the Untangle administrator password, or to a custom password especially for the purpose of unblocking. The following screenshot shows the Unblock functionaility:

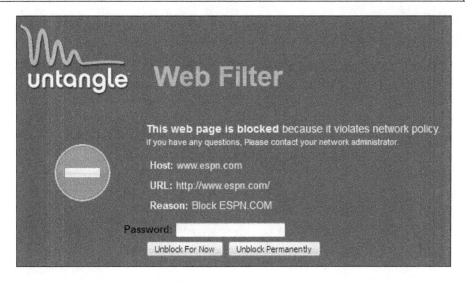

- **Clear category URL cache**: When a website is requested for the first time, Web Filter will query the zVelo online database about this website category and will save the result locally to enhance the upcoming queries. This temporary local cache will automatically be cleared when it gets old or stale. However, you can clear it for testing purposes, or if you feel that the results are incorrect.

Reviewing the history

We have many ways to review the web filter scan details; the first way is the application faceplate, which indicates the total scanned pages, the number of blocked/allowed pages, and the number of pages passed based on the policy. In addition, it shows a graph of the current scan as shown in the following screenshot:

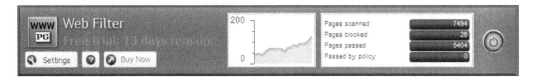

The second way is via the event logs. You can review each site's block/flag status and the reason for that (in the block list category, the file extension block list, the individual sites block list, because of using IP address, and so on) along with the details about the category and description associated with individual blocking. You can customize the fields you want to be displayed to include the timestamp, client IP, username, and so on.

You could review **All Web Events, Flagged Web Events, Blocked Web Events, All HTTP Events, All HTTPS Events**, and **Unblocked Web Events**:

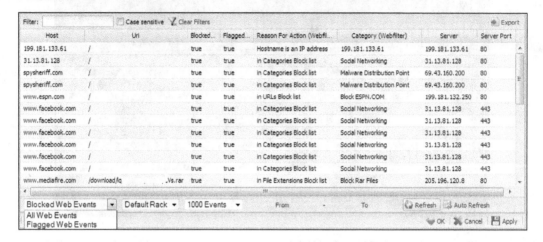

The third way is through the reports application, where we can find **summary reports**. The available reports are as follows:

- **Web Usage**: This provides a summary about the average and maximum hits/violations/blocks per hour

- **Total Web Usage**: This shows the total number of clean hits/violations/ blocked violations per day

- **Top Web Browsing Hosts (by Hits)**: This show the top clients based on the number of sessions

- **Top Web Browsing Hosts (by Size)**: This shows the top clients based on the traffic size

- **Top Web Browsing Users (by Hits)**: This shows the top users based on the number of sessions

- **Top Web Browsing Users (by Size)**: This shows the top users based on the traffic size

- **Top Categories of Violations (by Hits)**: This shows the categories that are classified as a violation

- **Top Categories of Blocked Violations (by Hits)**: This shows the categories that are set to be blocked

- **Top Websites (by Hits)**: This shows the top requested websites based on the number of hits

- **Top Websites (by Size)**: This shows the top requested websites based on the traffic size

- **Top Host Violators (by Hits)**: This shows the top clients that request a violation category
- **Top User Violators (by Hits)**: This shows the top users that request a violation category
- **Top Violations**: This shows the violated websites with the top number of hits
- **Top Blocked Violations**: This shows the blocked violated websites with the top number of hits

The following screenshot shows the Top Categories of Violations (by Hits) summary report:

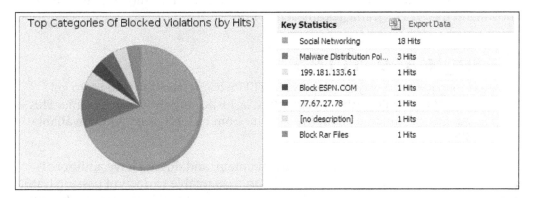

In addition to the summary reports, there are detailed reports such as all violation events, all scan events, all visited website events, and all unblocked website events. You could export these reports as a `csv` file and import them to an Excel file for extensive reviewing. The following screenshot shows the (**All Events**) detailed events:

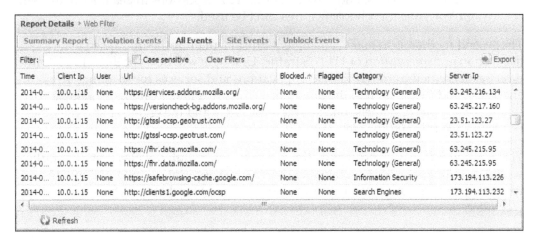

Utilizing HTTPS Inspector

HTTP over SSL (HTTPS) is used to create an encrypted channel between the client and server to protect the data transferred between them; also, it allows the client to validate the authenticity of the server.

Three years ago, most websites were running in HTTP and would allow firewalls to understand and inspect passing traffic. Nowadays, most websites tend to use HTTPS by default, such as Google and Facebook, which will shift the session to HTTPS even if it was initiated using HTTP. Using HTTPS results in firewalls being unable to understand or inspect the passing traffic, which affects the firewall's functionality as some of the blocked sites could be accessed by using HTTPS. Allowing firewalls to understand the HTTPS traffic became a necessity.

Untangle and HTTPS

Untangle provides two ways to deal with HTTPS traffic; the first is to try to get details about the website without decrypting or inspecting the passing traffic. This method can get information about the website from the SNI or IP, and is available in Web Filter.

This method is very simple to deploy and maintain, and doesn't have additional administrative headaches. However, as Untangle is unable to decrypt passing traffic and is only able to get information about the websites, it will block or pass the entire website. Thus, blocking certain games on Facebook is not possible anymore, and you have to entirely block or allow Facebook.

In addition, as modifying the passing traffic is not possible, Untangle will not be able to show the blocked pages, and it will rest the HTTPS sessions instead. Also, the Safe Search and YouTube for schools features can't be used.

The second method is to make Untangle perform a man-in-the-middle style decryption and encryption of HTTPS traffic. Untangle will decrypt the HTTPS traffic, pass the decrypted traffic (HTTP) to applications and services for scanning, re-encrypt it, and then pass it to the other party. This will make Untangle maintain two separate encrypted channels: one between Untangle and the end user and the other between Untangle and the web server.

This method is very powerful and allows you to get the full details about the traffic, so you can utilize the full functionality of Untangle applications and not only the web filter, and also use the Safe Search and YouTube for schools features inside the web filter.

The downside of this method is that it requires the use of a special certificate that must be installed on all clients behind Untangle; also, the decryption and encryption of the traffic will consume more server resources. In addition, some applications with certificate hardcoded on it, such as Dropbox, won't work with this method.

Working of HTTPS Inspector

The HTTPS Inspector allows Untangle applications and services to scan the HTTPS traffic as if it was HTTP traffic.

When a client makes an HTTPS request, the HTTPS Inspector will initiate a secure SSL connection to the external server on behalf of the client. While this session is being established, the HTTPS Inspector will capture information about the SSL certificate provided by the server. Once the server session is active, the HTTPS Inspector will use the details provided on the server certificate to create a new certificate that will be used to encrypt the session between the inspector and the client.

Thus, the traffic between the external server and Untangle NGFW is encrypted using the external server certificate, and the traffic between Untangle NGFW and the client is protected by a certificate issued by Untangle CA that replicates subject information contained on the external server certificate. As the new certificate is signed by the Untangle server's internal root CA, we will need to add the Untangle server's root CA certificate to the client's trusted root CAs.

 Each Untangle NGFW server will have a unique root CA certificate.

Configuring clients to trust Untangle's root CA

The HTTPS Inspector is turned off by default. Once you turn it on, a warning message will appear on your browser stating that the connection is untrusted. The reason for this is the certificate generated by Untangle, which is used to encrypt the traffic between Untangle and the client, so we need to make the client trust the Untangle root CA that issues on-the-fly certificates.

The manual method

The first way is to navigate to `http://<Untangle_IP>/cert`, which will allow you to download and install the certificate. This method is suitable for mobile users as it simplifies the process of getting and installing the certificate; the following screenshot shows this step on Firefox. You should check the **Trust this CA to identify websites** checkbox and click on the **OK** button, as shown in the following figure:

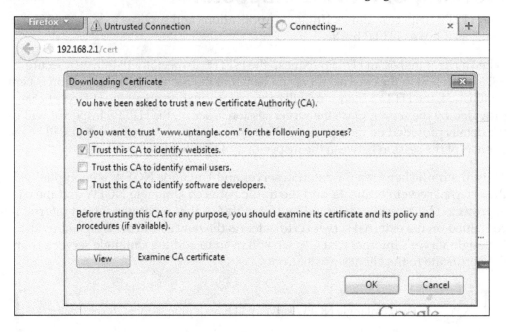

Importing the CA certificate to Firefox will not affect Internet Explorer or Google Chrome, as Internet Explorer and Google Chrome use the Windows certificates store, while Firefox uses its own certificate store, which can be reached from the **Certificate Manager** menu located under **Options | Advanced | certificates**. The following figure shows the Firefox Certificate Manager:

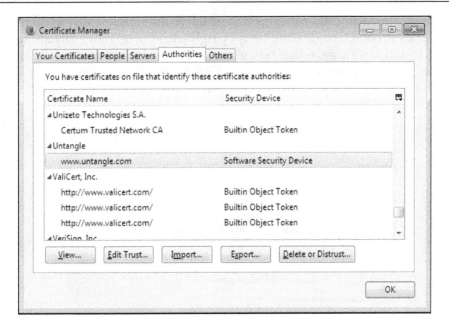

The second way is to manually download and import the certificate. You can get the certificate from the HTTPS Inspector's settings by clicking on the **Download Root Certificate** button, or by navigating to **Config** | **Administration** | **Certificates** by clicking on the **Download Root Certificate** button, as shown in the following screenshot:

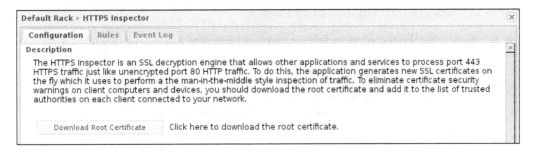

After you get the certificate, you'll need to install it; the simplest way to do this for Internet Explorer and Google Chrome is by right-clicking on the certificate and selecting **Install certificate**, which will open **Certificate Import Wizard**. From the **Certificate Store** page, select **Trusted Root Certification Authorities**, as shown in the following screenshot. For Firefox, you will need to import the certificate to the Firefox certificate's manager:

Deploying the root CA certificate using GPO

Using a group policy to deploy the Untangle root CA will remove some headache from the IT department; however this will import the certificate to the Windows certificates' store, which will not affect Firefox.

1. First, you'll need to manually download the certificate and put it on a shared folder.

2. After that, from the group policy settings under **Computer Configuration | Policies | Windows Settings | Security Settings | Public Key Policies**, right-click on **Trusted Root Certification Authorities** and then click on **Import**.

3. **Certificate Import Wizard** will be displayed; on the **File to Import** page, provide the certificate path, and on the **Certificate Store** page, click on **Place all certificates in the following store**. Then, finalize the wizard.

4. Now, after installing the Untangle root CA on the client PCs, when you navigate to any HTTPS website, it will be displayed as usual and no warning message will be displayed. The following screenshot shows a part of the on-the-fly certificate issued by Untangle for www.google.com:

Issued To	
Common Name (CN)	*.google.com.eg
Organization (O)	Google Inc
Organizational Unit (OU)	<Not Part Of Certificate>
Serial Number	14:06:04:22:67:00:00:01
Issued By	
Common Name (CN)	www.untangle.com
Organization (O)	Untangle
Organizational Unit (OU)	Security

Configuring HTTPS Inspector

The Untangle HTTPS Inspector comes with predefined settings; it only scans traffic from certain websites with high interest, such as Facebook, YouTube, Google, and Yahoo. Any other traffic will be ignored and will not be scanned by the HTTPS Inspector. This reduces the additional resource utilization caused by the decryption and re-encryption process, and prevents the problem caused by changing the certificate for some websites and applications while maintaining the scanning for traffic with high interest such as Facebook.

 Some applications, such as Dropbox, have their certificate hardcoded onto the application; thus, they will never accept the on-the-fly certificate generated by Untangle. Hence, we will need to make the HTTPS Inspector ignore traffic from these types of applications.

The following screenshot shows the default rules provided by Untangle, which are considered to be a safe start for you; allowing the inspection of all traffic can be done by checking rule number **4**:

Enabl...	Rule...	Description	Action	Reor...	Edit	Delete
✓	1	Ignore Microsoft Update	Ignore	⊕	📄	✕
✓	2	Ignore GotoMeeting	Ignore	⊕	📄	✕
✓	3	Ignore Dropbox	Ignore	⊕	📄	✕
☐	4	Inspect All Traffic	Inspect	⊕	📄	✕
✓	5	Inspect YouTube Traffic	Inspect	⊕	📄	✕
✓	6	Inspect Google Traffic	Inspect	⊕	📄	✕
✓	7	Inspect Facebook Traffic	Inspect	⊕	📄	✕
✓	8	Inspect Wikipedia Traffic	Inspect	⊕	📄	✕
✓	9	Inspect Twitter Traffic	Inspect	⊕	📄	✕
✓	10	Inspect Yahoo Traffic	Inspect	⊕	📄	✕
✓	11	Inspect Bing Traffic	Inspect	⊕	📄	✕
✓	12	Inspect Ask Traffic	Inspect	⊕	📄	✕
✓	13	Ignore Other Traffic	Ignore	⊕	📄	✕

Using rules for the HTTPS Inspector is similar to using rules for any other application as we already know that rules will be evaluated from top to bottom. Thus, the preconfigured rules will ignore traffic from Microsoft Update, GoToMeeting, and Dropbox, and inspect traffic from YouTube, Facebook, and so on. Any other traffic that is not listed will be ignored by rule number **13**.

 You should add the ignore rules before the inspect rules.

The HTTPS Inspector rules provide three new matchers that can be used to identify the traffic, which are as follows:

- **HTTPS: SNI Host Name**: This matches based on the provided SNI. This method is very effective as SNI is included in the initial packet of the HTTPS session.

- **HTTPS: Certificate Subject**: This matches any part of the certificate subject to a provided value. This method is useful when the application doesn't provide the SNI details. An example of a certificate subject for a certificate issued to Dropbox would be **CN=*.dropbox.com, O="Dropbox, Inc.", L=San Francisco, ST=California, C=US**.

- **HTTPS: Certificate Issuer**: This matches any part of the certificate issuer's **distinguished name (DN)** to a provided value. This method is useful when the application doesn't provide the SNI details. An example of an issuer DN that issued the certificate would be **CN=Thawte SSL CA, O="Thawte, Inc.", C=US**.

Creating the inspect or ignore rules is very simple; just click on the **Add** button, and then edit the rule to what best fits you. For example, a rule to ignore the inspecting of the Apple App Store traffic could be **HTTPS: SNI Host Name** is **apple.com* or **HTTPS: Certificate Subject** is **Apple**.

 The new rule will be placed at the bottom of the list. Remember to move it up before any inspect rule.

Additional HTTPS Inspector configurations located under the **Configuration** tab include:

- **Block invalid traffic**: This blocks any traffic directed to port 443 and is not HTTPS; if the HTTPS Inspector found that the traffic being directed to port 443 is not HTTPS, the default behavior is to not inspect that traffic and pass it to its destination.

 Remember that the HTTPS Inspector only scans HTTPS and doesn't scan any other SSL traffic such as SSL SMTP.

- **Trust all server Certificates**: This option allows Untangle NGFW to trust all certificates provided by external servers without checking their validity; this option is very dangerous and it's advised to *not* enable it. When not checked, Untangle will check the authenticity of certificates against a list of trusted CA that it has; you can add additional CAs to this list by clicking on the **Upload Trusted Certificate** button.

Reviewing the inspect activity

We can review the activities from the application faceplate or the application events.

The HTTPS Inspector faceplate includes a graph of the current traffic and the total number of inspected, ignored, untrusted, and abandoned sessions.

- **Inspected sessions**: This is determined based on your rule's settings; the inspected sessions are evaluated and scanned by Untangle applications.

- **Ignored sessions**: Untangle can't inspect the session. The session will continue between the server and the client without scanning from Untangle.

- **Untrusted sessions**: This type of session is for websites that don't provide a valid certificate or provide a certificate that is issued from CA that is not trusted by Untangle. Untangle will close the session and will not allow the client to proceed in the session unless the **trust all server certificates** option is checked.

- **Abandoned sessions**: Traffic will be blocked because of a problem of the underlying SSL, such as in the case of Dropbox.

The **Event Log** tab provides detailed information about the sessions; you could group sessions by all, inspected, ignored, blocked, untrusted, and abandoned. The most valued tab is the **Detail (HTTPS)** tab as it gives you information that can help you diagnose any problem and create suitable rules. The following screenshot shows the event log tab:

Timestamp	Client	Client port	Server	Server P...	Rule ID...	Status (Https)	Detail (Https)
2014-08-23 1:16:16 am	10.0.1.15	51126	192.30.252.129	443	0	ABANDONED	github.com
2014-08-23 1:16:14 am	10.0.1.15	51125	131.253.61.80	443	4	INSPECTED	login.live.com
2014-08-23 1:16:14 am	10.0.1.15	51124	131.253.61.80	443	4	INSPECTED	login.live.com
2014-08-23 1:16:13 am	10.0.1.15	51123	63.245.217.105	443	4	INSPECTED	www.mozilla.org
2014-08-23 1:16:13 am	10.0.1.15	51122	131.253.61.98	443	4	INSPECTED	login.live.com
2014-08-23 1:16:13 am	10.0.1.15	51121	63.245.217.105	443	4	INSPECTED	www.mozilla.org
2014-08-23 1:16:13 am	10.0.1.15	51120	131.253.61.98	443	4	INSPECTED	login.live.com
2014-08-23 1:16:10 am	10.0.1.15	51118	179.60.192.113	443	4	INSPECTED	www.facebook.com
2014-08-23 1:16:10 am	10.0.1.15	51116	179.60.192.113	443	4	INSPECTED	www.facebook.com
2014-08-23 1:16:08 am	10.0.1.15	51115	179.60.192.113	443	4	INSPECTED	www.facebook.com
2014-08-23 1:16:08 am	10.0.1.15	51114	179.60.192.113	443	4	INSPECTED	www.facebook.com
2014-08-23 1:16:08 am	10.0.1.15	51113	157.56.151.13	443	4	INSPECTED	login.microsoftonline.com
2014-08-23 1:16:08 am	10.0.1.15	51112	157.56.151.13	443	4	INSPECTED	login.microsoftonline.com
2014-08-23 1:16:08 am	10.0.1.15	51111	157.56.151.13	443	4	INSPECTED	login.microsoftonline.com
2014-08-23 1:16:08 am	10.0.1.15	51110	157.56.151.13	443	4	INSPECTED	login.microsoftonline.com
2014-08-23 1:11:19 am	10.0.1.15	51104	64.4.30.199	443	13	IGNORED	s.imp.microsoft.com
2014-08-23 1:11:14 am	10.0.1.15	51103	173.192.220.67	443	13	IGNORED	stags.bluekai.com
2014-08-23 1:11:11 am	10.0.1.15	51101	66.117.23.100	443	13	IGNORED	windowslive.tt.omtrdc.net
2014-08-23 1:11:10 am	10.0.1.15	51100	93.184.220.203	443	13	IGNORED	tags.bkrtx.com
2014-08-23 1:11:05 am	10.0.1.15	51099	54.194.194.17	443	13	IGNORED	msft.demdex.net
2014-08-23 1:11:03 am	10.0.1.15	51098	2.19.25.28	443	13	IGNORED	sc.imp.live.com

Untangle Application Control

Many modern applications are hard to block by using the port number as they are designed to avoid blocking (for example, by scanning and using any of the available open ports). Untangle Application Control deeply inspects the packets to identify the used protocol/application.

Untangle offers two versions of Application Control: the free Lite version, which is based on **L7-Filter Open project**, and the paid version, which is based on the **PROCERA networks Network Application Visibility Library (NAVL)** technology.

 While Untangle Application Control provides the ability to block websites, the best way to block websites is still through Web Filter. Using Application Control to block websites might not be sufficient for you.

Untangle Application Control Lite

The Lite version of the Application Control version is signature based; the signatures are regular expressions (see more on `http://en.wikipedia.org/wiki/Regular_expression` and `http://www.regular-expressions.info/tutorial.html`) that are used to match the desired protocol. An example of a signature used to block BitTorrent traffic is `^(\x13bittorrent protocol|azver\x01$|get /scrape\?info_hash=)`. As you see, the signatures are complex to build. In addition, it's hard to get the exact match signature. As a result, many undesired effects may appear, such as blocking legitimate traffic, and partially blocking the desired traffic; the application could also detect that it has been blocked and tries to evade this blocking and find another method for communication.

You can't add custom rules via paid Application Control, but you can do this by using Application Control Lite. You can find a signature for many protocols on `http://l7-filter.sourceforge.net/protocols`, and you can learn how to build an application control signature on `http://l7-filter.sourceforge.net/Pattern-HOWTO`. However, you need to be aware that undesired effects may appear and it's advisable to run the new signature in **LOG only** mode first before you start to use it in traffic blocking.

Adding Application Control Lite signatures

By default, Application Control Lite signatures are not preloaded. The user will need to go to the Wiki page to download them. This is an attempt to stop users from just enabling all signatures without understanding their side effects.

To get the Application Control Lite signatures, click on the **Help** button located under the Application Control Lite settings, as shown in the following figure:

This will open the Untangle Application Control Lite Wiki page; from there, under the signatures section, you'll find a warning that includes the link of the signatures (shown in the following screenshot). The direct link to the signatures is http://wiki.Untangle.com/images/8/8e/Application_Control_Lite_Bad_Signatures.json.

> **WARNING:** In previous and old versions of Untangle there was a default signature set. However, enabling block on some of the default signatures caused false positives and blocked legitimate network traffic. Despite big warnings in the user interface and help documentation, we found users often misconfigured Application Control Lite anyway and experienced network problems as a result. To avoid this issue there are now no default signatures. If you have read this warning and understand that misconfiguring Application Control Lite **will cause major network connectivity issues**, then you can download the original list of signatures here and import them into Signatures.

After downloading the signatures, we will need to import them to Untangle by navigating to **Settings | Signatures**. Click on the **Import** button and browse to the downloaded json file, as illustrated in the following screenshot:

After clicking on the **Done** button, the signatures will be imported to Untangle Application Control Lite, as shown in the following screenshot:

You will need to press **OK** on the display of the **Import Successful** message and then apply the changes.

Application Control Lite Status

The **Status** tab shows the total number of available signatures, how many signatures are set to be logged, and how many are set to be blocked:

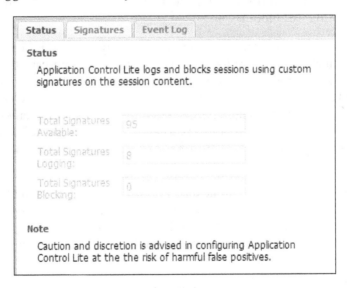

Blocking applications/protocols

We can configure the applications/protocols to be logged/blocked under the **Signatures** tab. Simply check the **Block/Log** checkboxes next to the desired traffic to block and/or log this traffic. You have the option to add a custom signature, and import/export those signatures, as shown in the following screenshot:

Protocol	Category ▲	Block	Log	Description	Edit	Delete
POP3	Email	☐	☐	Post Office Protocol version ...	📄	✗
IMAP	Email	☐	☐	Internet Message Access Pr...	📄	✗
SMTP	Email	☐	☐	Simple Mail Transfer Protoc...	📄	✗
TFTP	File Transfer	☐	☐	Trivial File Transfer Protocol ...	📄	✗
FTP	File Transfer	☐	☐	File Transfer Protocol - RFC ...	📄	✗
Jabber (XMPP)	Instant Messenger	☐	☑	open instant messenger pr...	📄	✗
MSN Messenger	Instant Messenger	☐	☑	Microsoft Network chat client	📄	✗

The paid version of Application Control

The paid version of Application Control is based on the PROCERA Networks NAVL classification engine, which performs Layer 7 classification and metadata extraction of the traffic. In addition, it does deep packet and deep-flow inspection of that traffic in multilayers of the OSI model.

The classification engine uses many methods including surgical pattern matching, conversation semantics, deep protocol dissection, heuristic analysis, future flow awareness, flow association, and statistical inspection. This allows the server to accurately identify thousands of today's common applications such as social networking, P2P, instant messaging, video streaming, file sharing, enterprise applications, Web 2.0, and much more. You can find a list of the defined applications on http://wiki.Untangle.com/index.php/Application_Control_Application_List.

There are many more classified applications under paid Application Control than in Application Control Lite (1140 versus 95). The paid version of the Application Control classification is more accurate and has rare false positives, which is not the case with Application Control Lite. Also, the paid version of Application Control can easily block evading programs.

The installation of both Application Control and Application Control Lite into the same rack is supported. However, this is not the recommended action and may lead to many conflicts.

The Application Control status

The following screenshot shows the **Status** tab which displays the traffic scanning statistics (scanned, allowed, flagged, and blocked sessions); it also shows the total number of known applications and how many of them are set to be flagged, blocked, and tarpitted. Finally, it shows the total number of the available rules and how many of them are active:

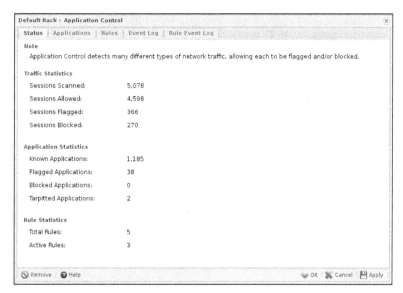

Blocking applications/protocols

The paid version of Application Control has two ways to block applications: the first is via the **Applications** tab, where you can simply select the desired application, and the other way is via the **Rules** tab, where you cloud set rules to block more complex traffic. The **Applications** tab (shown in the following screenshot) is the primary and preferred way to use Application Control to manage network traffic:

Default Rack ▸ Application Control									
Status	**Applications**	Rules	Event Log	Rule Event Log					
Application ▲	Block	Tarpit	Flag	Name	Category	Productivity	Risk	Description (click for f...	
FASP	☐	☐	☐	FASP	File Transfer	4	3	FASP (Fast and Secur...	▲
FATMEN	☐	☐	☐	Fatmen	Networking	3	1	Port 347/tcp and 347/...	
FBOOKAPP	☐	☐	☐	Facebook Apps	Social Networking	2	5	Add ons developed fo...	
FB_EVENT	☐	☐	☐	Facebook Event	Social Networking	2	2	Creating/editing Face...	
FB_MSGS	☐	☐	☐	Facebook Messages	Social Networking	2	2	Facebook E-mail and I...	
FB_POST	☐	☐	☐	Facebook Post	Social Networking	2	2	Interactions with Face...	
FB_SRCH	☐	☐	☐	Facebook Search	Social Networking	2	2	Searching within Face...	
FB_VDCHT	☐	☐	☐	Facebook Video Chat	Social Networking	2	3	Facebook Video Chat	
FB_VIDEO	☐	☐	☐	Facebook Video	Social Networking	2	3	Facebook streaming v...	
FC2	☐	☐	☐	FC2.com	Web Services	3	1	Traffic generated by b...	
FEDERATD	☐	☐	☐	Federated Media	Web Services	3	1	Visiting websites that...	

Simply select the desired application and then check the desired action. The different action is **Block**, which will reset the session if the traffic was TCP and drop the packets if the traffic was UDP. The **Log** action will flag traffic as violation in the reports and event logs but will not block it. The **Tarpit** action will keep the session between the client and the server open but will drop all the packets.

> The default behavior of Application Control is to forward the initial packets of the traffic to the client until it is certain about the used application. This may result in partly-loaded websites. Some applications have the ability to quickly reinitiate the sessions if they were blocked; this will allow the websites to download another part before the session is closed again. This will appear to the user as if Application Control is not blocking anything. So, it's preferred to use the trapit action in this case as it will let the session to remain open but will drop all the packets.

In addition, Application Control has classified the applications based on their effect on the productivity and their risk. The productivity has a value from 1 to 5 where 1 represents applications that badly affect productivity, such as online gaming, while 5 represents critical applications such as Active Directory and file transfer. The same goes for the risk, where 5 represents applications that could allow malware and other malicious traffic into your network, such as bit torrent, while 1 represents top trusted traffic such as LDAP.

> You can click on the description field to open a pop up for the full details of the traffic.

In addition, you can create custom rules to block complex traffic that can't be handled by the **Applications** tab. Application Control rules have normal rule properties such as they look for a matcher to match in the scanned traffic, and if a match is found, the defined action will be taken.

> The application control rules are only evaluated after the complete classification of the traffic. Thus, if the session was dropped/ blocked or reset before the complete classification of the traffic, the rules will not be evaluated.

By default, there are five precreated rules that could be used to block complex traffic. The five rules are shown in the following screenshot:

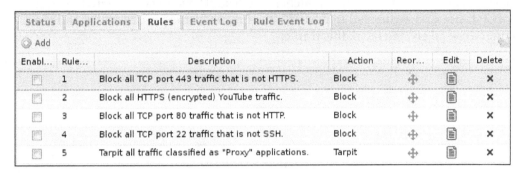

Status	Applications	Rules	Event Log	Rule Event Log				
Add								
Enabl...	Rule...	Description			Action	Reor...	Edit	Delete
☐	1	Block all TCP port 443 traffic that is not HTTPS.			Block	✛	📄	✕
☐	2	Block all HTTPS (encrypted) YouTube traffic.			Block	✛	📄	✕
☐	3	Block all TCP port 80 traffic that is not HTTP.			Block	✛	📄	✕
☐	4	Block all TCP port 22 traffic that is not SSH.			Block	✛	📄	✕
☐	5	Tarpit all traffic classified as "Proxy" applications.			Tarpit	✛	📄	✕

Application Control introduces some new matchers. In addition to risk and productivity, it introduces the following:

- **Application**: This is the name of the application/protocol that creates the session (for example, GMAIL, BITTORRE, and SSL).

- **Category**: This is the application category (games, mail, or social networking).

- **ProtoChain**: This is the stack (chain) of protocols leveraged by this session to communicate, for example, /IP/TCP/HTTP/GMAIL; thus, layer 3 protocol is IP, layer 4 protocol is TCP, the application layer protocol is HTTP, and the specific application is Gmail. Additional examples are /IP/UDP/BITTORRE and /IP/TCP/SSL.

- **Detail**: This is a string that stores application-specific parameters that vary depending on the application. For Facebook, it will store the Facebook application name (Farmville or wordswithfriends); for HTTP, it will store the content type (image/gif); and for SSL, it will store the hostname found on the certificate (mail.google.com); review the event logs section for more clearance.

- **Confidence**: This represents the percentage of the engine's certainty about the traffic classification; the classification engines continue to scan the traffic until they are certain about it. Thus, short sessions may get incomplete classifications, unlike the case of long sessions. A value of 50 indicates that the classification is only done based on the source and destination address and port information, while 100 indicates that the traffic has been fully classified based on the deep inspection techniques.

Let's investigate the **Block all HTTPS (encrypted) YouTube traffic** rule, which is shown in the following screenshot. This rule searches for three matchers and will match if and only if all the three matchers are true. The matchers are that the traffic is TCP traffic and is directed to port 433, the PrortoChain is */YOUTUBE*, and the action to be taken is to block this traffic.

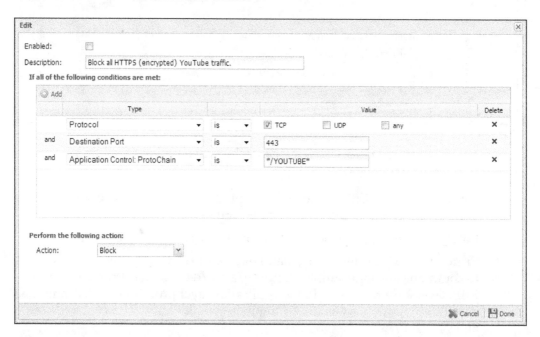

Reviewing the scanning history

As is the case with all apps, we can review the scanning and blocking history from the application's faceplate, event logs, and reports. The application's faceplate gives us a quick review of the scanning history since the last restart and also provides a graph that shows the real-time scan activity, as shown in the following screenshot:

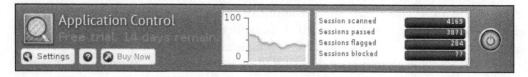

The event logs provide more detailed information about the traffic properties such as the detected application and protocol, server ports, and client IP. The Lite version provides one event log tab that covers the scanning activity against the defined signatures while the paid version provides two event log tabs, one for the application and the other for the rules. The application event log is shown in the following screenshot. The default view for the event logs is the classified sessions. In addition, there are the blocked and flagged views. There is also an All Sessions view as some could be unclassified.

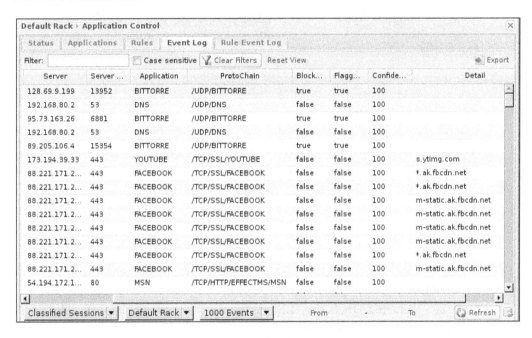

The rules event log only shows the traffic that matches any enabled rules. The following screenshot shows the traffic from blocking the YouTube rule:

The reports application provides complete event's details and a summary report. The available reports are:

- **Sessions**: This provides the average and maximum detections/blockage and flagging per hour.
- **Top Ten Blocked Applications (by Hits)**: This lists the top applications based on the number of hits that caused Application Control to block the traffic.
- **Top Ten Flagged Applications (by Hits)**: This lists the top applications based on the number of hits that caused Application Control to flag the traffic.
- **Top Ten Detected Applications (by Hits)**: This lists the top detected applications based on the number of hits.
- **Top Ten Blocked Protochains (by Hits)**: This lists the top protochains based on the number of hits that caused Application Control to block the traffic.
- **Top Ten Flagged Protochains (by Hits)**: This lists the top protochains based on the number of hits that caused Application Control to flag the traffic.
- **Top Ten Detected Protochains (by Hits)**: This lists the top detected protochains based on the number of hits.
- **Top Ten Blocked Hosts (by Hits)**: This lists the top hosts that the traffic is blocked from.
- **Top Ten Flagged Hosts (by Hits)**: This lists the top hosts that the traffic is flagged from.
- **Top Ten Detected Hosts (by Hits)**: This lists the top hosts based on the number of hits detected from them.
- **Top Ten Blocked Users (by Hits)**: This lists the top users that traffic is blocked from.
- **Top Ten Flagged Users (by Hits)**: This lists the top hosts that traffic is flagged from.
- **Top Ten Detected Users (by Hits)**: This lists the top users based on the number of hits detected from them.
- **Top Bandwidth Applications**: This lists the top applications based on their bandwidth usage.
- **Top Bandwidth Protochains**: This lists the top protochains based on their bandwidth usage.

The following screenshot shows the Sessions summary report:

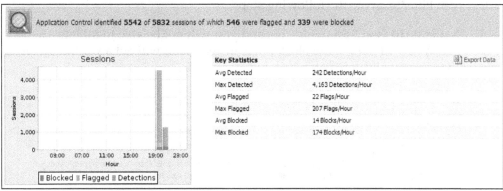

Lab-based training

In this lab, we will learn how to utilize Web Filter, the HTTPS Inspector, and Application Control to enhance users' productivity and block undesired access to certain websites. The lab only requires two PCs and one Untangle NGFW server. This lab assumes that Web filter, Application Control, and the HTTPS Inspector are not installed in your rack.

Configuring Web Filter settings

In this section, we will start setting the configurations for Untangle Web Filter to start filtering our network traffic:

1. Install the Web filter application.
2. Under **Block categories**, block **Social Networking**.
3. Under **Block Sites**, add ESPN.com.
4. Under Block File types, block the exe file extension.
5. Make sure that the **Enforce Safe Search on popular search engines** option is selected.
6. Check the checkbox of block pages from IP only hosts.
7. Set the **Unblock** settings to **permanent and global**, check the **password required** checkbox, and add any custom password you want.
8. Under **Pass Sites**, add Linkedin.com.
9. Under **Pass Clients**, add the IP address of the client machine for which you don't want Web Filter to scan traffic.

Testing the functionality of Web Filter

To test Web Filter, execute the following steps:

1. Navigate to `www.facebook.com`, and you will not be able to initiate a session in it. You will not get the block page; instead, you will get a warning page about an invalid certificate.

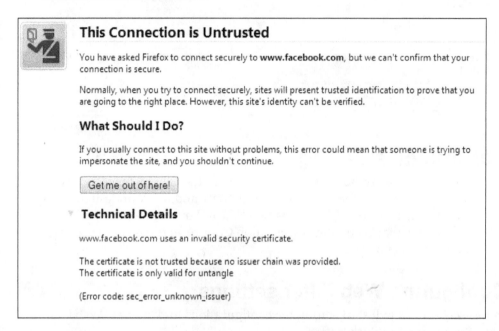

2. Navigate to `www.Hi5.com`; this time, you'll get the block page because it's on HTTP and not HTTPS.

3. Navigate to `www.LinkedIn.com`. It will be allowed even though it is considered as a social networking website because we added it to the pass list.

4. Navigate to `www.Espn.com`. Again, you will get the block page. Let's try to permanently allow this website. By reviewing the **Pass Sites** list, we will find it automatically added to the list as shown in the following figure:

Site ▲	Pass	Description	Edit	Delete
espn.com	✓	unblocked by user	▤	✗
linkedin.com	✓	Allow Linkedin	▤	✗

5. Let's get the IP address of www.ESPN.com from the event logs and try to navigate to it using this IP: 199.181.133.61. This time, access to the website will be blocked even though it is in the **Pass Sites** list.

6. Navigate to get.adobe.com/reader/ to download Adobe Reader. When you start the download process, you will get a block page.

7. Navigate to www.Bing.com (as it does not use HTTPS by default) and search for porn; you will get a page as shown in the following screenshot, as we have Safe Search enforced:

8. From the allowed client machine, navigate to any blocked content such as www.facebook.com; you will be allowed to access it.

Configuring HTTPS Inspector settings

Though Untangle Web Filter was able to block HTTPS traffic, we need to fully utilize its features with the HTTPS traffic such as YouTube for Schools and Safe Search on HTTPS traffic. We will need to perform the following configuration steps:

1. Disable the SNI options on Web Filter.

2. Install and enable the HTTPS Inspector.

3. Install the root CA certificate on the client computers.

4. Configure HTTPS Inspector to scan all the traffic.

5. Configure HTTPS Inspector to block invalid traffic.

Testing the functionality of Web Filter

Perform the following steps:

1. Try to download the Eicar test virus using HTTPS; this time, it will be blocked.

2. Try to navigate to www.facebook.com. This time, you'll get the block page.

3. Try to search for porn on Google (which uses HTTPS); this time, Google will apply Safe Search.

Configuring and testing Application Control settings

In this section, we will see how to configure and test the functionality of Untangle Application Control. Perform the following steps:

1. From the client PC, navigate to www.youtube.com; also try to download something via torrent clients.

2. Go to the Application Control settings, and under the **Applications** tab, set **BITTORRE** to **Tarpit**. Under the **Rules** tab, check **Block all HTTPS (encrypted) YouTube traffic**.

3. Now, go back to the client PC and try to navigate to www.youtube.com and resume your torrent download; they will fail and you can review this under the event logs.

4. From Web Filter, unblock Facebook for now, and under Application Control, block the **FBOOKAPP**.

5. Try to navigate to https://www.facebook.com/games/candycrush and select **Play Now**; the page will not load, and on the event log, you will see that the block was because you were trying to access the *Candy Crush* app.

The cat and mouse game

Since we completed our initial configurations, users started to search for ways to override our set filters. This section will cover the endless game between the network administrator and the users that want to evade the filtering.

This lab assumes that no other controls are taken by the network administrator, such as prohibiting normal users from installing applications on their PCs and blocking USB devices. However, in all the coming steps, the user is not able to get the proxy or the programs from inside the network as the proxy, anonymizer categories are blocked. The following figure shows the eventlogs for the application control when using the hidemyass proxy:

1. The user accessed www.hidemyass.com and got proxy details to use in their browser. The user will be able to access the websites they want as Web Filter will not be able to block the traffic. However, by using Application Control, the administrator will be able to classify the traffic and block it, as shown in the following figure:

Client	Client...	Server	Ser...	Application	ProtoChain	Blocked...	Flagged...	Confi...	Detail
172.16.1.10	37512	41.231.53.40	3128	TWITTER	/TCP/HTTP/HTTPTNNL/SSL/TWIT...	true	false	100	twitter.com
172.16.1.10	37511	41.231.53.40	3128	FACEBOOK	/TCP/HTTP/HTTPTNNL/SSL/FACE...	true	true	100	www.facebook.com
172.16.1.10	37510	41.231.53.40	3128	FACEBOOK	/TCP/HTTP/HTTPTNNL/SSL/FACE...	true	true	100	www.facebook.com
172.16.1.10	37509	41.231.53.40	3128	FACEBOOK	/TCP/HTTP/HTTPTNNL/SSL/FACE...	true	true	100	www.facebook.com
172.16.1.10	37508	41.231.53.40	3128	FACEBOOK	/TCP/HTTP/HTTPTNNL/SSL/FACE...	true	true	100	www.facebook.com
172.16.1.10	37507	41.231.53.40	3128	FACEBOOK	/TCP/HTTP/HTTPTNNL/SSL/FACE...	true	true	100	www.facebook.com
172.16.1.10	37506	41.231.53.40	3128	FACEBOOK	/TCP/HTTP/HTTPTNNL/SSL/FACE...	true	true	100	www.facebook.com
172.16.1.10	37505	41.231.53.40	3128	FACEBOOK	/TCP/HTTP/HTTPTNNL/SSL/FACE...	true	true	100	www.facebook.com
172.16.1.10	37504	41.231.53.40	3128	FACEBOOK	/TCP/HTTP/HTTPTNNL/SSL/FACE...	true	true	100	www.facebook.com
172.16.1.10	37503	41.231.53.40	3128	FACEBOOK	/TCP/HTTP/HTTPTNNL/SSL/FACE...	true	true	100	www.facebook.com
172.16.1.10	37502	41.231.53.40	3128	FACEBOOK	/TCP/HTTP/HTTPTNNL/SSL/FACE...	true	true	100	www.facebook.com
172.16.1.10	37500	41.231.53.40	3128	TWITTER	/TCP/HTTP/HTTPTNNL/SSL/TWIT...	true	false	100	twitter.com
172.16.1.10	37494	41.231.53.40	3128	TWITTER	/TCP/HTTP/HTTPTNNL/SSL/TWIT...	true	false	100	twitter.com
172.16.1.10	37492	41.231.53.40	3128	TWITTER	/TCP/HTTP/HTTPTNNL/SSL/TWIT...	true	false	100	twitter.com
172.16.1.10	37491	41.231.53.40	3128	FACEBOOK	/TCP/HTTP/HTTPTNNL/SSL/FACE...	true	true	100	www.facebook.com
172.16.1.10	37490	41.231.53.40	3128	FACEBOOK	/TCP/HTTP/HTTPTNNL/SSL/FACE...	true	true	100	www.facebook.com
172.16.1.10	37489	41.231.53.40	3128	FACEBOOK	/TCP/HTTP/HTTPTNNL/SSL/FACE...	true	true	100	www.facebook.com

2. The user tried to use **Hot Spot Shield**; Untangle Application Control can easily detect and block traffic from it, as shown in the following figure:

172.16.1.1...	55555	50.117.72.2...	706	HOTSPTSH	/TCP/HOTSPTSH	false	false	100	
172.16.1.1...	55554	50.117.72.2...	3028	TWITTER	/TCP/HTTP/HTTPTNNL/SSL/TWIT...	true	false	100	twitter.com
172.16.1.1...	55553	50.117.72.2...	706	HOTSPTSH	/TCP/HOTSPTSH	false	false	100	
172.16.1.1...	55552	50.117.72.2...	706	HOTSPTSH	/TCP/HOTSPTSH	false	false	100	
172.16.1.1...	55551	50.117.72.2...	706	HOTSPTSH	/TCP/HOTSPTSH	false	false	100	
172.16.1.1...	55550	50.117.72.2...	706	HOTSPTSH	/TCP/HOTSPTSH	false	false	100	
172.16.1.1...	55549	50.117.72.2...	706	HOTSPTSH	/TCP/HOTSPTSH	false	false	100	
172.16.1.1...	55548	50.117.72.2...	3028	FACEBOOK	/TCP/HTTP/HTTPTNNL/SSL/FACE...	true	true	100	*.facebook.com
172.16.1.1...	55547	50.117.72.2...	706	HOTSPTSH	/TCP/HOTSPTSH	false	false	100	
172.16.1.1...	55546	50.117.72.2...	706	HOTSPTSH	/TCP/HOTSPTSH	false	false	100	

3. The user tried to use **Tor**; Untangle Application Control is able to detect it during the session initiation and blocks the session creation, as shown in the following figure:. However, if the session is created the user can access whatever they want.

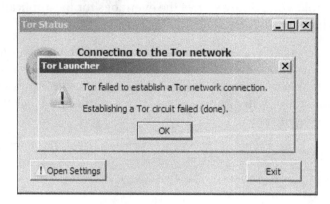

4. The user tried to use **Anonymizer**, which uses OpenVPN to create a VPN tunnel to a server; from there, they can access what they want. As the session will be encrypted, once created, the user will be able to access whatever they want. The administrator can detect such applications by reviewing the Application Control event log; they will notice the usage of OpenVPN on a machine that doesn't need to, as shown in the following figure:

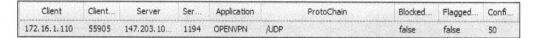

Client	Client...	Server	Ser...	Application	ProtoChain	Blocked...	Flagged...	Confi...
172.16.1.110	55905	147.203.10...	1194	OPENVPN	/UDP	false	false	50

In addition, after the session is completed, a web page to www.anonmyizer.com will be opened automatically on the client PC. Web Filter will block it, and the administrator can review it from the event logs, as shown in the following figure:

2014-09-...	172.16.1.1...	greenlight.anonymizer.c...	/vpn_status?service=au	147.203.108.50	80	true	true	in Categories Block list
2014-09-...	172.16.1.1...	greenlight.anonymizer.c...	/vpn_status?service=au	147.203.108.50	80	true	true	in Categories Block list
2014-09-...	172.16.1.1...	greenlight.anonymizer.c...	/vpn_status?service=au	147.203.108.50	80	true	true	in Categories Block list
2014-09-...	172.16.1.1...	greenlight.anonymizer.c...	/vpn_status?service=au	147.203.108.50	80	true	true	in Categories Block list
2014-09-...	172.16.1.1...	greenlight.anonymizer.c...	/vpn_status?service=au	147.203.108.50	80	true	true	in Categories Block list
2014-09-...	172.16.1.1...	greenlight.anonymizer.c...	/vpn_status?service=au	147.203.108.50	80	true	true	in Categories Block list

So the administrator can block using Anonymizer by blocking OpenVPN for undesired users.

5. The user tried to use **UltraSurf**. The old version from UltraSurf is very easy to detect and block, as shown in the following figure, while the detection of the new version is not completely possible, at the time of writing this book.

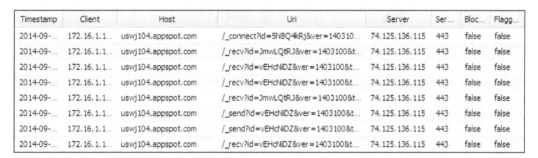

Client	Client...	Server	Ser...	Application	ProtoChain	Blocked...	Flagged...	Confi...	Detail
172.16.1.10	55069	173.194.39,...	80	ULTRASRF	/TCP/HTTP/ULTRASRF	false	true	100	
172.16.1.5	53273	205.251.19...	53	ULTRASRF	/UDP/DNS/ULTRASRF	false	true	100	
172.16.1.5	52747	205.251.19...	53	ULTRASRF	/UDP/DNS/ULTRASRF	false	true	100	
172.16.1.10	54852	173.194.39...	80	ULTRASRF	/TCP/HTTP/ULTRASRF	false	true	100	
172.16.1.10	54536	173.252.10...	443	FACEBOOK	/TCP/SSL/FACEBOOK	true	true	100	www.facebook.com
172.16.1.10	54535	173.252.10...	443	FACEBOOK	/TCP/SSL/FACEBOOK	true	true	100	www.facebook.com

However, when the user starts to use UltraSurf, the administrator can detect it by the amount of abnormal events coming from a certain machine, such as the following events on Application Control:

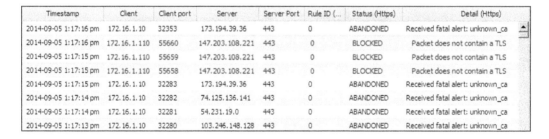

Timestamp	Client	Host	Uri	Server	Ser...	Bloc...	Flagg...
2014-09-...	172.16.1.1...	uswj104.appspot.com	/_connect?id=5N8Q4kRj&ver=140310...	74.125.136.115	443	false	false
2014-09-...	172.16.1.1...	uswj104.appspot.com	/_recv?id=JmwLQtRJ&ver=1403100&t...	74.125.136.115	443	false	false
2014-09-...	172.16.1.1...	uswj104.appspot.com	/_recv?id=vEHcNiDZ&ver=1403100&t...	74.125.136.115	443	false	false
2014-09-...	172.16.1.1...	uswj104.appspot.com	/_recv?id=vEHcNiDZ&ver=1403100&t...	74.125.136.115	443	false	false
2014-09-...	172.16.1.1...	uswj104.appspot.com	/_recv?id=JmwLQtRJ&ver=1403100&t...	74.125.136.115	443	false	false
2014-09-...	172.16.1.1...	uswj104.appspot.com	/_send?id=vEHcNiDZ&ver=1403100&t...	74.125.136.115	443	false	false
2014-09-...	172.16.1.1...	uswj104.appspot.com	/_send?id=vEHcNiDZ&ver=1403100&t...	74.125.136.115	443	false	false
2014-09-...	172.16.1.1...	uswj104.appspot.com	/_recv?id=vEHcNiDZ&ver=1403100&t...	74.125.136.115	443	false	false

6. In addition, you will find many Bad certificate Events on the HTTPS Inspector as shown in the next figure:

Timestamp	Client	Client port	Server	Server Port	Rule ID (...	Status (Https)	Detail (Https)
2014-09-05 1:17:16 pm	172.16.1.10	32353	173.194.39.36	443	0	ABANDONED	Received fatal alert: unknown_ca
2014-09-05 1:17:16 pm	172.16.1.110	55660	147.203.108.221	443	0	BLOCKED	Packet does not contain a TLS
2014-09-05 1:17:15 pm	172.16.1.110	55659	147.203.108.221	443	0	BLOCKED	Packet does not contain a TLS
2014-09-05 1:17:15 pm	172.16.1.110	55658	147.203.108.221	443	0	BLOCKED	Packet does not contain a TLS
2014-09-05 1:17:15 pm	172.16.1.10	32283	173.194.39.36	443	0	ABANDONED	Received fatal alert: unknown_ca
2014-09-05 1:17:14 pm	172.16.1.10	32282	74.125.136.141	443	0	ABANDONED	Received fatal alert: unknown_ca
2014-09-05 1:17:14 pm	172.16.1.10	32281	54.231.19.0	443	0	ABANDONED	Received fatal alert: unknown_ca
2014-09-05 1:17:13 pm	172.16.1.10	32280	103.246.148.128	443	0	ABANDONED	Received fatal alert: unknown_ca

Summary

In this chapter, we have learned about Untangle Web Filter, the HTTPS Inspector, Application Control, Bandwidth Control, and Web Cache applications.

We saw how Web Filter and Application Control can help to increase the employee's productivity by blocking certain sites and applications. Also, we learned how to utilize the HTTPS Inspector to decrypt the HTTPS traffic and pass it as HTTP to other applications for processing.

In the next chapter, we will learn about two new Untangle applications that are used to enhance and optimize your network traffic. The first application will be Bandwidth Control that can be used to prevent certain users from draining the whole bandwidth by setting quotas. You can also limit the bandwidth assigned to certain protocols (such as BitTorrent). The second application is the Web Cache that provides a local cache of the recently visited websites. This allows the users to download the data from the local cache instead of re-downloading the data when the user re-requests this web site, which could enhance their browsing experience.

9
Optimizing Network Traffic

Untangle's Bandwidth Control application can be used to enhance your bandwidth usage. Using Bandwidth Control, you can prevent certain users from draining the whole bandwidth by setting quotas. You can also limit the bandwidth assigned to certain protocols (such as BitTorrent). Untangle's Web Cache, provides a local cache of the recently visited websites. This can allow users when rerequesting this website to download the data from the local cache instead of redownloading the data, which could enhance their browsing experience.

The same method that was used to explain the applications in the previous chapters will be used here. We will first introduce the application, then cover how it works and any related technical details, see how we can review the event logs, and finally give some lab-based training. The list of topics that will be covered in this chapter is as follows:

- Untangle's Bandwidth Control
- Untangle's Web Cache

Bandwidth Control

Untangle's Bandwidth Control enables you to control, monitor, and prioritize your network's bandwidth consumption. It allows you to optimally share the network traffic among your users by prioritizing important sites (Salesforce) and time-critical traffic (VOIP), deprioritizing unimportant sites (YouTube), and limiting unauthorized usage (BitTorrent).

How does Bandwidth Control work?

Untangle's Bandwidth Control is similar to the **Quality of Service (QoS)** rules covered in *Chapter 4, Untangle Advanced Configuration*. In fact, when you enable Untangle's Bandwidth Control, you'll enable QoS rules. While QoS works with the bypassed traffic only, Untangle's Bandwidth Control can deal with traffic that enters the UVM. As a result, you can prioritize/deprioritize traffic based on its layer 7 information such as the used protocol, application, and destination sites. In addition, Untangle's Bandwidth Control enables you to set quotas for users to prevent network saturation.

Untangle's Bandwidth Control integrates with other Untangle applications to get the application/website-specific information. This includes Web Filter to provide website categorization, Application Control to provide protocol-profiling categorization, and the Directory Connector to provide username/group information.

Settings

This section covers the Untangle Bandwidth Control settings; first, we will cover how to set rules to prioritize/deprioritize and limit the traffic, then we will review the bandwidth monitor tool, and finally, we will review the quotas and penalty box for the users who overuse the network bandwidth.

Bandwidth Control rules

After installing Untangle's Bandwidth Control, it will be turned off by default. We have to run **Bandwidth Control Setup Wizard** before we turn it on. You can start the setup wizard from the **Run Bandwidth Control Setup Wizard** button located under the **Bandwidth Control Settings | Status**. The Bandwidth Control setup wizard will enable the QoS feature and create custom rules based on the configured settings on both QoS and Bandwidth Control.

Bandwidth Control setup wizard

The first window in the Bandwidth Control setup wizard is the welcome screen, which gives us a hint that to fully utilize the Bandwidth Control functionality, we may need to install other Untangle applications such as Web Filter, Application Control, and Directory Connector.

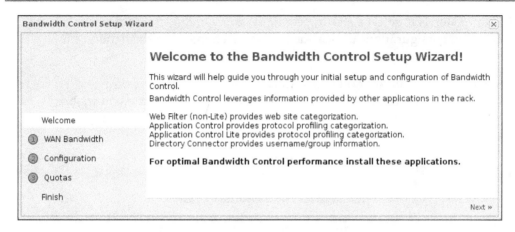

The second step is to configure the bandwidth rate on the WAN interfaces. Here, we only have one interface, which will be configured with a download rate of 8 Mbps and an upload rate of 1 Mbps. You should set the rate around 95 percent to 100 percent of the true rate. As the application sets the limit based on the percentage of the total available bandwidth, so if you have 1 Mbps and set the rate in the setup wizard to 10 Mbps, 10 percent will equal the 1 Mbps, which is the true bandwidth, and instead of limiting the usage, you will let the user fully utilize the bandwidth. If you set the value in the setup wizard to a very low value, the application will limit most traffic to this value even if there is an unallocated bandwidth. The following screenshot shows the configuration steps of the WAN interface:

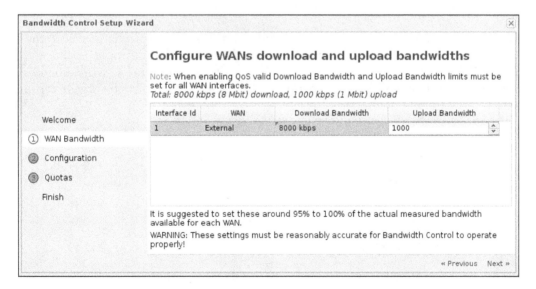

The third step is to select a starting configuration. Untangle provides many predefined configurations to ease the process of configuring the Bandwidth Control application.

The predefined configuration will automatically create the prioritizing, deprioritizing, and limiting rules. You can modify them anytime you wish, or even create your custom rules from scratch. However, starting with a predefined configuration is always a good idea.

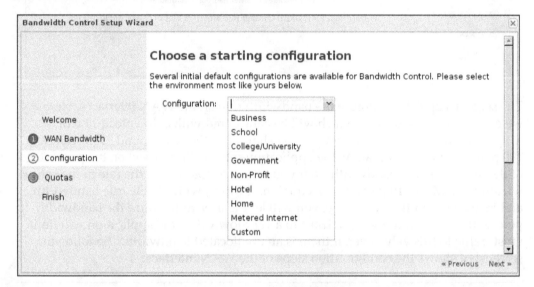

All configurations have common sense in between. They will optimize traffic in the interest of the plan users and deprioritize any other traffic. For example, business users will be more interested in search engines than any other traffic, while home users will need to have flawless experience while watching YouTube videos even if they have running downloads.

Common prioritizing rules are as follows:

- Interactive traffic and services (remote desktop, e-mail, DNS, and SSH)
- Interactive web traffic (based on the selected rule; thus, the school configuration will optimize traffic to education sites, while a hotel plan will optimize traffic to business-related sites)

Common deprioritizing/limit rules are as follows:

- Non-real-time background services (for example, Microsoft updates and backup services)
- Web traffic to download sites

- Any detected peer-to-peer traffic
- All web traffic in violation of the plan policy

Also, you can set quotas, which is useful in many cases. Quotas allow you to limit the assigned bandwidth for certain hosts if they exceeded their allowed bandwidth usage. Different settings that can be configured are as follows:

- **Quota Clients**: The quota can be applied to a certain host or a group of hosts. You will need to define the hosts using their IP.

- **Quota Expiration**: This defines how long the assigned quota will be in use before a host grants a new quota. The quota's expiration could be hourly, daily, or weekly.

- **Quota Size**: This specifies the allowed data usage before applying any limitation on the host. The default value is 1 GB.

- **Quota Exceeded Priority**: This specifies the priority given to hosts when they exceed their quota size. These priorities are the same as QoS priorities.

These settings are illustrated in the following screenshot:

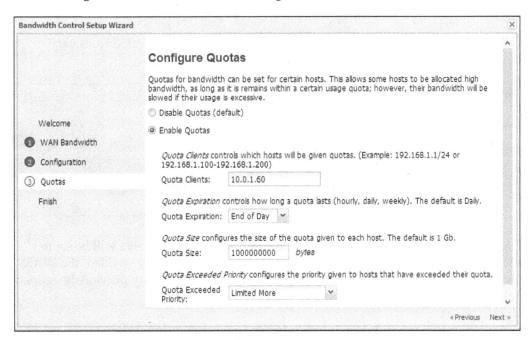

The default values will grant each host 1 GB per day. If the 1 GB limit is reached in a single day by a host, a bandwidth limitation will be applied to that host, which limits the upload and download to 2 percent of the available bandwidth (if there are any other hosts that use the bandwidth) and to 50 percent of the available bandwidth (if there isn't any other host that uses the bandwidth).

 When a client bandwidth is limited, all limited clients share the limitation level's available bandwidth. Thus, for the preceding example, the client will not grant the whole 2 percent of the available bandwidth, but it will share it with any other limited clients.

The final screen will inform you that the Bandwidth Control is now configured and enabled. After completing the setup wizard, the following statement will appear under the **Status** tab:

Preconfigured rules will be created under the **Rules** tab. The created rules vary depending on the configurations selected in the setup wizard:

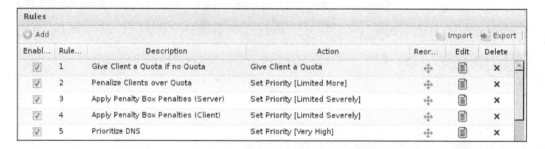

Also, the QoS rules will be enabled and the WAN bandwidth value will be set to the value defined in the setup wizard. If the QoS was previously enabled, the WAN bandwidth settings defined in the setup wizard will override any previously defined values as shown in the following screenshot:

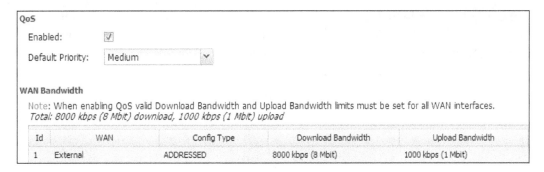

Rules

Basically, rules are what configure and control the behavior of Untangle's Bandwidth Control. You can create custom rules or use the preconfigured rules; the rules are evaluated in order and when a match is found, the action on this rule will be taken; if no match is found, no action will be taken and the traffic will take the default QoS priority, which is medium.

Unlike the other applications' rules, which are evaluated during the session formation only, Untangle's Bandwidth Control rules are evaluated during the session formation and on the first 10 packets of the session since some matchers such as **HTTP: Hostname** and **Application Control: Application** are not known until several packets have been transferred. In addition, all rules will be reevaluated if the host moved to the penalty box or exceeded its quota.

As the case with all rules, we will need to define a Matcher and an action to be taken if the traffic is matched. Matchers will mainly look for the traffic properties in layer 7 and can get details such as site category and application protocol from other applications. Actions can be **Set Priority**, **Send to Penalty Box**, or **Set Quota**. The **Set Priority** action will limit the matched traffic bandwidth based on the priority level. Different priorities and their limitation details were discussed in the *QoS* section of *Chapter 4*, *Untangle Advanced Configuration*. The **Send to Penalty Box** and **Set Quota** actions will be discussed in the upcoming sections.

An example of a rule that limits the traffic to `dropbox.com` is shown in the following screenshot. The used matcher is **HTTP: Hostname = dropbox.com,** and the action is to set this traffic priority to the more limited priority.

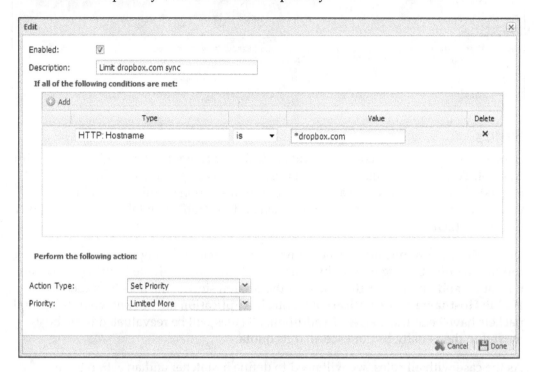

Bandwidth Monitor

The **Bandwidth Monitor** tool allows you to review the current sessions and their traffic usage. You can run the tool from the **Open Bandwidth Monitor** button located under **Settings | Status:**

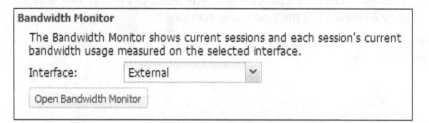

The tool is similar to the session viewer tool. However, it has additional columns that state the current bandwidth usage and the assigned priority to that traffic, as shown in the following screenshot:

Current Sessions											
Client ...	Server ...	Hostna...	Client (Pre...	Client Por...	Server (Post-...	Ser...	Applicatio...	Client KB...	Server K...	Tot...	Priority (Ba...
Servers	External	10.0.0.5	10.0.0.5	49270	202.12.27.33	53	UDP	0	0	0	Very High
Users	External	10.0.1....	10.0.1.15	49612	54.230.93.37	443	AMAZONWS	0	0	0	Medium
Servers	External	10.0.0.5	10.0.0.5	64834	216.239.38.10	53	UDP	0	0	0	Very High
Users	External	10.0.1....	10.0.1.15	49620	213.158.189....	443	GOOGLE	0	0	0	Medium
Servers	External	10.0.0.5	10.0.0.5	64737	96.7.49.129	53	DNS	0	0	0	Very High
Users	External	10.0.1....	10.0.1.15	49605	74.125.71.94	443	GOOGLE	0	0	0	Medium
Servers	External	10.0.0.5	10.0.0.5	53688	173.194.35.1...	80	YOUTUBE	0	0	0	Medium
Users	External	10.0.1....	10.0.1.15	49606	173.194.66.95	80	GOOGAPIS	0	0	0	Medium
Servers	External	10.0.0.5	10.0.0.5	53702	173.252.110....	80	FACEBOOK	0	0	0	Medium
Servers	External	10.0.0.5	10.0.0.5	61565	64.4.11.25	80	MICRSOFT	0.1	0.1	0.2	Medium
Servers	External	10.0.0.5	10.0.0.5	64267	74.115.250.1...	53	DNS	0	0	0	Very High

The penalty box

Sometimes, the default deprioritizing and limiting traffic rules are not the right way to punish the offending hosts, especially with hard-to-block and hard-to-control applications such as BitTorrent clients and Skype. Instead, if any unauthorized usage was detected from any host, the host will be sent to the penalty box for a period of time. While in the penalty box, we are able to apply rules to slow or block all traffic from this host. Thus, if any user was using a BitTorrent client instead of giving this traffic a low priority, we will slow down or block all traffic from this user to stop the user from trying to evade the default deprioritize rule.

First, we will need to set a rule to send the host to the penalty box if unauthorized usage such as torrent traffic was detected, as shown in the following screenshot:

Then, we should add another rule that applies to hosts on the penalty box to slow or block their traffic:

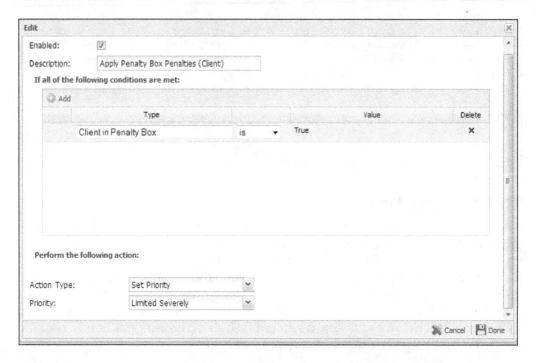

We can review the hosts on the penalty box via the **View Penalty Box** button located under **Settings | Status | Penalty Box**, which will open the host viewer window from where we can review the current hosts in the penalty box and the penalty box event log.

The following screenshot shows the IP addresses of currents hosts in the penalty box, the time they entered it, and the planned time to exit from it. You can also manually release the clients from the penalty box before the planned exit time.

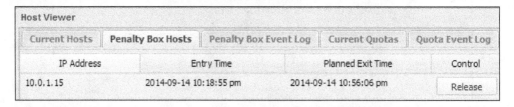

The **Penalty Box Event Log** tab provides historical data of the clients entered in the penalty box and when they left it, and the reason for that (the rule ID):

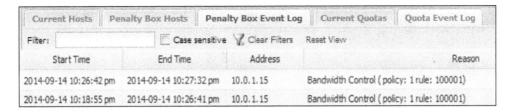

Quotas

You can review the current quotas by pressing the **View Quotas** button located under **Status | Quotas**, which will open the **Host Viewer** window from which we can review the current applied quotas and the quota event log. Configuring quotas is done under Rules.

The following screenshot shows the current applied quotas. The applied quota is 30 MB and the remaining quota is 29.9 MB. The quota was allocated at 10:59 p.m. and will expire at the end of the day, that is, at 11:59:59 p.m. You can refill the quota (give the user another 30 MB to download) or you can drop (the quota won't apply on the user until the traffic condition rematches).

The quota event logs give a detailed summary about the quota events: when they are applied, on which device, the quota size, and the reason for that:

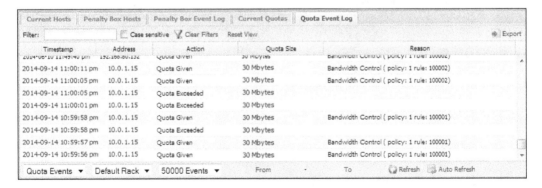

To set quota rules, we will need to apply quotas on a client, as shown in the following screenshot:

Then, we will need to limit the traffic if the client exceeds their quota:

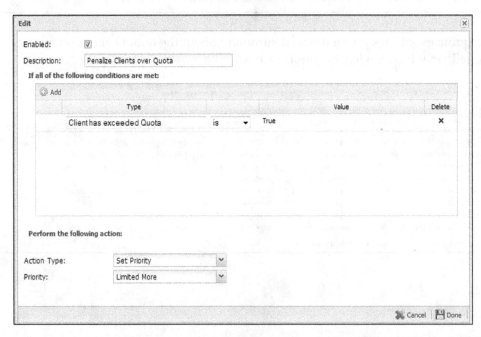

Reviewing the scan history

As you know, we can review the scan history via the application faceplate, event logs, or reports. The application faceplate gives a summary about what happened since the last server reboot and the real-time traffic processed by the application.

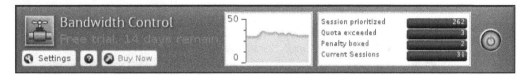

The Event logs give more details about the traffic such as its type, the used application, and the server and client address. They also show the priority assigned to the traffic and the rule that caused that. In addition to **Prioritize Event Log**, there are also the **Quota** and **Penalty Box Event Log**:

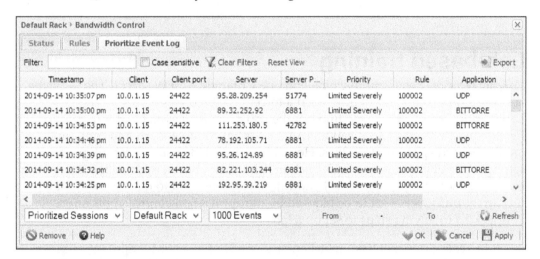

Finally, there are Reports, which provide summary reports about the Bandwidth and detailed Quota events. The available Reports are as follows:

- **Bandwidth Usage**: This gives the average data rate (KB/S) and the total data transferred per day

- **Top Bandwidth Hosts**: This shows the top hosts' utilization of the available bandwidth

- **Top Bandwidth Users**: This shows the top users based on their utilization of the available bandwidth

- **Top Bandwidth Ports**: This shows the top ports that used the available bandwidth

- **Bandwidth by Priority**: This shows the bandwidth consumed by each priority
- **Sessions by Priority**: This gives the number of sessions for each priority (for example, **Limited Severely** has 2000 sessions)

The following screenshot shows the **Bandwidth by Priority** summary report:

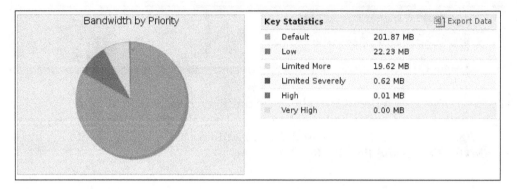

Lab-based training

This lab requires one client machine and one Untangle NGFW server. The lab steps are very simple. First, try to download a torrent file before applying Untangle's Bandwidth Control settings to find out the real download speed. After installing the Bandwidth Control application, run the configuration wizard and configure the WAN with appropriate values. Here, I have selected custom preconfiguration settings to be able to create simple custom rules. Also, I have selected the later option in order to not apply quota now. In addition, you will need to make sure that the BitTorrent traffic is not set to be blocked by the application control application. Perform the following steps to set up a lab:

1. Create a rule that has a matcher, `Application Control: Application is BITTORRE`, and set the action as **Set Priority** and select **Limited Severely**. When you start the download process, the BitTorrent application will be detected, and the **Limited Severely** priority will be applied on it. You'll notice that the download speed equals about 2 percent of the total available bandwidth.

2. Change the previous rule action to send the client to the penalty box and set the duration as 1800 seconds. We will need to create another rule that sets the clients' priority in the penalty box to **Limited Severely**. The matcher used in the second rule is **Client in Penalty Box Is True** and the action is **Set Priority** to **Limited Severely**. When the user starts the download process, the client will be sent into the penalty box, and the download limit will reach the 2 percent limit of the available bandwidth.

3. Again, we will change the first rule matcher to the **Source Address is <client IP>** and the action will be to **give client a Quota** with **End of Day** Quota Expiration and Quota size of **30,000,000** bytes (30 MB). The second rule will be **changed to client has exceeded quota is true** and let the **Set Priority** settings remain unchanged. Now, after starting the download, the download will be at full speed, but after the first 30 MB of download, the traffic will be throttled to 2 percent of the available traffic as the quota will be exceeded.

Web Cache

Untangle Web Cache helps companies to reduce the bandwidth usage and increase the sites' response time. Every time a user visits a website, its contents are stored locally on the Untangle NGFW server, and whenever the same site is requested either by the same user or by another user, the response will be provided from the cached version.

Untangle Web Cache is based on the Squid project, and it only works with the HTTP traffic. The local cache is kept on the server's hard disk and it's preserved even after system restart. Every cache query uses a fair amount of CPU resources and disk I/O, which when the server is fully utilized may lead to some latency.

To take full advantage of the Untangle Web Cache, you will need to run it on a network with at least one of the following: more than 100 users, slow/metered Internet connection, high duplicated traffic, and low dynamic website traffic (which is not cacheable).

Web Cache settings

Under the **Settings** tab, we can review the Untangle Web Cache status and configure the bypass list. However, there are not many settings to configure.

Status

Every client request is first directed to the Web Cache app, and if the content is available, it will be served through the local cache (which is called cache hit); otherwise, it will be called cache miss, and the traffic is downloaded directly from the Internet, and a local copy is saved for later usage.

This section provides the total count of the cache hits and misses. It also provides their size in bytes and the count of any bypass that occurred. The bypass could be a result of the bypass rule created under the **Cache Bypass** tab or because the HTTP session was determined to be incompatible with the Untangle Web Cache system.

If you feel that the cache contents become obsolete or corrupted, you can clear the current cache contents via the **Clear Cache** button. You will need to check the **I understand the risks** checkbox first as clearing the cache contents is done by restarting the cache engine, which will interrupt all the active sessions:

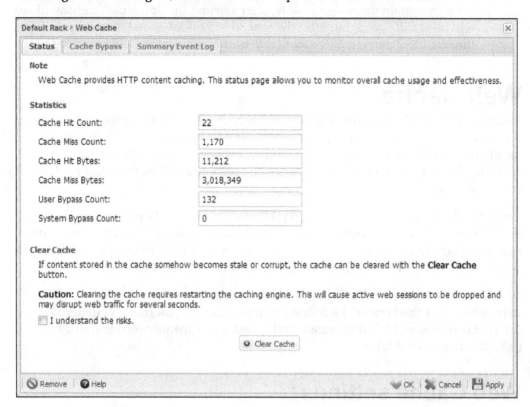

Cache Bypass

Some sites will not operate correctly when cached, for example, Google Maps, which is added by default. To add additional sites to this bypass list, simply click on the **Add** button and add the site domain name, as shown in the following screenshot:

Reviewing the caching history

Needless to say, we have three options to review the Untangle Web Cache application activity. The options are the application faceplate, application event logs, and the reports. The following screenshot shows the application's faceplate:

The **Summary Event Log** tab gives you a summary of the cache hit and misses and their sizes based on the time and not the requested site:

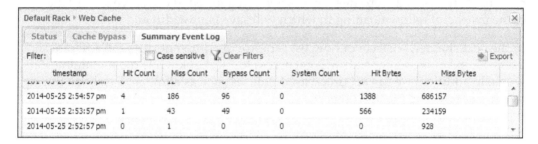

The reports also provide a complete overview over the Web Cache event. The available reports are as follows:

- **Hits**: This gives the average and maximum number of cache hits and misses
- **Size**: This gives the average and maximum MB/hours served from the cache or downloaded for the first time

Lab-based training

In this lab, we will prove the Web Cache functionality by trying to load a large image from the Web Cache and see how it can enhance the load time and save the network bandwidth. To do so, perform the following steps:

1. Browse to Google images.
2. Search for any term you wish.
3. From **Search Tools**, select the maximum size possible.
4. Open any picture you wish and notice the load time.

5. Clear your browser cache and try to open the image again and notice the load time.

6. In step 5, you'll notice that the image loaded much faster than the first time.

7. Open the same picture from another browser and you'll notice that it loads faster than the previous one.

Summary

In this chapter, we learned about Untangle Bandwidth Control and Web Cache and saw how they can save your network bandwidth and optimize its usage. Bandwidth Control is used to set priority for the traffic based on its criteria. Any violience traffic can be limited or can get a certain quota. The Web Cache is used to cache the static contents of the visited web sites; thus, when rerequested, it can serve it from the cache instead of redownloading it, which will save bandwidth and time.

In the next chapter, we'll cover how we can provide different rules for different users; for example, senior staff will get access to Facebook while the remaining staff won't. In addition, we can set time-based policies such as allowing Facebook during the dinner time and block it otherwise.

10
Untangle Network Policy

Up to this point, we have learned about different rules. There are the kernel-level rules that evaluate the traffic before being processed by the different applications. The kernel level rules include bypass rules, QoS rules, input filter rules, port forward rules, and so on.

When the traffic is passed to be processed by applications, different rules will be applied on the traffic. The first rule to be applied is the one that evaluates the traffic at the session initiation such as the Firewall rule. If the traffic passes the Firewall rule, it will be scanned by other applications such as Web Filter to determine whether to allow or block the traffic. After that, there are rules that will be applied after fully classifying the traffic, such as the Application Control and Bandwidth Control rules. In addition, each individual application has rules to not scan traffic from a certain website or from certain device.

All the previous rules are based on the traffic criteria. In this chapter, we will learn how we can set rules per user or per time of day. For example, we may want to provide executives with non-restricted access to the Internet, while blocking the remaining employees of the company unless in the break hour.

First, we will need to use Untangle's Directory Connector to identify the logged in user and their Active Directory group membership. Second, we will use the Policy Manager to assign different policies to the different users based on their membership and the time of day.

Untangle's Captive Portal can be used to provide authentication for mobile devices' users and to acknowledge those users with the **acceptable use policy** (**AUP**).

 The configurations done in this chapter is assumed to be done on Acme school's headquarter.

The topics that will be covered in this chapter are as follows:

- Untangle's Directory Connector
- Untangle's Captive Portal
- Untangle's Policy Manager

Directory Connector

The main functionality of Untangle's Directory Connector is to allow Untangle NGFW to communicate with Active Directory and Radius servers. Untangle's Directory Connector can be used with Captive Portal to authenticate users or to provide user details (such as the username and the security group) to other Untangle applications such as Policy Manager, Reports, and Rules (that is, username matcher).

> Captive Portal must be installed on Untangle NGFW after Directory Connector to work properly. If you have installed Captive Portal first, just uninstall and reinstall it.

The User Notification API

Untangle NGFW deals with clients based on their IP addresses. Thus, the discovered username will need to be mapped to the machine's IP address and stored in the host table so that other applications can use the information about this host.

The User Notification API is a web app that runs on Untangle NGFW. It is used to notify Untangle NGFW that a specific user is logged in to a specific IP address. The API can be updated as follows:

- Manually
- With the **User Notification Login Script** (**UNLS**)
- Through an Active Directory Server Login Monitor Agent
- Using a custom script or external program

To enable user notifications, we will need to enable the User Notification API from the **Enabled** radio button located under **Directory Connector Settings | User Notification API**. By default, any call from any source to the API is accepted. We can limit this by setting a secret key. Thus, the API will only accept calls that have this secret key as shown in the following screenshot:

The User Notification API URL is `http://<Server_IP>/userapi/registration`. The user-machine details can be defined by calling the API with the following arguments:

- `ClientIP`
- `Username`
- `Hostname`
- `Action (login, logout)`
- `SecretKey`

For example, if we want to notify Untangle that a user named JDoe is logged in to a machine whose IP address is `192.168.2.70` and its name is JDoe-PC, using the secret key of `P@$$w0rd`, we will use the following URL (assuming that our Untangle internal IP is `172.16.1.1`):

`http://172.16.1.1/userapi/registration?action=login&clientIP=172.16.1.106&username=JDoe&hostname=Acme-Client02&secretKey=P@$$w0rd`

To remove the mapping, we can use the following URL:

`http://172.16.1.1/userapi/registration?action=logout&clientIP=172.16.1.106&username=JDoe&hostname=Acme-Client02&secretKey=P@$$w0rd`

The previous actions will appear on the **Event Log** tab as shown in the following screenshot (the successive login actions will appear as and when updated):

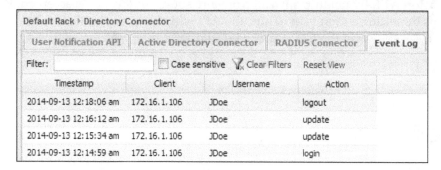

The previous method is the manual method as it is obviously clear that making users manually visit these URLs is not practical and many users may forget to do this. However, many organizations might want to script this and add it into their login/ logout scripts.

Untangle offers two automated ways to update the user-machine details. The first way is by using a login script that sends the username details to Untangle. The second way is by using Login Monitor Agent that is deployed on your DCs, which monitors login events and updates Untangle NGFW. Also, any automated script that uses the previously mentioned arguments will work fine.

UNLS

UNLS is a Visual Basic script that runs at the user login process. The script will get the username and the machine's IP data and send them to Untangle's User Notification API. The script helps to automatically update the mapping between usernames and the machine's IP address.

The UNLS script runs at the user's login and periodically after every 5 minutes. If no updates come to Untangle NGFW for 10 minutes, Untangle NGFW will drop the mapping from the host table. You can download the UNLS script by pressing the **Download User Notification Login Script** button located under **Directory Connector Settings | User Notification API**, which will open a new browser window that can also be reached via http://<Untangle_IP>/adpb/ or http://<Untangle_IP>/userapi/. Clicking on the **User Notification Login Script** link highlighted in blue in the new page will download the UNLS script, as shown in the following screenshot:

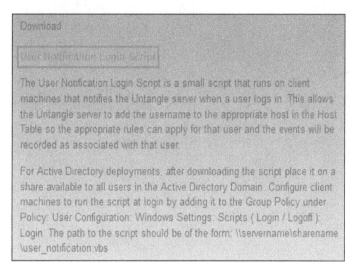

The downloaded script is preconfigured with server settings. However, some additional settings may be required such as the secret key.

A script that can be used with Mac OS X servers can be found at http://forums.Untangle.com/directory-connector/11157-using-ut-mac-os-x-server-ldap.html.

You can then cloud deploy this login script to your network computers via a group policy. You'll need to copy the script file to the shared NETLOGON folder and then configure a **Group Policy Object** (**GPO**) to run this script at user login. The desired configurations can be found under **User Configuration** | **Windows Settings** | **Scripts (Logon/Logoff)** as shown in the following screenshot:

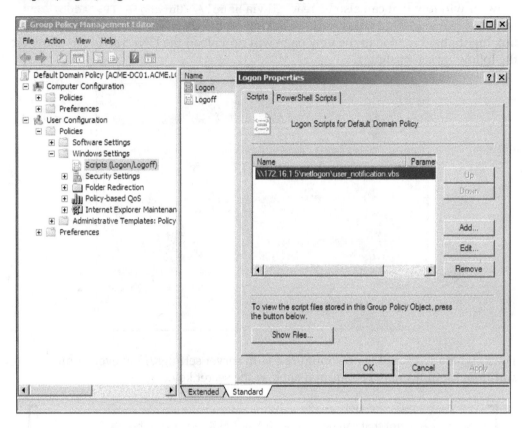

By default, Windows will try to run and complete all login scripts before allowing a user to log in (synchronously). This will cause problems with our script as it runs in loop and thus it never ends, so the user will wait until the login timeout occurs (about 20 minutes) before they can log in to their machine. In addition, the script may never complete with these default settings. Thus, we will need to modify additional GPO settings under **Computer Configuration** | **Policies** | **Administrative Templates** | **System** | **Scripts**. We will need to change the **Run logon scripts synchronously** configuration to **Disabled** and the **Run startup scripts asynchronously** configuration to **Enabled**, as shown in the following screenshot:

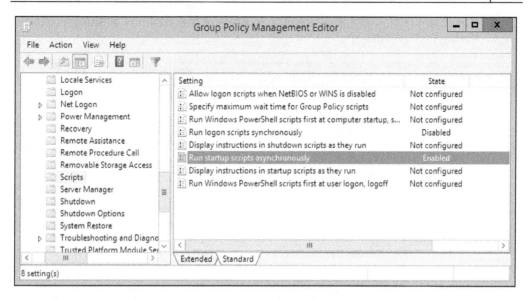

Also, you will need to make sure that the **Domain controller: LDAP server signing requirements** setting located under **Default Domain Controller Policy | Computer Configuration | Policies | Windows Settings | Security Settings | Local Policies | Security** is set to disabled or none.

We can only monitor the login and update events via the UNLS script. When a user logs out, the event will stop, and thus after 10 minutes, Untangle NGFW will remove the mapping. If we want to immediately remove the mapping and log the logout action, we can use another logout script for this purpose.

The new logout script can be the same as the login script but with some modifications:

1. Remove the loop (the Do While True loop).

2. Modify `keepLooping` to `False`.

3. Change `action` to `logout`.

4. Remove `SLEEP_PERIOD = 300000` to prevent logout delay as shown in the following screenshot:

```
                              user_notification_logout - Notepad
 File  Edit  Format  View  Help

Do While True
        Set AJAX = CreateObject("MSXML2.ServerXMLHTTP")
        Set wshNetwork = CreateObject("WScript.Network")
        strHostname = wshNetwork.ComputerName
        strDomain = wshNetwork.UserDomain

        'The next section gets username from function and checks that it isn't null
        sUserName = GetActiveUser(strHostname)
        If sUserName <> "" Then
            strUser = sUserName
        'MsgBox "Active user from function: " + sUserName
        Else
        'will default to user executing script if no active user
        strUser = wshNetwork.UserName
        End If

        command = urlProtocol + "://" + serverLocation + "/userapi/registration?username=" _
                              + strUser + "&domain=" + strDomain + "&hostname=" + strHostname _
                              + "&action=logout"
        'WScript.Echo "Hitting Url: " & command
        AJAX.Open "GET", command
        AJAX.Send ""
        If keepLooping Then
                'WScript.Echo "Sleeping..."
                WScript.sleep(sleepPeriodMs)
                AJAX.Abort
                Set AJAX = nothing
        Else
                AJAX.Abort
                Set AJAX = nothing
                Exit Do
        End If
Loop

' Function will return active user name from QWINSTA.EXE
```

We can review the user-machine mapping through the **Host Viewer** page as shown in the following screenshot:

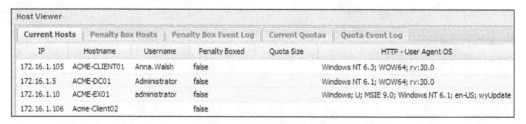

Host Viewer						
Current Hosts	Penalty Box Hosts	Penalty Box Event Log	Current Quotas	Quota Event Log		
IP	Hostname	Username	Penalty Boxed	Quota Size	HTTP - User Agent OS	
172.16.1.105	ACME-CLIENT01	Anna.Walsh	false		Windows NT 6.3; WOW64; rv:30.0	
172.16.1.5	ACME-DC01	Administrator	false		Windows NT 6.1; WOW64; rv:30.0	
172.16.1.10	ACME-EX01	administrator	false		Windows; U; MSIE 9.0; Windows NT 6.1; en-US; wyUpdate	
172.16.1.106	Acme-Client02		false			

We can review the login and logout events via the Directory Connector events as shown in the following screenshot:

Default Rack ▸ Directory Connector			
User Notification API	Active Directory Connector	RADIUS Connector	Event Log

Filter: [ ] ☐ Case sensitive ▼ Clear Filters Reset View

Timestamp	Client	Username	Action
2014-09-13 12:43:50 am	172.16.1.105	Anna.Walsh	update
2014-09-13 12:42:54 am	172.16.1.5	Administrator	update
2014-09-13 12:41:50 am	172.16.1.10	administrator	update
2014-09-13 12:41:46 am	172.16.1.110	JDoe	logout
2014-09-13 12:41:26 am	172.16.1.110	JDoe	logout
2014-09-13 12:38:50 am	172.16.1.105	Anna.Walsh	login
2014-09-13 12:37:54 am	172.16.1.5	Administrator	update
2014-09-13 12:36:50 am	172.16.1.10	administrator	login
2014-09-13 12:32:54 am	172.16.1.5	Administrator	login

The Active Directory Login Monitor Agent

The Active Directory Login Monitor Agent is a new feature in version 10.2 (only works with version 10.2 and higher). It's a tool that will be installed in your Domain Controllers to monitor the login events and will call the User Notification API to update the `host` table. The Login Monitor Agent has many advantages over the login script method. First, we won't need to create a GPO; also, we will evade the problem of some machines that don't process the group policy. Secondly, as the tool runs on the Domain Controllers, we could use the secret key so that the DC will only be able to update the user mapping. However, the users won't be able to do this as they don't have the secret key.

You can download the Monitoring agent from `http://www.Untangle.com/download/LoginMonitorSetup.exe`.

 Untangle web pages are hosted on Apache servers, so make sure from the capitalization on the URL.

You can install the Monitoring Agent on all of your DCs or only to one of your DCs. The installation process is very simple; after installing the agent, you will need to configure it as follows:

- **NGFW IP**: This is your Untangle server IP. If you have more than one server, you can add their IPs using the **More** button.
- **Domain**: This is the Active Directory domain that we want to record its user's login activity.

- **Secret Key**: The secret key to be used in communication with the User Notification API.

- **Prefix**: The protocol to be used in communication with the User Notification API. It can be either HTTP or HTTPS.

- **Exempt IP's**: Specify certain IPs or IP ranges from which any login activity won't be updated to Untangle NGFW. This can be useful with terminal servers.

- **Exempt Users**: Specify users whose login activities won't be updated to Untangle NGFW.

After setting the desired configuration, we will need to click on the **Save and Close** button.

There are some cases where many users connect to Untangle from the same machine IP such as Windows Fast Switching and terminal servers. Untangle is able to deal with the Windows Fast Switching feature by identifying the current active user on the console. As **remote desktop (RD)** sessions don't have console sessions, Untangle is not able to natively identify them. However, virtual IPs can be used through the Microsoft RD session host to override this limitation.

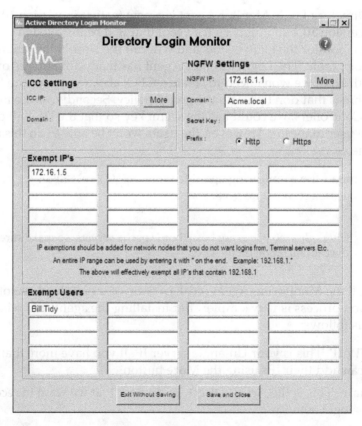

Configuring Active Directory Connector

Active Directory Connector allows users to log in to Captive Portal via their Active Directory credentials. Also, it allows Untangle NGFW to query Active Directory about the security groups that specific users belong to so that the User In Group matcher can be used. Untangle NGFW can only run with a single domain; multiple domain environments are not supported at this time.

We can configure Active Directory Connector located under the **Directory Connector Settings | Active Directory Connector**. First, we will need to enable the Connector, and then fill up the following required data:

- **AD Server IP or Hostname**: The IP or hostname of one of your Domain Controllers. Using IP is preferred to prevent any DNS issues.

- **Port**: By default, 389 is used, which is the default port for LDAP. If you have changed this on your **Active Directory Settings** page, you will need to change it here also.

- **Authentication Login**: This is the Active Directory user that has the ability to read all user information. You can use the administrator account or a normal account with the read-all user information delegation over the desired **organization unit** (OU).

- **Authentication Password**: The password of the user account used as the authentication login.

- **Active Directory Domain**: The **Fully Qualified Domain Name** (FQDN) of your domain.

- **Active Directory Organization**: The Active Directory OU that contains the desired users. By default, this field is blank, which will query Active Directory for all user accounts. If you want to limit it to a specific OU, you can add this OU (for example, to limit a query to the Sales OU that is located under the Users OU, we will use OU=Users and OU=Sales).

All these settings are illustrated in the following screenshot:

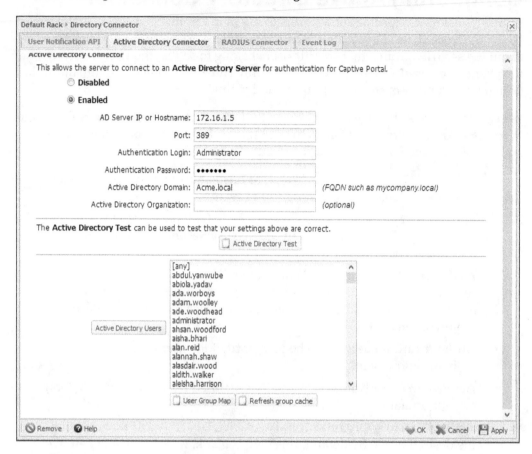

After configuring Active Directory Connector, we can test our settings via the **Active Directory Test** button. If our settings are correct, we will get the success message as shown in the following screenshot:

You can query the Active Directory users by clicking on the **Active Directory Users** button. All of your Active Directory users will be displayed in the box next to the button.

> The default setting of Active Directory is to return only 1000 user accounts. So, if your organization users are more than 1000, you will need to run the following commands on your Domain Controller to increase the returned user account to 5000:
>
> ```
> ntdsutil.exe
> LDAP policies
> Connections
> Connect to server <Your_Domain_FQDN>
> Quit
> Set MaxPageSize to 5000
> Commit Changes
> Quit
> Quit
> ```

In addition, you can query the security groups those users belong to via the **User Group Map** button. The user group mapping will be displayed in a new window as shown in the following screenshot:

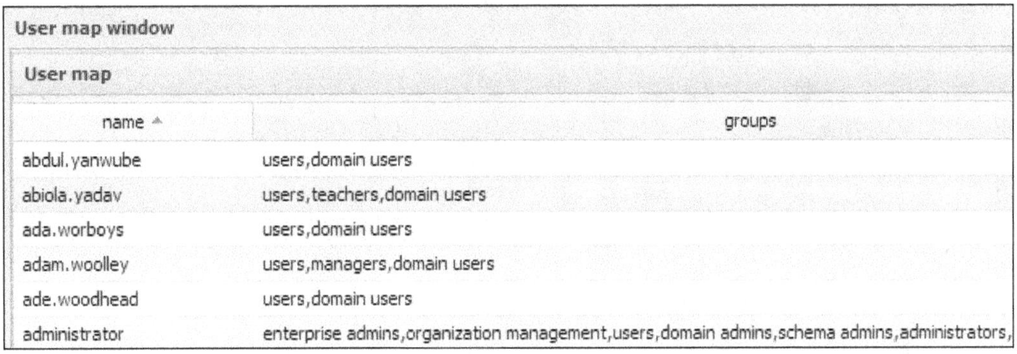

User map window	
User map	
name ▲	groups
abdul.yanwube	users,domain users
abiola.yadav	users,teachers,domain users
ada.worboys	users,domain users
adam.woolley	users,managers,domain users
ade.woodhead	users,domain users
administrator	enterprise admins,organization management,users,domain admins,schema admins,administrators,

By default, Untangle updates the user group mapping every 30 minutes. You can force user group mapping updates before this default period via the **Refresh Group Cache** button.

Connecting Untangle to a RADIUS server

Untangle is able to communicate with RADIUS servers using Directory Connector. It allows users to authenticate via the RADIUS server. You can configure the connection to RADIUS servers from **Directory Connector Settings | RADIUS Connector**. You can enable the connector through the **Enabled** radio button. Then, you'll need to configure the connector settings. The different settings are as follows:

- **RADIUS Server IP or Hostname**: The IP or hostname of your RADIUS server. Using IP is preferred to prevent any DNS issues.

- **Port**: By default, **1812** is used, which is the default port. If you have changed this on your RADIUS server, you will need to change it here also.

- **Shared Secret**: The shared secret configured on the RADIUS server to secure the connection with Untangle.

- **Authentication Method**: The authentication method used with the RADIUS server. **Password Authentication Protocol (PAP)** is clear text authentication while **Challenge Handshake Authentication Protocol (CHAP)** is a more secure method. The specified authentication method should match the method on the RADIUS server.

These settings are illustrated in the following screenshot:

You can test your configuration via the **RADIUS Test** button. You may need to enter user credentials to complete the test. If the authentication is successful, you'll get the following message on your screen:

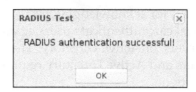

Directory Connector reports

There are different summary reports available for the Directory Connectors. The reports are as follows:

- **AD Events**: These show a summary about authentication events related to Active Directory such as the number of logins per hour
- **Top AD Users**: These give the number of logins done by Active Directory users
- **Total Sessions**: These give the total number of identified and unidentified sessions
- **Sessions**: These show a summary about the identified and unidentified login events per hour

The following screenshot shows the **Top AD Users** summary report:

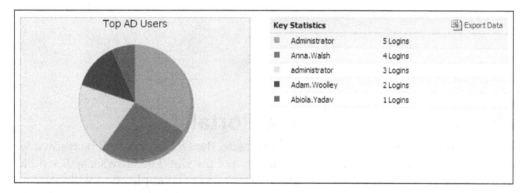

Untangle's Captive Portal

Captive Portal is used to enforce users' authentication before they can use the Internet. This is helpful in many cases, as follows:

- To ensure that users read and accept the AUP before they can access the Internet
- To enforce different Internet usage policies based on the username and/or device type such as wireless connected devices, BYOD, and smartphones

Captive Portal can just be used for acknowledging users, or to enforce users' authentication. Captive Portal can authenticate users against the Untangle NGFW local directory, RADIUS servers, or Active Directory. The ability to authenticate users against RADIUS servers and Active Directory requires the usage of the Directory Connector application.

The working of Captive Portal

When an unauthenticated user requests a website, the DNS query will be resolved as usual and the browser will get the IP address of the site. The browser will send a HTTP request to this IP address. Untangle's Captive Portal application will intercept any HTTP and HTTPS (requires the usage of the HTTPS Inspector application) traffic and redirect it to the Captive Portal page for acknowledging or authentication.

The Captive Portal page will only be displayed if the user was using a web browser. Untangle doesn't have the ability to open a web browser page to authenticate traffic from other sources. For example, your antivirus application won't be able to update its database until you first open a web browser and complete the authentication process. The same is true for your smartphone where all your applications won't be able to connect to the Internet till the Captive Portal authentication does.

Most modern smartphones are able to detect Captive Portals and will display notifications about additional steps that are required to complete the connection to the Internet. However, if the steps didn't get completed in a certain amount of time, the smartphone will fall back to the 3G/4G connection.

Configuring Captive Portal

You have to configure Captive Portal before starting. The configuring of Captive Portal is a really simple process. The required steps are as follows:

1. We need to set up capture rules to define the traffic we want to be captured by Captive Portal (that is, the Captive Portal page will appear for traffic matching a certain criteria while any other traffic will be able to connect normally). For example, we can set traffic from wireless devices to be captured while traffic from wired devices to be passed. We will also capture traffic from students while allowing teachers to bypass Captive Portal.

 There is a default capturing rule that will capture traffic from all devices connected to the Untangle NGFW internal interface.

2. We need to configure the server bypass list. We can allow clients to access certain servers without authenticating via Captive Portal. This can be useful if you have web servers in your DMZ. The servers will be listed in **Pass Listed Server Addresses**.

3. We need to configure the client bypass list. We can allow a certain client (which is included in the capture rule clients range) to connect directly to the Internet without authentication. This can be useful when all clients are located in the same subnet. The clients will be listed in **Pass Listed Client Addresses**.

4. We need to customize the Captive Portal page. In this step, we can configure whether the Captive Portal page will be an informative page or will be used for authentication and against which directory.

Setting traffic capture rules

Traffic capture rules are located under **Captive Portal Settings | Capture Rules**. There is a default rule that will capture any traffic coming from any device connected to the Untangle NGFW internal interface.

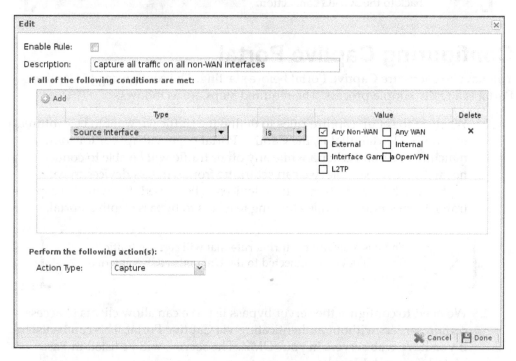

The capture rules have the same properties as other rules. We will define a traffic matcher that when met, Captive Portal will capture this traffic. The available matchers are Destination Address, Destination Port, Destination Interface, Source Address, Source Interface, Protocol, Username, Client Hostname, Client in Penalty Box, Server in Penalty Box, Client has exceeded Quota, Server has exceeded Quota, Directory Connector: User in group, HTTP: Client User Agent, and HTTP: Client User OS. The available actions are to capture or pass the traffic.

Common traffic capture rules

In this section, we will review common traffic capture rules. For the complete utilization of the mentioned rules, you may need to utilize the Directory Connector and Policy Manager applications.

One of the most common rules is to pass traffic from authenticated users (in the case of using Directory Connector) and capture traffic from unauthenticated users, which will be useful with guest devices. The matcher to be used in this case is *Username is unauthenticated*.

Another rule that will be common if you are running a public Wi-Fi is to prohibit devices access to the Internet till they read and accept the AUP. The easiest way to achieve this is by connecting your Wi-Fi access point to Untangle NGFW on an Ethernet port that is different from the wired traffic. The matcher to be used is the Source Interface matcher.

You can also display a custom Captive Portal page to users who are in the penalty box or have exceeded their quota to notify them about that.

Another interesting use will be to run Captive Portal on the traffic coming through the WAN interface. This gives you the ability to authenticate users before they'll be able to use your internal services. For example, when you set a rule on the WAN interface, users try to access the **Outlook Web App (OWA)**. To access their e-mails, we'll need to authenticate against Captive Portal before they are allowed to access the OWA.

HTTP: Client User Agent and HTTP: Client User OS can be used. To define smartphones, we will use *Phone* as the matcher value for iPhone and *android* for Android devices. It's preferred to try to match the traffic using both matchers.

 Review the host table to get the accurate value of the client user agent and client user OS.

Configuring the passed hosts

As mentioned previously, certain hosts can bypass Captive Portal. To bypass traffic directed to a certain external server, we will use **Pass Listed Server Addresses**, which will be useful if we have our server on another subnet. To bypass traffic from certain hosts to any external destination, we will use **Pass Listed Client Addresses**. You can find both lists under **Captive Portal Settings | Passed Hosts**.

 You have to define the hosts by their IP; using URL and FQDN is not supported.

You can add the hosts via the **Add** button. You will need to define the IP address and whether to enable and log this traffic or not. Also, you can add a description, which is recommended. You also have the option to export the host list and import them to another Untangle server.

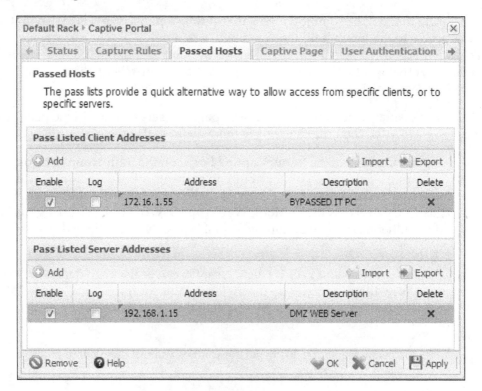

Customizing the captive page

You can configure the captive page settings under **Captive Portal Settings | Captive Page**. There are two default pages; the basic message page, which can be used to provide the AUP, and the basic authentication page, which can be used to provide user authentication.

You can customize these two pages by modifying the **Page Title**, **Welcome Text**, **Message Text**, and **Lower Text** fields. The basic message page has an option to include a checkbox that the user must have read and agreed to the AUP. The basic authentication page has two additional fields: **Username Text** and **Password Text**. The authentication method to be used with Captive Portal is defined under the **User Authentication** tab:

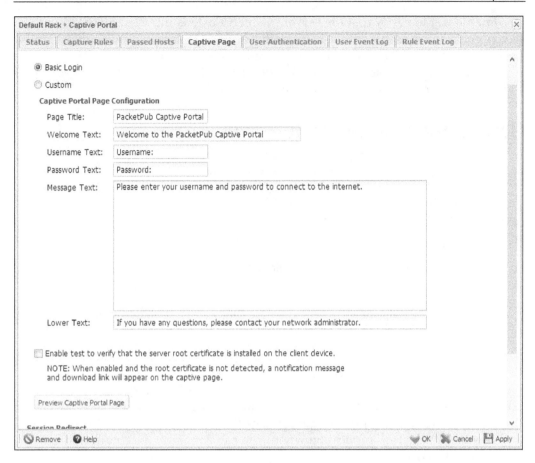

In addition, you can upload your custom page to provide additional functionality such as integrating with PayPal and charging users for Internet usage. This requires that you have good knowledge of HTML, Python, and JavaScript.

You can find simple custom pages that can help you to create your own one on `http://wiki.Untangle.com/index.php/Captive_Portal#Custom_Pages`.

You have the ability to preview how the Captive Portal page will look through the **Preview Captive Portal Page** button. Also, you can set a redirect URL to which the users will be routed after successful authentication. If you left the **Redirect URL** field blank, the users will be directed to their original destination.

 You must enter the redirect URL in the full form such as `http://www.google.com`; any other form won't work.

The **Enable test to verify that the server root certificate is installed on the client device** checkbox is useful with HTTPS traffic. Thus, if Untangle provided the Captive Portal page in HTTPS and the server certificate was not installed on the client, a warning page will be displayed to the client. This option allows Untangle to provide the download link for the root certificate in the Captive Portal page.

Setting the user authentication method

In this section, we will configure the authentication method to be used with the basic authentication page. The available options are as follows:

- Untangle local directory
- RADIUS server
- Active Directory server
- None, which is used with the basic message page

> The usage of RADIUS and Active Directory requires the existence of the Directory Connector application.

Under each authentication method, there is a button that will direct you to the directory configuration page. Thus, the **Configure Local Directory** button will direct you to **Config | Local Directory** where you can manage the local directory, while the **Configure RADIUS** and **Configure Active Directory** buttons will direct you to the Directory Connector application where you can configure the connection to the RADIUS and Active Directory servers.

Untangle can auto logout devices based on the standard authentication timeout or the idle timeout. The **Idle Timeout** option is triggered if no traffic is received from the client for the specified time, while the **Timeout** option is trigged after the specified time has elapsed regardless of whether the device is active or not.

The **Allow Concurrent Logins** option enables users to log in from different machines using the same credentials. Simultaneously, disable this option if you want users to have one session only, as shown in the following screenshot:

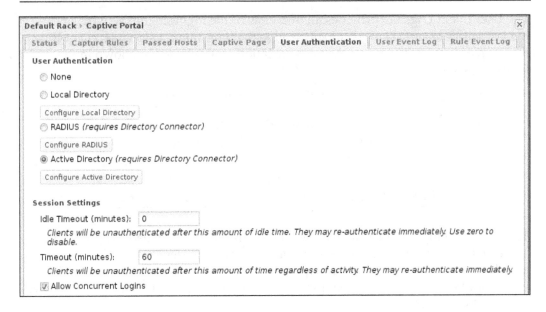

Reviewing Captive Portal events

The current active sessions can be monitored from **Captive Portal Settings | Status**. This tab provides the username and the IP address of the machine the user logged in from. It also shows the login time and the total number of user sessions. You are able to enforce user logout through the **X** button. Anonymous will be the username of any user accessed through the basic message page, while the name of any authenticated user will be displayed as shown in the following screenshot:

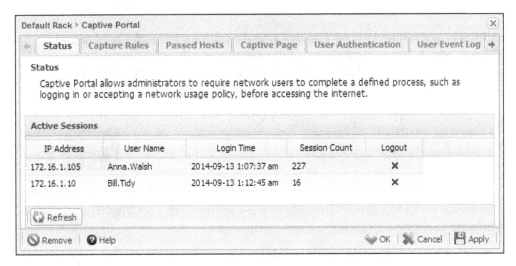

The **User Event Logs** tab provides an overview of the login/logout activity since the last server restart. The event logs provide the timestamp, username, client IP, the login or logout action, and the authentication method used as shown in the following screenshot:

Timestamp	Client	Username	Action	Authentication
2014-09-13 1:20:56 am	172.16.1.105	Anna.Walsh	Idle Timeout	Active Directory
2014-09-13 1:12:45 am	172.16.1.10	Bill.Tidy	Login Success	Active Directory
2014-09-13 1:07:37 am	172.16.1.105	Anna.Walsh	Login Success	Active Directory
2014-09-13 1:07:09 am	172.16.1.105	Anonymous	Admin Logout	Active Directory
2014-09-13 1:05:40 am	172.16.1.105	Anonymous	Login Success	None

The rule event log provides an overview of the traffic that matched a capture rule. The event log provides the timestamp, client IP and port, destination IP and port, and the rule ID of the matched rule, and if the traffic was captured or passed. The passed traffic will only be logged if the log checkbox is selected on the rule, as shown in the following screenshot:

Timestamp	Client	Client port	Server	Server ...	Rule ID (Ca...	Captured
2014-09-13 1:12:28 am	172.16.1.10	28060	192.232.216.151	80	100001	true
2014-09-13 1:07:25 am	172.16.1.105	49439	93.184.221.133	80	100001	true
2014-09-13 1:07:15 am	172.16.1.105	49437	179.60.192.113	80	100001	true
2014-09-13 1:05:42 am	172.16.1.5	49539	63.245.217.36	80	100001	true
2014-09-13 1:05:42 am	172.16.1.5	49537	213.158.175.27	80	100001	true
2014-09-13 1:05:40 am	172.16.1.105	49414	93.184.221.133	80	100001	true
2014-09-13 1:05:37 am	172.16.1.105	49412	179.60.192.113	80	100001	true

In addition, we can review the Captive Portal summary from the application faceplate, which gives an overview of the number of allowed/blocked sessions, number of DNS lookups done by the clients, and the number of successful logins done via the Captive Portal page as shown in the following screenshot:

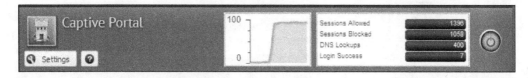

Reports also provide a good summary of the Captive Portal activity. The available reports are as follows:

- **Usage**: This shows a summary about the number of login/timeout/logout events per hour.

- **Top Captive Portal Users**: This shows the top users to authenticate via Captive Portal.

- **Top Blocked Clients**: This shows the clients who tried to access the Internet before authentication. The sessions will be blocked and the client will be directed to the Captive Portal page.

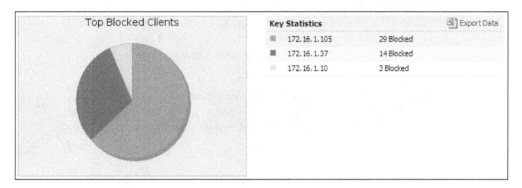

Untangle's Policy Manager

Untangle's Policy Manager allows you to set different policies based on the username, date, and time. For example, you can provide teachers with a spam filtering feature and allow them to access Facebook and YouTube anytime and use BitTorrent applications, while completely blocking all of this for students, and for the administrative users, you can allow them to access Facebook and YouTube during break time only.

We have already covered a whole set of applications settings for different users or based on different dates and times. A complete set of applications is known as a rack. So, to set different policies for teachers, students, and administrative users, we will need to use three different racks.

Achieving the desired different polices is very simple with Policy Manager. Without Policy Manager, you have to manually add exceptions on each application, and you may have had to use IP reservation. The whole process will be complex and not practical. In addition, without Policy Manager, you won't be able to set different rules based on the time of day or the day of the week.

In Untangle NGFW, we will need to create policies (or racks) and rules. Policies contain the configuration for an application while the rules contain the routing criteria to different racks.

Configuring Policy Manager policies

Using the previous example, we will need to create three different racks (that is, teachers, students, and administrative). By default, there is a default rack, which we have been using throughout the book. It can be renamed, but not removed.

When a rule is matched, the traffic will be directed to the appropriate rack. However, if no rule is matched, the traffic will be directed to the rack with ID 1, which will probably be your default rack unless you have changed the order. Thus, it's advisable to set the rack with ID 1 to the most restrictive settings.

 You can change the rack IDs by changing the **ID** field next to each rack. However, you still have to have a rack with ID 1. So, when you change the default rack ID to something else than 1, you have to give another rack the ID 1.

We have two options to deploy our scenario: the first is to use the firewall application on the default rack and configure it to block any traffic, and use three separate racks. The second option is to use the default rack as the students rack as it would be the most restrictive one and just create two additional racks.

Parent and child racks

Instead of configuring the new racks from the beginning, you can use the parent and child racks. The child rack will inherent all settings from the parent rack. However, you can still customize the child rack by adding additional applications that do not exist in the parent rack or change individual application settings. This is useful to replicate Virus Blocker and Spam Blocker settings, which will probably not change between racks, while also having the ability to set different settings for other applications such as Web Filter.

For our scenario, we will use the default rack as the students rack. Create a child rack for the administrative rack with the students rack as the parent rack. The administrative and students racks will have the same settings unless in the break time. We will create a new rack (with no parent) for the teachers. To add a new rack, press the **Add** button located under **Policy Manager Settings | Policies**. A new screen will appear from which you can customize your rack settings, as shown in the following screenshot:

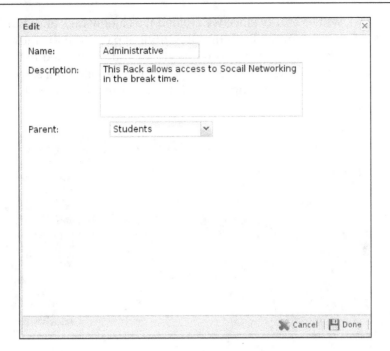

The different racks will be the same as shown in the following screenshot:

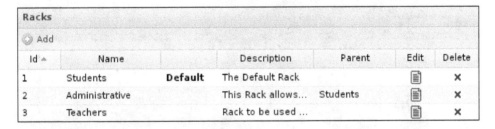

Configuring the racks is not done through Policy Manager, but in the rack itself, which we have done in the default rack throughout the book. You can switch between racks from the menu located at the top of the screen:

The teachers rack will be empty since we created it as a new rack and didn't use a parent rack. However, you will still find the services part from the rack as it is shared between racks and any change on it is global and not limited to the rack unlike the application part, which is rack dependent. The following screenshot shows the teachers rack after adding the Web Filter, Virus Blocker, and Spam Blocker applications:

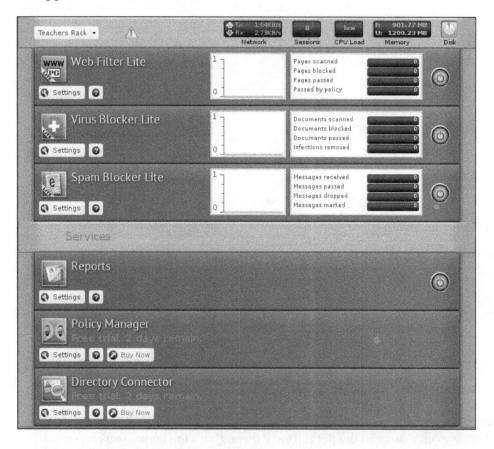

The administrative rack by default will have the same applications and services as the students rack. However, the applications will be grayed out and you can't configure them from the child rack. Any general modification on the applications will be done from the parent rack.

Instead of using the inherited application settings, you can configure rack-specific settings by adding additional applications, or enable modification to grayed out applications by installing them to the rack (they are available for installation from the apps list).

The students rack has the paid Web Filter and Application Control and Bandwidth Control applications. The following screenshot shows the administrative rack after installing the paid Web Filter and Phish Blocker applications (notice the applications inherited from the parent rack as available for installation):

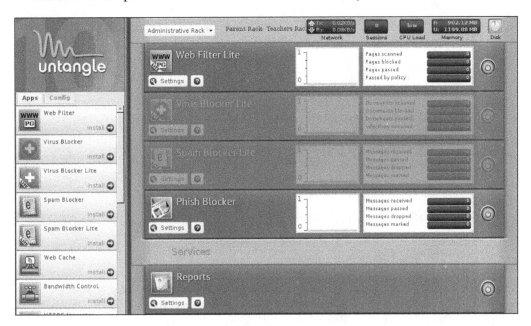

After the illustration of the different rack options, you are able to configure the racks' applications the way you want. For our demo, we will set the students rack to block social networking, allow social networking for teachers anytime, and allow social networking for the administrative rack between 12:00 p.m. and 1:00 p.m. Thus, both the administrative and teachers racks will have social networking enabled in Web Filter.

Configuring Policy Manager rules

After setting up the new racks and completing their configurations, we shall start to set rules that will direct traffic for the appropriate rack. The different available matchers include Destination Address, Destination Port, Destination interface, Source address, Source Interface, Protocol, Username, Time of Day, Day of week, Client Hostname, Client in Penalty Box, Server in Penalty Box, Client has exceeded Quota, Server has exceeded Quota, Directory Connector: User in group, HTTP: Client Use Agent, and HTTP: Client User OS.

Policy Manager will periodically check for traffic criteria changes to redirect the traffic to the new appropriate rack. You can add rules from the **Add** button located under **Policy Manager Settings | Rules**. For our scenario, we will need to add the following rules:

- Rules for teachers rack:
    ◦ Directory Connector: user in group is a teacher
    ◦ Target Rack: teachers

- Rules for administrative rack:
    ◦ Directory Connector: user in group is an administrative user
    ◦ Time of day is 12:00-13:00
    ◦ Target Rack: administrative

- Rules for students and administrative users within business hours:
    ◦ Directory Connector: user in group is a student and administrative users
    ◦ Target Rack: students

Other traffic that doesn't match the preceding criteria (for example, username is administrator, which is not a member of the preceding groups) will be processed by the default rack and the default rack settings will be applied on it.

The **> No Rack** Target Rack option will let the traffic assigned to it be processed as if it was generated from the Untangle NGFW server itself. Thus, no restrictions will be applied on it. The rack name will be displayed in the events as a Services rack.

Reviewing the Policy Manager events

The Policy Manager events can help us to diagnose our rules setup and ensure that our policies are working right. You can find the event logs under **Policy Manager Settings | Event Log**. The main points on the event logs are the username, IP address, and the assigned rack. The following screenshot shows a sample event log:

Timestamp	Client	Client ...	Username	Policy Id	Server	Server Port
2014-09-14 4:14:31 pm	172.16.1.10	54418	Abiola.Yadav	Teachers Rack	192.168.1.1	53
2014-09-14 4:14:31 pm	172.16.1.10	11677	Abiola.Yadav	Teachers Rack	173.194.113.224	443
2014-09-14 4:14:31 pm	172.16.1.10	59842	Abiola.Yadav	Teachers Rack	192.168.1.1	53
2014-09-14 4:14:22 pm	172.16.1.105	49517	Anna.Walsh	Students Rack	173.194.113.227	443
2014-09-14 4:14:22 pm	172.16.1.105	49516	Anna.Walsh	Students Rack	173.194.113.227	443
2014-09-14 4:14:22 pm	172.16.1.105	49515	Anna.Walsh	Students Rack	173.194.113.227	443

In addition to the preceding event logs, other applications' (which are set as matchers) event logs may be helpful for tracking whether the Active Directory authentication is done correctly or not.

We can also get a summary report about the Policy Manager activities via the Reports application. The available reports are as follows:

- **Bandwidth Usage**: This gives the average KB/sec per rack and the total amount of downloaded data per rack
- **Sessions By Policy**: This gives the average and total MB/hour per rack
- **Traffic By Policy**: This shows the average and total KB/sec per rack
- **Top Policies By Sessions**: This shows the number of sessions per rack
- **Top policies By Bandwidth**: This shows the amount of downloaded data per rack

The following screenshot shows the **Top Policies By Sessions** summary report:

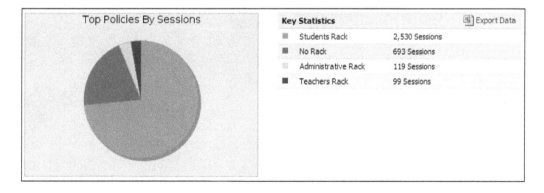

Summary

In this chapter, we covered three powerful tools from Untangle that allow us to control user privileges on the network by identifying the user and giving them the appropriate level of access based on their membership details. Directory Connector allowed us to integrate Untangle NGFW with external RADIUS and Active Directory servers to collect user data. Captive Portal allowed us to prohibit any access to the Internet until the user authentication, which greatly helps in public Wi-Fi and guest network scenarios. Policy Manager allowed us to apply different policies and settings on different users based on their criteria such as username and group membership. Also, it allowed us to control these policies based on time.

In the next chapter, we'll cover WAN-related services. Untangle provides two applications to help us to provide highly available, stable, and reliable WAN connection. Untangle's WAN Balancer allows us to provide higher throughput to our network by distributing the load between the different WAN NICs. Untangle's WAN Failover allows Untangle NGFW to provide an undisturbed WAN connection by failing over to one NIC when the second one fails.

11
Untangle WAN Services

This chapter covers the services provided by Untangle to allow you to get the full utilization of multiple Internet connections. With Untangle WAN services, you can use multiple cheap ADSL lines instead of one expensive leased line, which, when goes down, will disconnect you from the Internet.

WAN Failover allows you to use multiple WAN interfaces and get a continuous Internet connection. It detects disconnected interfaces and redirects their traffic to another available interface. WAN Balancer allows you to maximize bandwidth utilization by distributing your network traffic among multiple WAN interfaces.

WAN Balancer has some dependencies on the WAN Failover; thus, Untangle offers WAN Failover with no additional charge for the purchases of the WAN Balancer.

To utilize the functionality of multiple WAN interfaces, your Untangle NGFW internal interface should be in addressed mode and not bridged mode.

A list of topics that will be covered in this chapter are as follows:

- Untangle WAN Failover
- Untangle WAN Balancer

WAN Failover

With Untangle WAN Failover, you can provide a redundant Internet connection to your network. Untangle WAN Failover runs connectivity tests on each WAN interface; you have to determine its status. If any test failed for a certain amount of time, the WAN interface will be considered to be down, and the traffic will be rerouted to the WAN interface with the lower ID.

Setting up interface tests

For Untangle Failover to work properly, you should configure the connectivity test for each WAN interface you have. Untangle NGFW provides different tests that could be used to determine WAN interface connectivity:

- **Ping test**: Untangle NGFW will ping a configured IP address
- **ARP test**: Untangle NGFW will request the MAC address of the interface's gateway using the **Address Resolution Protocol (ARP)**
- **DNS test**: Untangle NGFW will try to query the DNS server configured in the interface settings
- **HTTP test**: Untangle NGFW will try to create an HTTP connection to a specific site

You should select the test to be used carefully. For example, if you used an HTTP test and the website you're running your test against is down while your Internet connection is up, Untangle NGFW will consider the interface to be disconnected as the configured test will fail.

You can create a new test by pressing the **Add** button located under **WAN Failover settings | Tests**. You will need to configure the following settings:

- **Interface**: Select the interface you wish to run the test on.
- **Description**: Enter a suitable description for your test.

 Adding the description will help you identify the tests in the event logs.

- **Testing Interval**: The test will run based on the defined time interval. The default interval is 5 seconds.
- **Time Out**: This is the time that Untangle NGFW will wait for a response before it considers the test as a failed test. The default time-out is 2 seconds.

 It's important to select a time-out that is lower than the time interval.

- **Failure Threshold**: This is the number of failed tests (out of 10) to consider the interface to be down. The default value is 3 tests out of 10.
- **Test Type**: Select the test type you want to use (that is, **Ping, ARP, DNS,** and **HTTP**).

These settings are illustrated in the following screenshot:

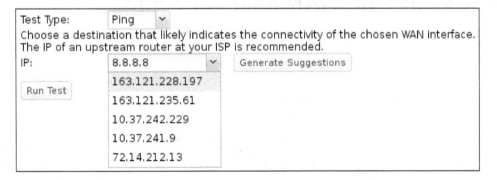

The default value for the Ping Test IP is **8.8.8.8**, which is the Google's DNS server. You can use the default value as it represents a high available destination for your test. However, Untangle recommends the usage of an upstream router of your ISP, as when the router is down, your connection will probably be down.

The **Generate Suggestions** button will perform a trace route to **8.8.8.8** that will return the routers between you and Google. Select an appropriate router from the **IP** drop-down menu. The higher the IP in the list, the closer the router is to you. The **Run Test** button could be used to test your settings and check whether the configured test would work properly or not:

The ARP test will try to get the MAC address of the gateway configured in the interface settings. There is nothing to configure here.

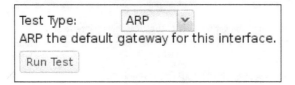

The DNS test will run a query using the DNS server configured in your interface settings. Also, there is nothing to configure here.

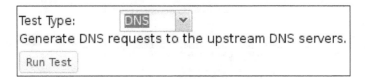

The HTTP test will try to connect to a website that you will configure. You can use a hostname or an IP address to complete this test. However, using an IP address is better as a DNS query would not be required.

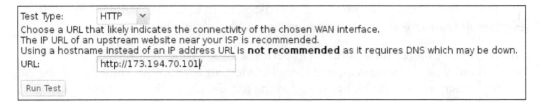

Reviewing the WAN Failover events

You can review your WAN interface's connection status from different sources. The first place to achieve this is the WAN Failover application faceplate, which will provide you with the total number of current connected and disconnected WAN interfaces. In addition, it shows the total number of state changes, and whether a WAN interface state has changed from connected to disconnected or vice versa, as shown in the following screenshot:

The second place to achieve this is under **WAN Failover Settings | Status**, which shows the different interfaces and their current status (online or offline), and the total number of tests that are completed and how many passed and failed:

WAN Status						
Interface ID	Interface Name	System Name	Online Status	Current Tests Count	Tests Passed	Tests Failed
1	External	eth0	false	81	77	4
3	WAN 2	eth2	true	81	26	55

The third place is the WAN Failover application event logs. There are two different event logs. The test event log shows when individual tests were run and whether they failed or succeeded:

Timestamp	Interface	Success	Test Description
2014-07-04 5:36:21...	External	true	WAN1 Ping Test
2014-07-04 5:36:20...	WAN 2	false	
2014-07-04 5:36:16...	External	true	WAN1 Ping Test
2014-07-04 5:36:15...	WAN 2	false	

The event log shows the interface status change events:

Timestamp	Interface	Action
2014-07-04 3:03:58 pm	External	CONNECTED
2014-07-04 3:03:48 pm	WAN 2	CONNECTED
2014-07-04 3:03:39 pm	External	DISCONNECTED
2014-07-04 2:58:50 pm	WAN 2	DISCONNECTED
2014-07-04 2:56:43 pm	WAN 2	DISCONNECTED
2014-07-04 2:53:50 pm	WAN 2	CONNECTED
2014-07-04 2:52:32 pm	WAN 2	DISCONNECTED

The fourth place is the Reports application from which we can find the following summary reports:

- **WAN Availability**: This gives us a percentage of the number of times we were fully connected or partially connected or not connected to the Internet
- **WAN Interfaces With Downtime**: This indicates for how long the interface was down

- **WAN Interfaces With Failure**: This indicates the number of times the interface was down

The following screenshot shows the **WAN Interfaces With Downtime** summary report:

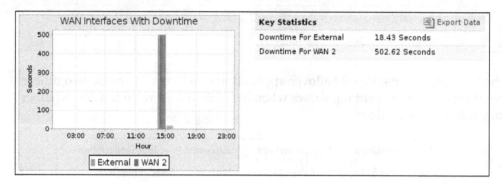

WAN Balancer

With Untangle's WAN Balancer, you can distribute your traffic across multiple ISPs to provide a higher bandwidth for your network. Untangle NGFW will dynamically distribute the traffic to different WAN interfaces based on the set rules. Untangle NGFW distributes the traffic based on the number of sessions and not bytes.

Untangle's WAN Balancer will not increase the total available speed for one session, but it will increase the available bandwidth for your entire network. For example, if you have 1 Mbps and 2 Mbps connections, no individual session can use the 3 Mbps. Instead, a session can use the 2 Mbps connection and another session can use the 1 Mbps connection.

Configuring traffic allocation

You could set the weights of traffic to be directed to each WAN interface under the **WAN Balancer Settings | Traffic Allocation** tab. By default, Untangle will divide the load equally on the different interfaces. Thus, if you have two interfaces, each interface will get 50 percent of the traffic, as shown in the following screenshot:

Interface Weights		
Interface	Weight	Resulting Traffic Allocation
External	50	50% of Internet traffic on the External interface
WAN 2	50	50% of Internet traffic on the WAN 2 interface

It's recommended to set the interfaces' weights based on their bandwidth. Thus, if you have 1.5 Mbps and 6 Mbps connections, you will set the weights as 15 and 60. The resulting traffic allocation ratio will automatically be changed to reflect the percentage of traffic that will be processed by each interface, as shown in the following screenshot:

Interface Weights		
Interface	Weight	Resulting Traffic Allocation
External	60	80% of Internet traffic on the External interface
WAN 2	15	20% of Internet traffic on the WAN 2 interface

When a new connection is to take place, the WAN interface to be used is determined based on the weights assigned for each interface. Once the connection is established, Untangle NGFW will cache that route (the connection between two specific IPs is done through a specific interface). If any new session is to be established and there is a cached route for it, that cached route would be used (that is, the previously used interface will be used again). Thus, the weights are applied on new sessions with no cached routes. The preceding behavior is also known as sticky sessions, which are used to prevent SSL-enabled websites and some cloud services from breaking down.

HTTPS sessions are sticky, while HTTP cloud services that are based on multiple load-balanced web servers need to use sticky sessions.

It is common for a web application to need to track a user's progress between pages. Some examples include keeping track of login information or the progress through a test with correct/incorrect totals, the items in a shopping cart, and so on.

The track is simple if the web application was using only one web server. When the application starts to use multiple load-balanced web servers, it is a must to use sticky sessions.

 Sometimes, when a change is done on any of the connection endpoints, the session will break down and issues can occur. The cause of the changes in the endpoints could be that the load balancer was forced to shift users to a different server or because the user was using a WAN failover, or in the case that the user was using a WAN Balancer solution that does not support sticky sessions.

The resultant issues are related to the loss of user's session data; the effects of this will vary depending on the application and what the user was doing at that time. Perhaps, they can get booted back to a login prompt, or maybe they lose the contents of their shopping cart, or maybe they suddenly lose their place in the test and are forced back to the beginning. All of these cases make the application appear defective to the end user.

For more information, visit `http://www.chaosincomputing.com/2012/05/sticky-sessions-are-evil/`.

Setting Route Rules

Sometimes, you want certain traffic to always use a certain interface. For example, if you have an e-mail server and you have two connections, one of which is an ADSL line in which the outgoing SMTP traffic is blocked by ISP, you will set a rule that will make the internal e-mail server always use the other connection for outgoing SMTP traffic. Also, VOIP sessions need to be sticky to the same interface, or they will fail.

Route Rules are similar to other Untangle NGFW rules in that they are evaluated from above downward, and if a match is found, the rule will be applied. If no match is found or the rule is set to balance the traffic, the traffic will be randomly assigned to a WAN interface based on its weight. There are five matchers that could be used with Route Rule, which are as follows:

- **Source Address**
- **Source Port**

- **Destination Address**
- **Destination Port**
- **Protocol**

The following screenshot shows a route rule that will direct any outbound SMTP traffic to WAN 2 interface:

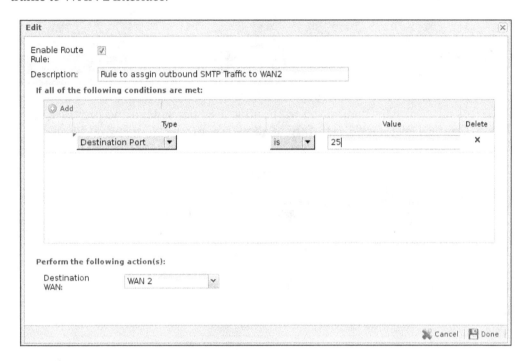

If the Routes configured under **Config | Network | Routes** are in conflict with the Route Rules, the Routes configured under **Config | Network | Routes** will always override any Route Rule. Also, if the interface selected in the Route Rules was detected to be down by the WAN Failover, WAN Balancer will assign the traffic to an interface based on the defined weights.

 WAN Failover is necessary for the WAN Balancer functionality as you won't distribute traffic to a failed-down interface.

As sessions are sticky, when the sessions interface goes down and a failover occurs, any new session will be processed by a new interface, but the old opened sessions will remain sticky to the down interface and won't change the interface; thus, the user of the computer that is running those individual sessions needs to reset them.

Reviewing the WAN Balancer status

As with all Untangle applications, we could review the status of the application from its faceplate, or from its status and event logs tab, and from the Reports application.

The WAN Balancer faceplate shows the total number of sessions processed by each WAN interface:

The **Status** tab shows the configured traffic allocation percentage and provides a link to **Config | Network | Interface** to allow you to configure any additional WAN interfaces.

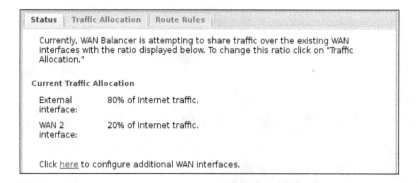

The Reports application provides a summary report about the maximum and average bandwidth usage by each interface. Also, it provides many summary reports related to the sessions' activity on each WAN interface. The reports are as follows:

- **Bandwidth Usage**: This shows the maximum and the average bandwidth usage for each WAN interface in KB/sec

- **Active Sessions**: This shows the maximum number of sessions at any single time, and the average number of sessions during the day

- **Sessions By WAN**: This shows the maximum and the average number of sessions/hour for each WAN interface

- **Traffic By WAN**: This gives you the maximum and the average KB/hour for each WAN Interface

- **Total Sessions By WAN**: This shows the number of sessions processed by each WAN interface

- **Bandwidth by a WAN interface**: This gives you the amount of the bandwidth usage for each WAN interface

The following screenshot shows the **Total Sessions By WAN** summary report:

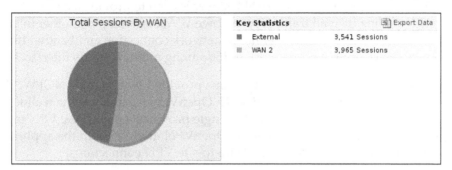

Troubleshooting

This troubleshooting part applies for both Untangle WAN Failover and Untangle WAN Balancer as the troubleshooting steps for both are similar. Besides the normal troubleshooting listed in *Chapter 4, Untangle Advanced Configuration*, if you have a problem with the WAN connection, you should do the following tasks:

- Check whether the modem/router is up.
- Check whether Untangle NGFW is able to reach the modem/router. Try to ping the modem/router from the Untangle NGFW administration console.
- Check whether the clients behind Untangle NGFW are able to reach the modem/router. Try to ping each of your modem routers from the clients.
- Make sure that each ISP's interface is configured to be a WAN interface under **Config | Networking | Interfaces**. Also, ensure that the interfaces have all of the required information properly entered.
- Verify that the WAN Failover has tests set up for each WAN connection.
- If you're only using WAN Failover, you'll need to disconnect your primary WAN to get traffic to flow over the secondary one.
- If you're using WAN Balancer, make sure your weights are set properly.
- You can test the WAN Balancer functionality by going to any of the show my IP sites.
- When you're using WAN Balancer beside WAN Failover and have connection problems, ensure that the WAN Balancer does not distribute traffic to a down interface as the WAN failover might be turned off or uninstalled.

Summary

In this chapter, we covered two Untangle applications related to WAN interfaces. The two applications allow us to utilize multiple WAN interfaces and get all the benefits from this setup. Untangle WAN Failover is used to provide a constant Internet connection by failing over all traffic from a down WAN interface to another interface. Untangle WAN Balancer is used to enhance network connection and bandwidth utilization by distributing your network traffic among multiple WAN interfaces.

The next chapter will cover the VPN solutions provided by Untangle NGFW. Open VPN is a free module using SSL-based VPN. OpenVPN is based on the well-known open source project (OpenVPN). Also, Untangle provides a paid IPsec VPN module that has some additional features over the OpenVPN module. Both the applications provide remote access (user-to-site) and site-to-site VPN connections.

12
Untangle VPN Services

This chapter covers the Untangle solutions used to provide **virtual private network (VPN)** services. Untangle provides two solutions: OpenVPN and IPsec. OpenVPN is an SSL/TLS-based VPN, which is mainly used for remote access as it is easy to configure and uses clients that can work on multiple operating systems and devices. OpenVPN can also provide site-to-site connections (only between two Untangle servers) with limited features in comparison to IPsec.

IPsec, a paid module from Untangle, Inc., is mainly used for site-to-site connections as it provides great features and performance in comparison to OpenVPN. It can also be used to provide a remote access service by leveraging L2TP/IPsec, which is more complex to set up and configure than the OpenVPN client.

A list of topics that will be covered in this chapter are as follows:

- Understanding VPN
- OpenVPN
- IPsec VPN

Understanding VPN

VPN allows you to extend your internal private network across a public network such as the Internet. VPN clients outside the company can access resources inside your company as if they were located inside the company. There are two general VPN types: remote access (client-to-site), which allows your road warriors to connect to your internal network while traveling on the road, and the site-to-site type, which is used to connect geographically-distributed branches of your organization. Any PC inside the branch office can connect to any resource located inside the main branch and vice versa with no connection required on the client side. The connections and configurations are done on the gateways of each branch.

A VPN provides a secure connection between the endpoints as it provides authentication, data integrity, and confidentiality. These terms are explained as follows:

- **Authentication**: The client ensures that the VPN server is not a rogue server, using a **preshared key (PSK)** or digital certificates. Also, the server authenticates the client before allowing it to initiate a connection to the internal network using a username and password or digital identity certificates.

- **Data integrity**: A VPN uses hashing protocols to ensure that no data manipulation will happen while the data will transfer between the two ends.

- **Confidentiality**: The transferred data between the two ends will be encrypted. Thus, if anyone intercepted the traffic, they will not be able to read it in plain text. Symmetric shared keys are used to encrypt the transferred data. However, to negotiate and transfer this symmetric key between the two ends, asymmetric algorithms are used (public and private keys or Diffie-Hellman key exchange).

 If you are interested in VPNs and the cryptography techniques and protocols such as public/private keys and Diffie-Hellman key exchange, and want to learn more about them, a great course by Prof. Dan Boneh from Stanford University might be your best choice. The course is available at https://www.coursera.org/course/crypto.

OpenVPN

Untangle's OpenVPN is an SSL-based VPN solution that is based on the well-known open source application, OpenVPN. Untangle's OpenVPN is mainly used for client-to-site connections with a client feature that is easy to deploy and configure, which is widely available for Windows, Mac, Linux, and smartphones. Untangle's OpenVPN can also be used for site-to-site connections but the two sites need to have Untangle servers. Site-to-site connections between Untangle and third-party devices are not supported.

How OpenVPN works

In reference to the OSI model, an SSL/TLS-based VPN will only encrypt the application layer's data, while the lower layer's information will be transferred unencrypted. In other words, the application packets will be encrypted. The IP addresses of the server and client are visible; the port number that the server uses for communication between the client and server is also visible, but the actual application port number is not visible. Furthermore, the destination IP address will not be visible; only the VPN server IP address is seen.

Secure Sockets Layer (SSL) and **Transport Layer Security (TLS)** refer to the same thing. SSL is the predecessor of TLS. SSL was originally developed by Netscape and many releases were produced (V.1 to V.3) till it got standardized under the TLS name.

The steps to create an SSL-based VPN are as follows:

1. The client will send a message to the VPN server that it wants to initiate an SSL session. Also, it will send a list of all ciphers (hash and encryption protocols) that it supports.

2. The server will respond with a set of selected ciphers and will send its digital certificate to the client. The server's digital certificate includes the server's public key.

3. The client will try to verify the server's digital certificate by checking it against trusted certificate authorities and by checking the certificate's validity (valid from and valid through dates).

4. The server may need to authenticate the client before allowing it to connect to the internal network. This could be achieved either by asking for a valid username and password or by using the user's digital identity certificates. Untangle NGFW uses the digital certificates method.

5. The client will create a session key (which will be used to encrypt the transferred data between the two devices) and will send this key to the server encrypted using the server's public key. Thus, no third party can get the session key as the server is the only device that can decrypt the session key as it's the only party that has the private key.

6. The server will acknowledge the client that it received the session key and is ready for the encrypted data transformation.

Configuring Untangle's OpenVPN server settings

After installing the OpenVPN application, the application will be turned off. You'll need to turn it on before you can use it.

You can configure Untangle's OpenVPN server settings under **OpenVPN Settings | Server**. The settings configure how OpenVPN will be a server for remote clients (which can be clients on Windows, Linux, or any other operating systems, or another Untangle server). The different available settings are as follows:

- **Site Name**: This is the name of the OpenVPN site that is used to define the server among other OpenVPN servers inside your origination. This name should be unique across all Untangle servers in the organization. A random name is automatically chosen for the site name.

- **Site URL**: This is the URL that the remote client will use to reach this OpenVPN server. This can be configured under **Config | Administration | Public Address**.

 If you have more than one WAN interface, the remote client will first try to initiate the connection using the settings defined in the public address. If this fails, it will randomly try the IP of the remaining WAN interfaces.

- **Server Enabled**: If checked, the OpenVPN server will run and accept connections from the remote clients.

- **Address Space**: This defines the IP subnet that will be used to assign IPs for the remote VPN clients. The value in **Address Space** must be unique and separate across all existing networks and other OpenVPN address spaces. A default address space will be chosen that does not conflict with the existing configuration:

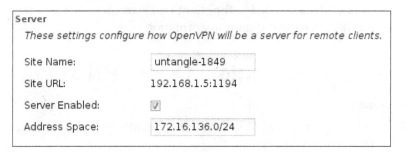

Configuring Untangle's OpenVPN remote client settings

Untangle's OpenVPN allows you to create OpenVPN clients to give your office employees, who are out of the company, the ability to remotely access your internal network resources via their PCs and/or smartphones. Also, an OpenVPN client can be imported to another Untangle server to provide site-to-site connection. Each OpenVPN client will have its unique IP (from the address space range defined previously). Thus, each OpenVPN client can only be used for one user. For multiple users, you'll have to create multiple clients as using the same client for multiple users will result in client disconnection issues.

Creating a remote client

You can create remote access clients by clicking on the **Add** button located under **OpenVPN Settings | Server | Remote Clients**.

A new window will open, which has the following settings:

- **Enabled**: If this checkbox is checked, it will allow the client connection to the OpenVPN server. If unchecked, it will not allow the client connection.

- **Client Name**: Give a unique name for the client; this will help you identify the client. Only alphanumeric characters are allowed.

- **Group**: Specify the group the client will be a member of. Groups are used to apply similar settings to their members.

- **Type**: Select **Individual Client** for remote access and **Network** for site-to-site VPN.

The following screenshot shows a remote access client created for JDoe:

After configuring the client settings, you'll need to press the **Done** button and then the **OK** or **Apply** button to save this client configuration. The new client will be available under the **Remote Clients** tab, as shown in the following screenshot:

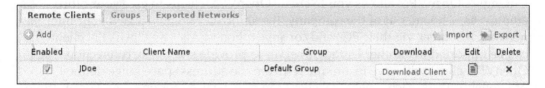

Understanding remote client groups

Groups are used to group clients together and apply similar settings to the group members. By default, there will be a **Default Group**. Each group has the following settings:

- **Group Name**: Give a suitable name for the group that describes the group settings (for example, full tunneling clients) or the target clients (for example, remote access clients).

- **Full Tunnel**: If checked, all the traffic from the remote clients will be sent to the OpenVPN server, which allows Untangle to filter traffic directed to the Internet. If unchecked, the remote client will run in the split tunnel mode, which means that the traffic directed to local resources behind Untangle is sent through VPN, and the traffic directed to the Internet is sent by the machine's default gateway.

> You can't use **Full Tunnel** for site-to-site connections.

- **Push DNS**: If checked, the remote OpenVPN client will use the DNS settings defined by the OpenVPN server. This is useful to resolve local names and services.

- **Push DNS server**: If the OpenVPN server is selected, remote clients will use the OpenVPN server for DNS queries. If set to **Custom**, DNS servers configured here will be used for DNS queries.

- **Push DNS Custom 1**: If the Push DNS server is set to **Custom**, the value configured here will be used as a primary DNS server for the remote client. If blank, no settings will be pushed for the remote client.

- **Push DNS Custom 2**: If the Push DNS server is set to **Custom,** the value configured here will be used as a secondary DNS server for the remote client. If blank, no settings will be pushed for the remote client.

- **Push DNS Domain**: The configured value will be pushed to the remote clients to extend their domain's search path during DNS resolution.

The following screenshot illustrates all these settings:

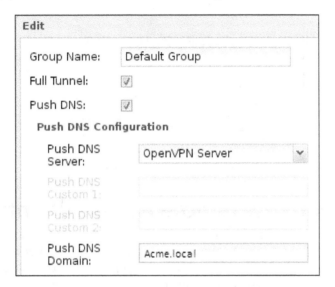

Defining the exported networks

Exported networks are used to define the internal networks behind the OpenVPN server that the remote client can reach after successful connection. Additional routes will be added to the remote client's routing table that state that the exported networks (the main site's internal subnet) are reachable through the OpenVPN server. By default, each static non-WAN interface network will be listed in the **Exported Networks** list:

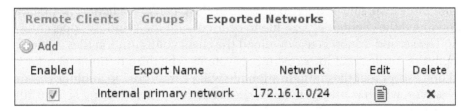

You can modify the default settings or create new entries. The **Exported Networks** settings are as follows:

- **Enabled**: If checked, the defined network will be exported to the remote clients.

- **Export Name**: Enter a suitable name for the exported network.

- **Network**: This defines the exported network. The exported network should be written in CIDR form.

These settings are illustrated in the following screenshot:

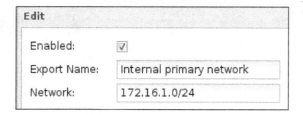

Using OpenVPN remote access clients

So far, we have been configuring the client settings but didn't create the real package to be used on remote systems. We can get the remote client package by pressing the **Download Client** button located under **OpenVPN Settings | Server | Remote Clients**, which will start the process of building the OpenVPN client that will be distributed:

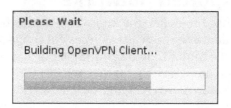

There are three available options to download the OpenVPN client. The first option is to download the client as a .exe file to be used with the Windows operating system. The second option is to download the client configuration files, which can be used with the Apple and Linux operating systems. The third option is similar to the second one except that the configuration file will be imported to another Untangle NGFW server, which is used for site-to-site scenarios. The following screenshot illustrates this:

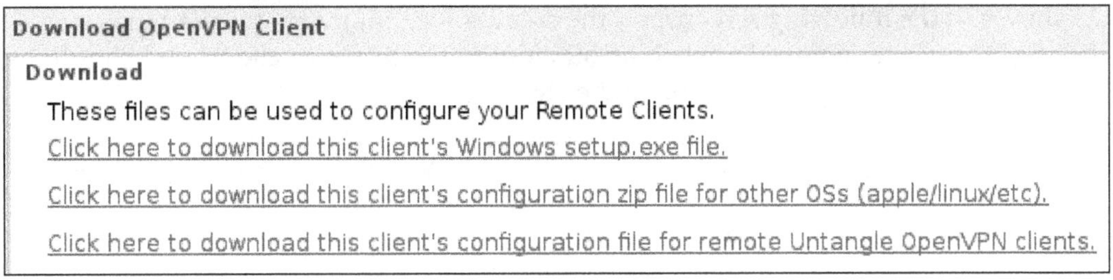

Download OpenVPN Client

Download

These files can be used to configure your Remote Clients.

Click here to download this client's Windows setup.exe file.

Click here to download this client's configuration zip file for other OSs (apple/linux/etc).

Click here to download this client's configuration file for remote Untangle OpenVPN clients.

The configuration files include the following files:

- `<Site_name>.ovpn`
- `<Site_name>.conf`
- `Keys\<Site_name>.-<User_name>.crt`
- `Keys\<Site_name>.-<User_name>.key`
- `Keys\<Site_name>.-<User_name>-ca.crt`

The certificate files are for the client authentication, and the `.ovpn` and `.conf` files have the defined connection settings (that is, the OpenVPN server IP, used port, and used ciphers). The following screenshot shows the `.ovpn` file for the site Untangle-1849:

```
client
resolv-retry 20
keepalive 10 60
nobind
mute-replay-warnings
ns-cert-type server
comp-lzo
verb 1
persist-key
persist-tun
dev tun
proto udp
port 1194
cipher AES-128-CBC
cert keys/untangle-1849-siteconnection.crt
key keys/untangle-1849-siteconnection.key
ca keys/untangle-1849-siteconnection-ca.crt
remote 192.168.1.5 1194 # public address
```

As shown in the following screenshot, the created file (openvpn-JDoe-setup.exe) includes the client name, which helps you identify the different clients and simplifies the process of distributing each file to the right user:

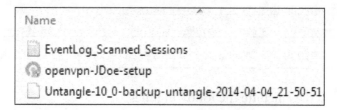

Using an OpenVPN client with Windows OS

Using an OpenVPN client with the Windows operating system is really very simple. To do this, perform the following steps:

1. Set up the OpenVPN client on the remote machine. The setup is very easy and it's just a next, next, install, and finish setup.

 To set up and run the application as an administrator is important in order to allow the client to write the VPN routes to the Windows routing table. You should run the client as an administrator every time you use it so that the client can create the required routes.

2. Double-click on the OpenVPN icon on the Windows desktop:

3. The application will run in the system tray:

4. Right-click on the system tray of the application and select **Connect**. The client will start to initiate the connection to the OpenVPN server and a window with the connection status will appear, as shown in the following screenshot:

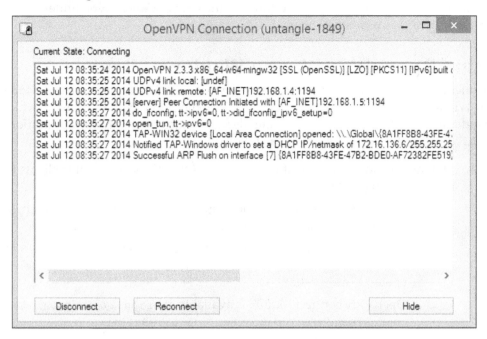

5. Once the VPN tunnel is initiated, a notification will appear from the client with the IP assigned to it, as shown in the following screenshot:

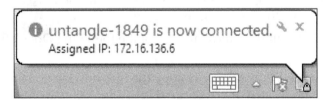

If the OpenVPN client was running in the task bar and there was an established connection, the client will automatically reconnect to the OpenVPN server if the tunnel was dropped due to Windows being asleep.

By default, the OpenVPN client will not start at the Windows login. We can change this and allow it to start without requiring administrative privileges by going to **Control Panel | Administrative Tools | Services** and changing the OpenVPN service's **Startup Type** to **automatic**. Now, in the **start** parameters field, put `--connect <Site_name>.ovpn`; you can find the `<site_name>.ovpn` under `C:\Program Files\OpenVPN\config`.

Using OpenVPN with non-Windows clients

The method to configure OpenVPN clients to work with Untangle is the same for all non-Windows clients. Simply download the `.zip` file provided by Untangle, which includes the configuration and certificate files, and place them into the application's `configuration` folder. The steps are as follows:

1. Download and install any of the following OpenVPN-compatible clients for your operating system:

    ◦   For Mac OS X, Untangle, Inc. suggests using Tunnelblick, which is available at `http://code.google.com/p/tunnelblick`

    ◦   For Linux, OpenVPN clients for different Linux distros can be found at `https://openvpn.net/index.php/access-server/download-openvpn-as-sw.html`

    ◦   OpenVPN connect for iOS is available at `https://itunes.apple.com/us/app/openvpn-connect/id590379981?mt=8`

    ◦   OpenVPN for Android 4.0+ is available at `https://play.google.com/store/apps/details?id=net.openvpn.openvpn`

2. Log in to the Untangle NGFW server, download the `.zip` client configuration file, and extract the files from the `.zip` file.

3. Place the configuration files into any of the following OpenVPN-compatible applications:

    ◦   **Tunnelblick**: Manually copy the files into the `Configurations` folder located at `~/Library/Application Support/Tunnelblick`.

    ◦   **Linux**: Copy the extracted files into `/etc/openvpn`, and then you can connect using `sudo openvpn /etc/openvpn/<Site_name>.conf`.

    ◦   **iOS**: Open iTunes and select the files from the `config` ZIP file to add to the app on your iPhone or iPad.

° **Android**: From OpenVPN for an Android application, click on all your precious VPNs. In the top-right corner, click on the folder, and then browse to the folder where you have the OpenVPN .Conf file. Click on the file and hit **Select**. Then, in the top-right corner, hit the little floppy disc icon to save the import. Now, you should see the imported profile. Click on it to connect to the tunnel. For more information on this, visit http://forums.untangle.com/ openvpn/30472-openvpn-android-4-0-a.html.

4. Run the OpenVPN-compatible client.

Using OpenVPN for site-to-site connection

To use OpenVPN for site-to-site connection, one Untangle NGFW server will run on the OpenVPN server mode, and the other server will run on the client mode. We will need to create a client that will be imported in the remote server. The client settings are shown in the following screenshot:

We will need to download the client configuration that is supposed to be imported on another Untangle server (the third option available on the client download menu), and then import this client configuration's zipped file on the remote server. To import the client, on the remote server under the **Client** tab, browse to the .zip file and press the **Submit** button. The client will be shown as follows:

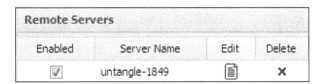

You'll need to restart the two servers before being able to use the OpenVPN site-to-site connection. The site-to-site connection is bidirectional.

Reviewing the connection details

The current connected clients (either they were OS clients or another Untangle NGFW client) will appear under **Connected Remote Clients** located under the **Status** tab. The screen will show the client name, its external address, and the address assigned to it by OpenVPN. In addition to the connection start time, the amount of transmitted and received MB during this connection is also shown:

Connected Remote Clients

Address	Client	Pool Address	Start Time	Rx Data	Tx Data
192.168.1.7	JDoe	172.16.136.6	2014-07-20 5:19:19 am	0 Mb	0 Mb
192.168.1.6	siteconnection	172.16.136.10	2014-07-20 4:58:03 am	0 Mb	0 Mb

For the site-to-site connection, the client server will show the name of the remote server, whether the connection is established or not, in addition to the amount of transmitted and received data in MB:

Remote Server Status

Name	Connected	Rx Data	Tx Data
untangle-1849	true	0 Mb	0 Mb

Event logs show a detailed connection history as shown in the following screenshot:

Start Time	End Time	Client Name	Client Address	Pool Address	KB Sent	KB Receiv...
2014-07-20 5:13:19...	2014-07-20 5:14:50...	JDoe	192.168.1.7		5.5	12.2
2014-07-20 4:58:03...	2014-07-20 5:14:50...	siteconnection	192.168.1.6		23.1	23.1
2014-07-20 4:52:26...	2014-07-20 5:00:50...	JDoe	192.168.1.7		235.8	406.4

In addition, there are two reports available for Untangle's OpenVPN:

- **Bandwidth usage**: This report shows the maximum and average data transfer rate (KB/s) and the total amount of data transferred that day
- **Top users**: This report shows the top users connected to the Untangle OpenVPN server

Troubleshooting Untangle's OpenVPN

In this section, we will discuss some points to consider when dealing with Untangle NGFW OpenVPN.

- OpenVPN acts as a router as it will route between different networks. Using OpenVPN with Untangle NGFW in the bridge mode (Untangle NGFW server is behind another router) requires additional configurations. The required configurations are as follows:

  ○ Create a static route on the router that will route any traffic from the VPN range (the VPN address pool) to the Untangle NGFW server.

  ○ Create a Port Forward rule for the OpenVPN port 1194 (UDP) on the router to Untangle NGFW.

  ○ Verify that your setting is correct by going to **Config | Administration | Public Address** as it is used by Untangle to configure OpenVPN clients, and ensure that the configured address is resolvable from outside the company.

- If the OpenVPN client is connected, but you can't access anything, perform the following steps:

  ○ Verify that the hosts you are trying to reach are exported in **Exported Networks**

  ○ Try to ping Untangle NGFW LAN IP address (if exported)

  ○ Try to bring up the Untangle NGFW GUI by entering the IP address in a browser

- If the preceding tasks work, your tunnel is up and operational. If you can't reach any clients inside the network, check for the following conditions:

  ○ The client machine's firewall is not preventing the connection from the OpenVPN client.

  ○ The client machine uses Untangle as a gateway or has a static route to send the VPN address pool to Untangle NGFW.

  ○ In addition, some port forwarding rules on Untangle NGFW are needed for OpenVPN to function properly. The required ports are 53, 445, 389, 88, 135, and 1025.

- If the site-to-site tunnel is set up correctly, but the two sites can't talk to each other, the reason may be as follows:

  ○ If your sites have IPs from the same subnet (this probably happens when you use a service from the same ISP for both branches), OpenVPN may fail as it consider no routing is needed from IPs in the same subnet. You should ask your ISP to change the IPs.

- To get DNS resolution to work over the site-to-site tunnel, you'll need to go to **Config | Network | Advanced | DNS Server | Local DNS Servers** and add the IP of the DNS server on the far side of the tunnel. Enter the domain in the **Domain List** column and use the FQDN when accessing resources. You'll need to do this on both sides of the tunnel for it to work from either side.

- If you are using site-to-site VPN in addition to the client-to-site VPN. However, the OpenVPN client is able to connect to the main site only:

  ○ You'll need to add **VPN Address Pool** to **Exported Hosts** and **Networks**

Lab-based training

This section will provide training for the OpenVPN site-to-site and client-to-site scenarios. In this lab, we will mainly use Untangle-01, Untangle-03, and a laptop (192.168.1.7).

The ABC bank started a project with Acme school. As a part of this project, the ABC bank team needs to periodically access files located on Acme-FS01. So, the two parties decided to opt for OpenVPN. However, Acme's network team doesn't want to leave access wide open for ABC bank members, so they set firewall rules to limit ABC bank's access to the file server only.

In addition, the IT team director wants to have VPN access from home to the Acme network, which they decided to accomplish using OpenVPN.

The following diagram shows the environment used in the site-to-site scenario:

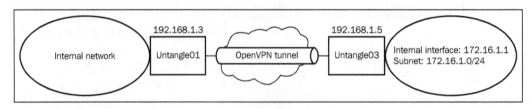

To create the site-to-site connection, we will need to do the following steps:

1. Enable OpenVPN Server on Untangle-01.

2. Create a network type client with a remote network of 172.16.1.0/24.

3. Download the client and import it under the **Client** tab in Untangle-03.

4. Restart the two servers.

5. After the restart, you have a site-to-site VPN connection. However, the Acme network is wide open to the ABC bank, so we need to create a firewall-limiting rule.

6. On Untangle-03, create a rule that will allow any traffic that comes from the OpenVPN interface, and its source is **172.16.136.10** (Untangle-01 Client IP) and is directed to **172.16.1.7** (Acme-FS01). The rule is shown in the following screenshot:

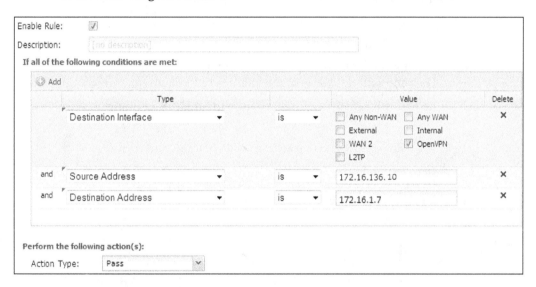

7. Also, we will need a general block rule that comes after the preceding rule in the rule evaluation order.

The environment used for the client-to-site connection is shown in the following diagram:

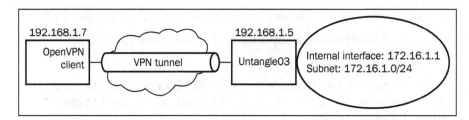

To create a client-to-site VPN connection, we need to perform the following steps:

1. Enable the OpenVPN server on Untangle-03.

2. Create an individual client type client on Untangle-03.

3. Distribute the client to the intended user (that is 192.168.1.7).

4. Install OpenVPN on your laptop.

5. Connect using the installed OpenVPN and try to ping Acme-DC01 using its name. The ping will fail because the client is not able to query the Acme DNS.

6. So, in the **Default Group** settings, change **Push DNS Domain** to **Acme.local**.

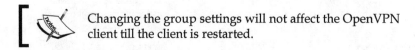 Changing the group settings will not affect the OpenVPN client till the client is restarted.

7. Now, the ping process will be a success.

IPsec VPN

The Untangle IPsec VPN is mainly used to provide site-to-site connections, which have many advantages over site-to-site solutions provided by OpenVPN including (but not limited to) better support for sharing, replication, LDAP protocols, and higher speed. Untangle IPsec VPN also provides the client-to-site connection method based on L2TP/IPsec. These features come at an additional cost as Untangle, Inc. provides the IPsec VPN as a paid module.

How the IPsec VPN works

The IPsec VPN works on the OSI layer 3 (the network layer), which allows the encryption of information from layer 3 and the above layers. Thus, any eavesdropper will not be able to get any information about the packet, including the used ports and the IP addresses.

Unlike SSL/TLS VPN, the IPsec parties have no prior knowledge of each other, and the connection initiation process will not include any server certificates. The connection between the two parties is established using the **Internet Key Exchange** (**IKE**) protocol, which has two phases:

- **IKE phase 1**: This phase authenticates the IPsec peers and establishes a secure channel that will be used in phase 2 for IPsec tunnel negotiation and building. In this phase, only the IPsec peers can talk to each other and no network-to-network or client-to-network communication is possible. IKE phase 1 includes the following negotiations:
  - **Hashing**: This determines the hash protocol that will be used to validate the data integrity.
  - **Authentication**: This method will be used for the IPsec peers to authenticate each other. A PSK or digital certificate can be used.
  - **Diffie-Hellman group**: The Diffie-Hellman key exchange method allows two parties that have no prior knowledge of each other to jointly establish a symmetric shared secret key over an insecure communications channel, which can be used to encrypt subsequent communications.
  - **Lifetime**: This determines IKE phase 1's tunnel time to live.
  - **Encryption**: This is the symmetric encryption protocol to be used.

  After completing the negotiation, the peers will run the Diffie-Hellman key exchange to generate the shared key; then, they will authenticate each other using the methods agreed in the negotiation.

- **IKE Phase 2**: This is also known as an IPsec tunnel. This phase will build the IPsec tunnel that allows network-to-network and client-to-network communication. IKE phase 2 tunnels' lifetimes are shorter than those of IKE phase 1. Thus, multiple IKE phase 2 tunnels are created in the same IKE phase 1 tunnel. IKE phase 2 negotiation settings are as follows:
  - **Lifetime**: This is the IKE phase 2 tunnel's lifetime.
  - **Hashing**: This is the Hash protocol to be used.

○ **Diffie-Hellman group**: The Diffie-Hellman group will be used to create the symmetric key for IKE phase 2 tunnels. If **perfect forward secrecy (PFS)** is used, each phase 2 key is derived independently through a separate Diffie-Hellman exchange. With PFS, if a single key is compromised, the integrity of the subsequently-generated keys is not affected.

○ **Encryption**: This is the encryption protocol to be used.

After completing the negotiation, the peers will build and use the IPsec tunnel using the methods agreed on the negotiation.

The default values used by Untangle NGFW are PSK for authentication, MD5 for hashing, 3DES for encryption, the Diffie-Hellman group 2 (1,024 bit), phase 1 lifetime of 28,800 seconds, and phase 2 lifetime of 3,600 seconds.

IKE phase 1 is done over UDP port 500. If any NAT/PAT device is located between the IPsec peers and this device can't forward the IPsec protocol (protocol number 50), we will use NAT traversal, which allows the encapsulation of IPsec packets inside UDP 4500 packets; TCP 10000 can also be used.

By default, IPsec only provides the site-to-site connection and works with IP networks. To allow the client-to-site connection and provide the ability to transport protocols other than IP, **Layer 2 Tunneling Protocol (L2TP)** over IPsec (L2TP/IPsec) can be used, which encapsulates L2TP packets between the two ends using IPsec.

Configuring Untangle's IPsec VPN

This section will cover how to create IPsec tunnels, and will describe the different options available for L2TP.

Creating IPsec tunnels

The NAT traversal can be enabled or disabled under **IPsec VPN Settings | IPsec Options**. This will be applied on all tunnels.

Tunnels can be configured under **IPsec VPN Settings | IPsec Tunnels**; there are two existing default disabled tunnels that can help you understand how to configure IPsec tunnels; you can modify them if you wish. To create a new tunnel, press the **Add** button located under the **IPsec tunnels** tab. The tunnel editor screen will appear with the following configurable settings:

• **Enable**: This determines if you wish to enable or disable this tunnel.

- **Description**: Include a description that can help you identify the tunnel in future. For example, if you have multiple branch sites and you want to create a tunnel for each site, it's recommended to set the description for each tunnel with the name of the branch site.

- **Connection Type**: IPsec has two connection types (**Tunnel** and **Transport**):
  - ○ **Tunnel**: This is used with site-to-site connections. It can support NAT traversal and it encrypts the payload and the IP header.
  - ○ **Transport**: This is used with client-to-site connections. It can't support NAT traversal; it only encrypts the payload and doesn't encrypt the IP header. L2TP can be used with this connection type. In addition, this type is usually used for encrypted traffic that will end at the tunnel endpoint (for example, if you're establishing an SSH connection to the endpoint server) as the endpoint server will need to read the IP header. In short, if the encrypted traffic is not to the endpoint of the tunnel, the **Tunnel** mode will be used.

- **Auto Mode**: This specifies the IPsec tunnels' starting behavior. There are two modes available:
  - ○ **Start Mode**: The tunnel is automatically loaded, inserts routes, and initiates a connection. This mode always provides a connected tunnel.
  - ○ **Add Mode**: The tunnel load is in standby mode, waiting to respond to an incoming connection request. This mode provides an on-demand tunnel.

- **Interface**: This allows you to choose the interface that you want to associate with the IPsec tunnel. When you select an interface, the IP of this interface will automatically be populated to the **External IP** field. If you wish to not use the interface's current IP, selecting **Custom** allows you to set the custom IP on the **External IP** field.

- **External IP**: This field determines the external IP that will be associated with the IPsec tunnel.

- **Remote Host**: This determines the IP or the hostname of the other endpoint of the tunnel.

- **Local Network**: This determines the networks (behind this endpoint) that will be reachable from the other endpoint. The current internal network is selected by default.

- **Local IP**: This determines the IP of the internal interface of Untangle NGFW that will be available for the remote endpoint.

- **Remote Network**: This determines the internal network located behind the remote endpoint.

- **Shared Secret**: Untangle NGFW uses a PSK to authenticate the two endpoints; the two endpoints must have the same key to be able to create the tunnel. The longer and more complex the key, the higher level of security you get.

- **Perfect Forward Secrecy (PFS)**: This determines if you want to use PFS or not. PFS is enabled by default and leaving it this way is suggested to provide higher security. Don't disable PFS unless you have a purpose for this.

- **Dead Peer Detection (DPD) Interval**: This determines the interval during which Untangle NGFW tries to detect if the other endpoint is still available.

- **DPD Timeout**: This determines the time with no response from the other endpoint before trying to re-initiate the tunnel.

- **Authentication and SA/Key Exchange**: IPsec automatically does the IKE negotiation with the remote peer. However, some peers require specific settings (usually when connecting Untangle to the third-party appliance); you can configure Untangle to use these specific settings on the tunnel initiation by manually choosing the desired settings for both IKE phase 1 and IKE phase 2. The available settings are encryption, hashing, the Diffie-Hellman key group, and lifetime.

Untangle can establish IPsec tunnels with third-party firewalls and appliances. Each firewall will have its required specific negotiation settings, a list of the settings required to successfully establish IPsec tunnels between Untangle and pfSense, M0n0wall, Cisco, Endian, Watchguard, eSoft InstaGate, and SonicWall are located at `http://wiki.untangle.com/index.php/IPsec_VPN`.

 If your device is not included in the preceding list of devices, Untangle may still be able to connect to your device. However, this has not been tested before.

Configuring L2TP options

L2TP options found under IPsec VPN settings are used to configure the Untangle NGFW server to support L2TP VPN client connections. The different settings are as follows:

- **Enable L2TP Server**: This enables Untangle to serve the L2TP VPN clients.

- **Listen addresses**: The external interface on which the server will listen for the incoming L2TP connections.

- **Address pool**: This configures the pool of addresses that will be assigned to the L2TP clients. The server will take the first IP in the pool and the clients will be assigned IPs dynamically when they connect to the Untangle server.

- The default pool is `192.18.0.0/16`, which is a private network that is generally reserved for internal network testing. It was chosen as the default because it is used less frequently than other RFC-1918 address blocks, and thus, it is less likely to conflict with existing address assignments on your network. You should not change this default address pool unless you have to, and don't set the pool to the same address block used by your internal network.

- **Custom DNS**: Here, you can configure the DNS servers to be used by the client. If kept blank, the client will send the DNS queries to Untangle NGFW.

- **IPsec Secret**: This is the secret used to establish the IPsec tunnel that will encapsulate the L2TP packets.

- **Configure Local Directory**: In addition to the secret key, the client must authenticate using a valid username and password stored in the local directory; clicking on the **Configure Local Directory** button will open **Config | Local Directory** from where you can manage the local users.

Reviewing the connection events

All enabled IPsec tunnels will be shown under **Enabled IPsec Tunnels** located under the **Status** tab. The tunnel details in addition to its status (active or not) are displayed as shown in the following screenshot:

Enabled IPsec Tunnels					
Local IP	Remote Host	Local Network	Remote Network	Description	Status
192.168.1.5	192.168.1.6	172.16.1.0/24	172.16.2.0/24	to UT04	Active

The IPsec **State** tab shows the status of the established connections. Each tunnel will have two entries, one for the local side and one for the remote side, as shown in the following screenshot:

```
src 192.168.1.6 dst 192.168.1.5
    proto esp spi 0x1b9b9efa reqid 16385 mode tunnel
    replay-window 32 flag af-unspec
    auth hmac(sha1) 0xda6e530ffebbed9c247573ed5d74f293c740764f
    enc cbc(aes) 0xd0e1d63034fca059a721e7b5a9f5e7da
src 192.168.1.5 dst 192.168.1.6
    proto esp spi 0xe1fc9d1a reqid 16385 mode tunnel
    replay-window 32 flag af-unspec
    auth hmac(sha1) 0xd68cbbd6f9b5da48c6cf00577f7909a46e1657c2
    enc cbc(aes) 0x8f67a0941261 3b3174a75e6123004905
```

The IPsec **Policy** tab shows the routing table associated with each IPsec VPN, as shown in the following screenshot:

```
src 172.16.1.0/24 dst 172.16.2.0/24
      dir out priority 2344 ptype main
      tmpl src 192.168.1.5 dst 192.168.1.6
            proto esp reqid 16385 mode tunnel
src 172.16.2.0/24 dst 172.16.1.0/24
      dir fwd priority 2344 ptype main
      tmpl src 192.168.1.6 dst 192.168.1.5
            proto esp reqid 16385 mode tunnel
src 172.16.2.0/24 dst 172.16.1.0/24
      dir in priority 2344 ptype main
      tmpl src 192.168.1.6 dst 192.168.1.5
            proto esp reqid 16385 mode tunnel
```

The IPsec **Log** tab provides low-level status messages that are generated by the underlying IPsec protocol components. This information can be very helpful when attempting to diagnose connection problems or other IPsec issues.

An active L2TP session can be found under the **Status** tab:

Active L2TP Sessions					
IP Address	Username	Interface	Connect Time ▲	Elapsed Time	Disconnect
198.18.0.2	test	ppp0	2014-09-06 11:06:33 pm	00:02:50	✖

The L2TP event log shows detailed connection events as follows:

Address	Usern...	Login Time	Logout Time	Elapsed	Interface	RX Bytes	TX Bytes
198.18.0.2	test	2014-09-06 11:10:5...	2014-09-06 11:12:0...	00:01:09	ppp0	3093	24784
198.18.0.2	test	2014-09-06 11:06:3...	2014-09-06 11:09:5...	00:03:18	ppp0	48201	25608

Lab-based training

The Acme network administrator decided to use Untangle IPsec to provide their branch office with a VPN connection to the HQ as it provides better performance than the OpenVPN module. In addition, they decided to use it with devices that support L2TP for remote access cases while sticking with OpenVPN for the other device. In this section, we will learn how to create site-to-site VPN and remote access VPN using the Untangle IPsec module.

In this lab, we will use Untangle-03, Untangle-04, laptop (192.168.1.7), and any internal clients you wish in the Acme sites.

The site-to-site lab network topology is shown in the following diagram:

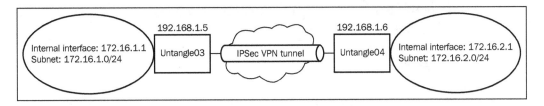

In Untangle-03, we will need to create the IPsec tunnel. We will keep the defaults and only change the following settings:

- **Interface**: External
- **Remote Host**: 192.168.1.6
- **Remote Network**: 172.16.2.0/24
- **Shared Secret**: asd123@

In Untangle-04, we will need to do the same, but this time, with the following settings:

- **Interface**: External
- **Remote Host**: 192.168.1.5
- **Remote Network**: 172.16.1.0/24
- **Shared Secret**: asd123@

Now, the IPsec tunnel is established and running. You can test connectivity by trying to ping a device in the 172.16.2.0/24 network from the 172.16.1.0/24 network or vice versa.

The client-to-site connection lab can be done with a network diagram as the one shown previously in the OpenVPN client-to-site lab.

The server-side configuration will be done as follows:

- **Enable L2TP server**: This will be checked
- **Address pool**: This will be kept as the default settings
- **IPsec Secret**: P@$$w0rd
- **Local Directory**: We have a local user (test) whose password is 123
- **Server Listen addresses**: This will be kept as the default settings, which include the server's external IP (192.168.1.5)

The client-side configuration on Windows can be done as follows:

1. From **Control Panel | All Control Panel Items | Network and Sharing Center**, choose **Set up a new connection or network**:

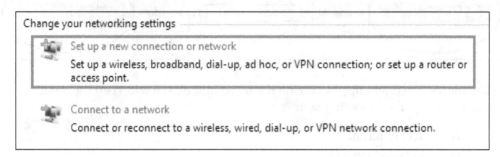

2. A new wizard is displayed, from which you need to select **Connect to a workspace**:

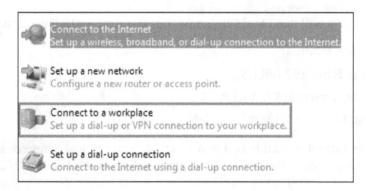

3. In the next step, select **Use my Internet connection (VPN)**:

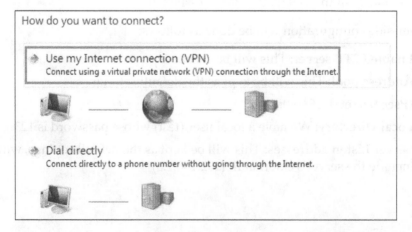

4. Now, select **I'll set up an Internet connection later**:

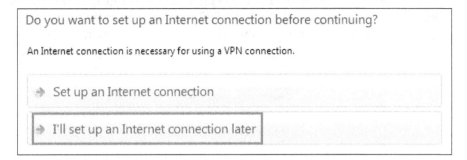

5. Enter the server's IP address and description for the connection:

6. Next, you will need to provide the username and the password of the user created on the Untangle NGFW local directory:

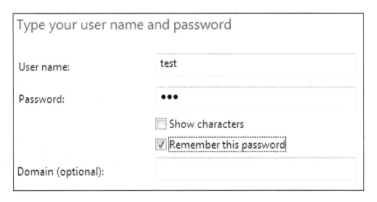

7. From **Control Panel | Network and Internet | Network Connections**, right-click on the newly-created VPN connection and select **Properties**. Under **Security**, change **Type of VPN** to **L2TP/IPsec**, and press the **Advanced Settings** button to add the pre-shared key used for the connection:

8. Now, you can connect to Untangle's local network using the created VPN connection:

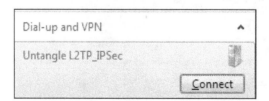

9. Now, try to open the Untangle-03 administration GUI using its internal IP (172.16.1.1). The GUI will open, which means that the client is able to access Acme's local resources.

Summary

In this chapter, we covered the VPN services provided by Untangle NGFW. We went deeply into understanding how each solution works. This chapter also provided a guide on how to configure and deploy the services. Untangle provides a free solution that is based on the well-known open source OpenVPN, which provides an SSL-based VPN. IPsec is also provided from Untangle as a paid service. Both applications can be used for client-to-site and site-to-site connections. The site-to-site service provided by IPsec is much better than the one provided by OpenVPN. The client-to-site connection provided by IPsec is based on L2TP/IPsec.

In the next chapter, we'll discuss the Untangle NGFW Reports and how the administrator can manage them. We'll also see how we can rebrand Untangle NGFW to our company brands using the Branding Manager. The Live Support service allows the administrator to get Untangle support when they face an issue with their server. The Configuration Backup service automatically creates daily backups of the server configurations and stores them in the data center of Untangle, Inc.

13

Untangle Administrative Services

This chapter will cover the applications that can be used to help administrators with their daily tasks. Untangle Reports is a necessary tool for every administrator, as it helps them to get an overview of what's going on in the network, and administrators can provide reports to non-IT staff such as the CEO. The Branding Manager helps organizations that prefer to customize their Untangle NGFW pages, which will interact with the end users to include the company-specific details and the support persons' contacts. Live Support allows the Untangle administrators to get help from Untangle support when they face an issue with their server. Configuration Backup provides an automated backup tool that stores Untangle NGFW configuration into the Cloud, which is a good place for off-site backups.

In this chapter, we'll cover the following topics:

- Untangle's Reports
- Untangle's Branding Manager
- Untangle's Live Support
- Untangle's configuration backup

Untangle's Reports

Untangle's Reports is used to help administrators monitor users' behavior and understand network usage. Also, it's a great tool to help administrators investigate security incidents. Untangle provides a summary, detailed, and reports per user.

Untangle's Reports application collects the application's event logs, which contain the real-time detailed data, and provides a summary report about the event logs' activity displayed in graphs and charts. Also, the detailed event logs can be accessed from Untangle's Reports application (if they are in the retention period range).

Untangle's Reports is available in PDF and HTML formats and can be automatically e-mailed to administrators.

Configuring the settings of Untangle's Reports

Untangle NGFW provides daily, weekly, and monthly reports. The reports generation schedule can be configured under **Reports Settings | Generation**.

- **Daily Reports**: These are the reports generated for the previous day. For example, the daily report generated on Monday will cover Sunday's events.

- **Weekly Reports**: These (including 7 days' data) will be created for the checked days of the week. For example, if Sunday and Wednesday are checked, you'll get two weekly reports, one from Sunday to Sunday and the other from Wednesday to the next Wednesday.

- **Monthly Reports**: If checked, a report that covers the previous month will be created on the first of each month.

- **Generation Time**: When Untangle NGFW generates reports, the generation process takes up resources on the Untangle server, which may slow down your network until it is finished. So, it's better to generate reports at non-working hours; 2 a.m. is the default value.

- **Data Retention**: This controls the duration for which the reports application will keep the event logs data that has been used on the generated reports on the server hard disk. Increasing the number will increase the amount of disk required to save the additional data. The default value of Untangle is **7**, which can provide full details for weekly reports. For monthly reports, you'll need to change the value to **30**.

 When you review reports that are older than the set value, you will be able to review the report summary but not the events' details as they would have been removed.

You can give users access to the generated reports by adding those users under **Reports Settings | Email**. The **Email Reports** option will send a summary PDF to the users, while **Online Reports** will give them access to the online reports.

In addition to the administrators, reports can be sent to normal users. You need to configure the e-mail settings by going to **Config** | **Email** to be able to send Untangle NGFW reports via e-mails.

Pressing the **Add** button will open a window where you can create the report users. The different configurations available on this page are as follows:

- **Email Address (username)**: This is the e-mail address of the user who needs access to the reports. This e-mail address is used to send reports to the user and also to authenticate the user when online access is selected.

- **Email Summaries**: This determines whether to send a summary PDF report to this user or not.

- **Online Access**: This determines whether to give this user access to the online reports or not.

- **Password**: This is the password to be used by the user to access the reports. A password is required if online access is selected.

These configurations are illustrated in the following screenshot:

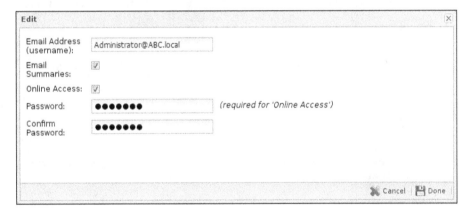

The events are stored in CSV files, which are used by online reports to generate tables and graphs in the reports. Sending the CSV files to administrators allows them to keep track of all events and return the detailed events any time they wish. Untangle can send CSV files to the report users by checking the **Attach Detailed Report Logs to Email (CSV Zip File)** checkbox. The CSV files will be sent in the .zip format.

> If you want to set a small data retention period for events located on the Untangle hard disk in order to ensure that your hardware performance is not degraded, and you also wish to keep the detailed logs for a longer period, you can use the attachment of CSV files feature to store the detailed events on an external storage device.

The **Attachment size limit** field sets the maximum size of the CSV ZIP file that can be attached to an e-mail. All e-mail servers have a maximum attachment size that they can accept. If the attached files are larger than this maximum size, the e-mail server will not accept the message. Therefore, you should limit the CSV ZIP file size to the maximum size that your e-mail server can accept. If the CSV ZIP file is larger than the **Attachment size limit** setting, the zipped file will not be attached and a warning will be appended to the e-mail:

Email Attachment Settings

☑ Attach Detailed Report Logs to Email (CSV Zip File)

Attachment size limit (MB): `10`

An example of Untangle Daily Report Summary is shown in the following screenshot:

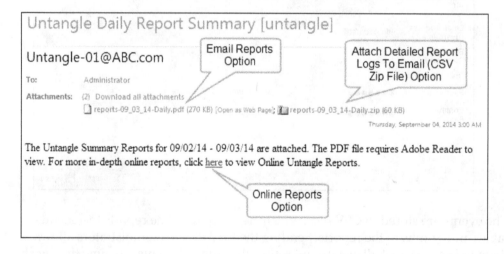

From the provided link, you can review the summary reports and the events details. The attached PDF only contains the summary reports, and the zipped file only contains the event logs. The following screenshot shows a summary report for the server-free memory from the PDF file:

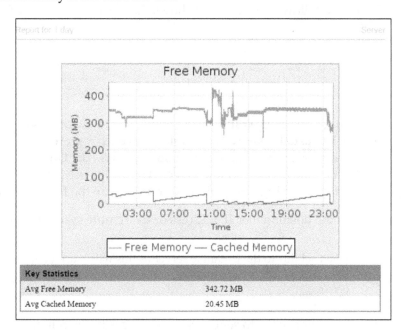

The following screenshot shows the detailed event logs from the Reports web page:

Time	User	Url	Blocked	Flagged	Category
2014-09-12 8:59:59 am	None	http://hotmail.com/	None	None	Web-based Email
2014-09-12 8:59:59 am	None	http://www.google.com/	None	None	Search Engines
2014-09-12 8:59:59 am	None	http://www.cnn.com/	None	None	News
2014-09-12 8:59:59 am	None	http://cnn.com/	None	None	News
2014-09-12 8:59:58 am	None	http://playboy.com/	true	true	Pornography

The ZIP file contains the event logs for the different applications. Each application's events are collected under one directory. For example, Untangle's Paid Virus Blocker has three CSV files (`ftp-events.csv`, `mail-events.csv`, and `web-events.csv`). The three CSV files are stored under the `untangle-node-commtouchav` folder located inside the ZIP file. The following screenshot shows the `mail-events.csv` file opened in Microsoft Excel:

A	B	C	D	E	F	G	H
time_stamp	hostname	username	commtouchav_name	subject	addr	c_client_addr	c_client_port
58:51.9	10.0.0.10		W32/Malware!9219	Test Virus Blocking (ABC>Acme)	administrator@acme.net	10.0.0.10	12443
46:04.0	192.168.1.5		W32/A-d7709921!Eldorado	Test Virus Blocking (Acme>ABC) Virus Blocker OFF	administrator@ABC.com	192.168.1.5	45248

Syslog is a way for network devices and *nix servers to send event messages to a logging server, which is usually known as a syslog server. For more information, visit `www.networkmanagementsoftware.com/what-is-syslog`. Untangle can send the events in real time to the remote syslog server. The syslog settings are located under **Reports Settings | Syslog**. You will need to configure the following options:

- **Host**: This is the hostname or IP address of the remote syslog receiver

> Don't set this to the Untangle server as this will cause your hard disk to fill up very quickly, and a server crash may occur.

- **Port**: This is the port used to send syslog messages to the remote syslog receiver. UDP 514 is the default syslog port.
- **Protocol**: This is the protocol used to send the syslog messages. UDP is the default protocol.

> Kiwi, which is available at `http://www.kiwisyslog.com`, is a common syslog receiver for Windows administrators, while RSYSLOG, available at `http://www.rsyslog.com`, is a common choice for the Linux administrators.

The following screenshot shows the syslog configurations on Untangle-03, which send the event logs to the syslog server located on ABC-EX01:

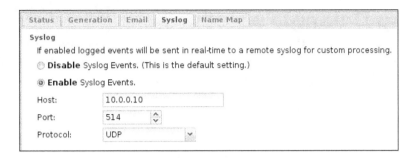

The following screenshot shows the received syslog on 3CDaemon installed on ABC-EX01:

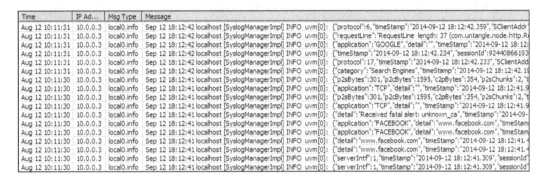

By default, Untangle will show the reports with the client device's IP details. The device names can be used by Untangle in the reports if they are available for Untangle (for example, Untangle can identify the device name through its internal DHCP, DNS, or through the Directory Connector, and so on). However, you can manually map the IP address to hostnames under the Name Map tab.

Adding a name map will not change the past reports; it will only affect the new events occurred after creating the name map.

To add a name map, press the **Add** button located under the **Name Map** tab. You will need to provide the client machine's IP and the name to be given to it.

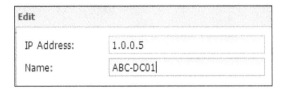

Viewing Untangle's Reports

Administrators can access the reports anytime via the **View Reports** button located under the **Status** tab. The reports page can also be accessed from outside the organization by using `https://<IP address of Untangle external interface>/reports` and from inside the company using `http://<IP address of Untangle internal interface>/reports`.

In addition to viewing the previously created reports, you can generate up to the moment partial report by using the **Generate Today's Reports** button located under the **Status** tab.

The Reports interface is easy to go through, and all you have to do is click on some hyperlinks; the Reports main page will open the last created report and show a summary of all events.

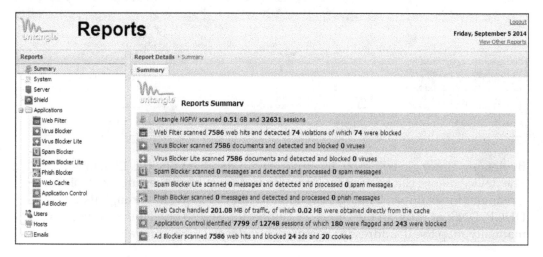

A list of older reports can be accessed via the **View Other Reports** link. On clicking this link, **View Report** will display a specific report. Reports older than the retention period can be opened for viewing. However, only the summary report is available; any detailed events will not be available.

Generated	Date Range	View	Range Size (days)	Per Host/User/Email Reports
09/12/14	Thursday, September 11 2014	View Report	1	Available
09/11/14	Wednesday, September 10 2014	View Report	1	Available
09/10/14	Tuesday, September 9 2014	View Report	1	Available
09/09/14	Monday, September 8 2014	View Report	1	Available
09/08/14	Sunday, September 7 2014	View Report	1	Available
09/07/14	Sunday, August 31 2014 - Saturday, September 6 2014	View Report	7	Unavailable
09/07/14	Saturday, September 6 2014	View Report	1	Available
09/06/14	Friday, September 5 2014	View Report	1	Unavailable
09/05/14	Thursday, September 4 2014	View Report	1	Unavailable

Available Reports

Report Details

Clicking on any node from the side menu will open this node-specific report. Each node will have a summary report displayed in charts and graphs, and also it will contain all detailed event logs. This report can be printed by clicking on the **Print** hyperlink. The **Export Data** button will output a CSV file with the application-specific events, as shown in the following screenshot:

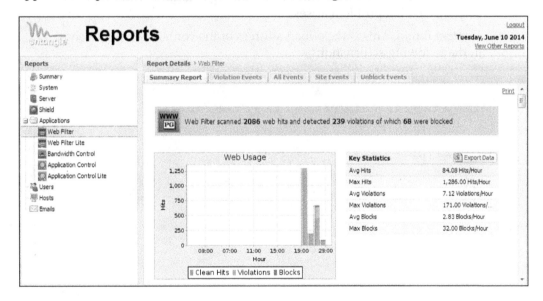

Branding Manager

Branding Manager allows you to rebrand user-facing components (including block pages, quarantine digest e-mails, and so on) by replacing all Untangle branding in all user-facing interactions with your company's logo, name, URL, and contact e-mail, which help you to provide the end users with a consistent look and feel between all your services, and the right contact details to call you when a problem arises.

Using Branding Manager, you can customize the following options:

- **Logo**: Replace the Untangle logo with that of your company. The recommended resolution for logos is 150 x 100; the maximum resolution is 166 x 100. All image types are supported, but using animation is not recommended as it may affect the PDF reports.

- **Company Name**: Replace the Untangle company name with your company name; all text fields have a limit of 256 characters.

- **Company URL**: Replace Untangle URL with your company URL.

- **Contact Name**: Enter the name of the Untangle administrator who should be contacted if a problem arises.

- **Contact Email**: This is the e-mail address of the contact person, as shown in the following screenshot:

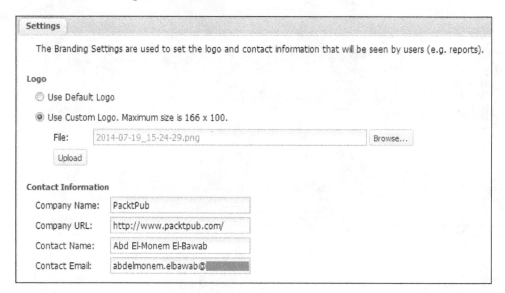

The modified settings will affect the following locations:

- Main GUI (virtual rack)
- Reports
- User-facing block pages (Web Filter, Spyware Blocker, and so on)
- Admin login page

An example of a customized block page is shown in the following screenshot:

The following screenshot shows a customized admin login page:

Live Support

Got a problem with your Untangle NGFW server and want expert help? Untangle provides commercial live expert technical support that will help you solve your Untangle NGFW issues. Untangle support will mainly help you with Untangle issues, but if the problem was somewhere else on your network, they can let you know what they think it is as well as make suggestions on how to fix it. However, they cannot help you do things such as reconfigure non-Untangle devices.

 If you are a nonpaid user and have a problem with your Untangle server, you can still open a support ticket to Untangle support, but they will serve you when there are no paid users on the queue.

In addition, when you purchase a paid application, you get premium support for this app.

When you have a problem, you can open a support ticket either through the Live Support application, by e-mail, by phone, or manually from the support page.

From the Live Support application, press the **Get Support!** button, which will open a new web page where you can create a new support ticket.

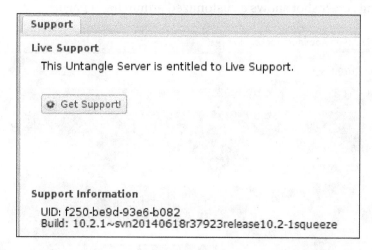

In the support ticket, you will need to enter your e-mail address, subject, and a description of the problem. You'll also need to add the UID (for the Untangle team to validate your license and identify your server) and provide any attachments that can help the support team to understand the problem:

This can also be done manually by browsing to `https://support.untangle.com` and selecting **Submit a request**.

 The support web page includes some solved tickets that you can review before opening a new ticket.

You can reach the Untangle support via e-mail by mailing your problem (with the necessary details and your UID) to `support@untangle.com`, which will automatically create a support ticket.

Also, you can contact Untangle support by phone. Untangle support phone numbers are as follows:

- **U.S. toll free**: +1.866.233.2296
- **International**: +1.408.598.4299
- **Australia**: +61.2.9191.7458
- **Brazil**: +55.11.3711.9278
- **Canada**: +1.866.920.0791
- **Mexico**: +52.33.4624.2961
- **New Zealand**: +64.9.973.5893
- **South Africa**: +27.10.500.1963
- **U.K.**: +44.870.490.0619
- **Skype users**: `untangle.skype`

Untangle support is based in Sunnyvale, CA (USA), so support is available from Monday to Friday, 6 a.m. to 5 p.m., US Pacific time.

 In addition to the Untangle support, you can get help anytime through the Untangle forum, which is an active community full of members, including some of Untangle employees, who really want to help you.

Untangle can only support installation done with the standard installation path. Using expert installation, installing any additional software to the Untangle NGFW server or manually modifying your server using the command line will make your server ineligible for the support.

Configuration backup

In addition to the manual backup feature available under **Config | System | Backup**, Untangle provides an automated solution that backs up your Untangle NGFW server's configuration (with the exception of report data) every night and stores the backup on the Untangle data center. The Untangle Configuration backup is included in the Live Support license.

 Remember that apart from this automated solution, you have an option to manually back up all your server configurations under the **Config | System | Backup** tab. Also, you have the option to back up individual applications' settings using the **Import/Export** buttons inside each application.

You can retrieve backups by accessing your Untangle account and selecting the **Servers** tab and then pressing **View Backups**. The backups will be listed by the date and time, as shown in the following screenshot:

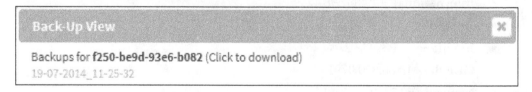

Clicking on the desired backup will download it. After downloading it, you can restore it by going to **Config | System | Restore**.

 Untangle officially supports restoring backups within the same version (for example, using the V10.2 backup with another V10.2 server). Restoring an old version to a new version within the same major version is also fine (for example, restoring from V10.1 to V10.2). Restoring from different major versions is not supported (for example, from V9 to V10).

The **Status** tab of the Configuration Backup application will show the date and time of the last successful backup, as shown in the following screenshot:

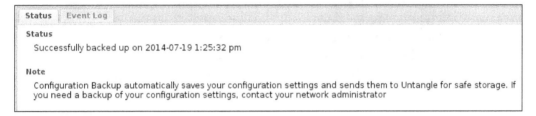

The **Event Log** tab shows the time when a backup event occurred and whether it was successful or not, as shown in the following screenshot:

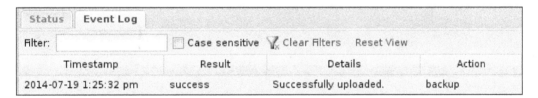

Summary

In this chapter, we covered four Untangle applications. Reports collects applications' event logs and gives the administrator an easy-to-read summary report that is presented in charts and graphs, while the event logs are suitable for detailed information about a specific user/machine. Branding Manager allows the rebranding of pages that end users will interact with, such as the block page, which helps to give your users a consistent look and feel among your services and provides them with your contact details. Live Support is a paid service that lets Untangle help you when you have a problem with your server. Configuration Backup is an application that comes with the Live Support that will back up your configuration daily to the Untangle data center.

In the next chapter, we will cover some regulatory compliance that affects the IT field. Also, we will see the advantages of Untangle NGFW over its rivals. Eventually, we will introduce some case studies on how Untangle helped SMBs, not-for-profit, healthcare, education, and government organizations to achieve network security with minimal cost and minimal administration efforts.

14
Untangle in the Real World

A regulatory compliance is a critical thing to know for IT professionals. The first section in this chapter will discuss the common regulatory compliances related to the IT field. Untangle had lead the **small and medium business (SMB)** market with its secure, easy-to-use, low-cost solutions. The second section will cover the advantages of Untangle NGFW over its rivals. Later, the chapter will cover the usage of Untangle in the SMB, education, healthcare, government, and nonprofit fields, including why they chose it and how they implemented it.

We will cover the following topics in this chapter:

- Understanding the IT regulatory compliance
- Untangle in real life

Understanding the IT regulatory compliance

Since the Enron scandal in 2001, governments all over the world have taken up the job of protecting consumers and companies against the poor management of sensitive information by issuing laws and regulations that require organizations to take the necessary steps to ensure the protection of sensitive information.

Regulatory compliance is an organization's adherence to laws, regulations, guidelines, and specifications relevant to its business. Violations of regulatory compliance regulations often result in legal punishment, including federal fines.

Regulatory compliance requires organizations to take proactive measures to establish network security processes to detect network anomalies, attacks, and other vulnerabilities that can put organizations' sensitive data in the risk of being compromised. Also, organizations are required to provide network compliance audit reports to auditors when demanded.

The following are some of the laws and regulations that have immediate impact on the IT field. This includes the well-known US laws and some national and international laws. Additional laws may affect you depending on your country and your business field:

- The **Sarbanes-Oxley (SOX)** Act of 2002 requires that the annual reports of public companies include an end-of-fiscal-year assessment of the effectiveness of internal control over financial reporting. This report includes the entire IT infrastructure (servers, network security, and IT practices and operations).

- Similar to the SOX in US, there is also Japan's Financial Instrument and Exchange Law (commonly referred to as J-SOX) and Canada's Keeping the Promise for a Strong Economy Act (Budget Measures), 2002 (commonly known as C-SOX or Bill 198).

- The Financial Services Modernization Act of 1999 (better known as the **Gramm-Leach-Bliley Act (GLBA)**) protects the privacy and security of individually identifiable financial information collected, held, and processed by financial institutions. The individuals' information can become exposed during online banking.

- The **Federal Information Security Management Act (FISMA)** of 2002 requires that all government agencies, government contractors, and organizations that deal and exchange data with government systems have to monitor, retain, and maintain audit records of all security events.

- **Information Security Management System (ISMS)** Compliance (ISO 27001) is an international standard for securing information assets from threats. The standard provides precise requirements for a holistic information security management. The standard has great worldwide acceptance by organizations both large and small, especially in the United Kingdom, Japan, India, and United States.

- The **Health Insurance Portability and Accountability Act (HIPAA)** was implemented to protect the confidentiality and integrity of electronic personal health information (ePHI), including protecting against unauthorized use or disclosure of information. Although the regulation focuses on the healthcare industry, other companies can be impacted if they engage in certain activities such as the management of employee group health plans, or if they provide services to companies that are directly impacted by the regulation.

- The **Payment Card Industry Data Security Standard (PCI-DSS)** is intended to protect cardholder data, wherever it resides, ensuring that members, merchants, and service providers maintain the highest information security standard.
- The **Children's Internet Protection Act (CIPA)** addresses concerns about access to offensive content over the Internet on school and library computers. Schools and libraries subject to CIPA need to certify that they have an Internet safety policy and technology-protection measures in place.

When it comes to Untangle NGFW and its role to achieve the regulatory compliance inside organizations, Untangle NGFW can help to achieve the required compliance through its rich features that could protect the network and provide detailed reports.

However, Untangle NGFW alone can't achieve the required compliance; additional policies and procedures and even computing aspects need to be employed to achieve the required compliance. Examples of bad procedures and controls include using noncomplex passwords (especially dictionary words) and allowing remote laptops to have VPN sessions to your facility that don't force human authentication, which would be a great risk if the laptop is stolen.

Untangle in real life

Untangle's integrated suite of security software and appliances that offer enterprise-grade capabilities and consumer-oriented simplicity are trusted by over 400,000 customers, and protect nearly 5 million clients.

Untangle mainly targets the SMB as more than 99 percent of Untangle customers have fewer than 100 employees. This includes accounting firms, professional services firms, retail franchises, and small government agencies/offices. Untangle is also popular for schools, especially private middle and high schools.

In 2014, Untangle started to extend its market to just-below-enterprise businesses and large campuses by releasing the IC Control and providing an HA option for Untangle NGFW.

This section will explore the advantages that Untangle NGFW offers over its rivals and how Untangle was able to lead the SMB market. After that, this section will introduce case studies for some companies and how Untangle NGFW helped them to reduce the administration headache and time, and increase the network's overall security.

Untangle's advantages

As most of the Untangle customers are SMBs, this section will discuss Untangle's advantages with SMBs in mind. The advantages could be extended to other markets and fields.

SMBs need affordable secure networking, which is largely out of reach of proprietary products, and open source projects were just too complex to implement and manage. Untangle provided a comprehensive network management solution that leverages the best open source network applications, which are designed for ease-of-use, and features just for small businesses. In short, Untangle makes it easy for small businesses to acquire, deploy, and install a network security solution.

SMBs will spend money, but only for something they really need. Untangle was able to understand the SMB market needs and achieve them to lead this market. The common advantages are as follows:

- **Strong platform**: Untangle brought together the best open source projects to create its comprehensive network management solution, which provides a cheaper and better alternative for the proprietary appliances. In addition, Untangle commercial modules are based on the industry-leading applications.

- **Cheap solution**: Untangle offers many free, open source applications. Advanced features and applications based on commercial applications are charged for competitive prices.

- **Reduction in the administration headache**: Most of the SMBs don't have dedicated IT personnel; for example, a computer teacher could be responsible for administrating Untangle NGFW for their school, besides their normal duties. Untangle provides an easy-to-use, pre-tuned solution that will need minimal administration after being deployed. In addition, the reports reduce the amount of time needed by the administrator to investigate and analyze the users' usage.

- **Modular selections**: Customers are able to purchase only the modules they need/want.

- **Generic hardware**: In addition to the appliances provided by Untangle, Untangle NGFW can be installed on any generic Intel/AMD PC.

- **Special pricing**: Untangle offers 60 percent discount for the software's complete package, and 20 percent for appliances with the complete package. The discount is available for schools and educational institutions, nonprofit organizations, and government entities.

- **Great support**: Most of the customers' inquiries are answered within hours, irrespective of whether it is in the forum or to the support team.

Untangle for SMB

When used well, Untangle can be leveraged to improve network security and performance while reducing administration efforts, which are the main needs for the SMBs. A few examples of how SMBs have been able to take advantage of Untangle are explored in this section.

South Mountain Creamery is a delivery services company that has seven computers for employees and free Wi-Fi for in-store customers who bring in their smartphones and computers. In 2012, Donald Koch joined the company as an IT manager. He started to build a fully qualified domain environment instead of the existing sneaker-net environment. Also, he wanted to secure the environment from external threats, so he replaced the existing Netgear appliance with Untangle NGFW. After running Untangle for a few years, Donald was approached by his CDW account representative to have a vendor-sponsored audit. The company went through the security services threat check from Symantec. The result was that the network had no botnets, malware, viruses, spyware, or even access to known unsafe sites. One of the Symantec engineers mentioned to Donald that in all the time he has been performing these tests, he has never seen zero results returned on the scan. With the strong security provided by Untangle NGFW, Donald freed up time for his other duties including managing various databases, file management, backup monitoring, Active Directory, and Exchange Online.

The Catania Hospitality Group is an award-winning collection of restaurants, hotels/resorts, and spas. The average network size is four sites with 250 employees and 200 computers for employees and guests. The group was using SonicWALL to protect their network. However, the cost to continue using it was downright offensive, as said by Robert Topolski—the only IT resource for the group. So, he decided to look for other solutions with similar functionality but at a much lower price point. Hence, he decided to use Untangle, which was implemented alongside an existing Cisco ASA. In addition to the price point, Robert found Untangle to be more familiar, and he was quickly able to use and manage the product. Using Untangle helped Robert to automate his day-to-day tasks and diagnose trouble areas on the network.

Bank of New Glarus and Sugar River Banks is an independent bank that provides financial guidance and solutions. The average network size is six area locations with about 60 users. After joining the bank, the IT veteran Jeff Armstrong quickly realized that he needed a solution that provides site-to-site VPN, bandwidth control, and web filtering in addition to protection against malware and phishing. After some research, he decided to use Untangle, which satisfied his needs simply. Jeff purchased two u10 appliances, which run flawlessly. The investment paid off for the bank by reducing administration headaches for Jeff and his team.

Portlandia IT, LLC, is a comprehensive **managed services provider** (**MSP**) with customers throughout Portland, Oregon. Portlandia IT used to provide Cisco solutions for their customers who often require spam blocking and web content filtering as top priorities. Portlandia IT decided to head to Untangle because of the level of power it introduced, great flexibility, and great saving over competitive devices. Providing Untangle solutions helped Portlandia IT to serve customers with low budgets and sell to markets that would normally not even look outside the box. Some other points that interested Portlandia IT about Untangle were the reports, the ability to monitor the overall network or certain machines, Untangle's speed, and the ability to provide it as a software-only solution or as an appliance.

Shoreline Business Machines Ltd. (SBM Tech Ltd.) is a Canadian IT services company that serves in the computer networking and office automation fields. In addition, it provides network security recommendations for its customers, which include legal firms, medical clinics, schools, and nonprofit organizations. Jeff Hope, IT manager for SBM, found Untangle online and decided to try it on his own network. After familiarizing himself with the product, he felt that it would be a great fit not only for SBM Tech but also for their customers. Most of the SBM Tech customers are small businesses, and their needs include antivirus, antispam, web filtering, and reporting, all of which are provided by Untangle and at a price that is palatable to businesses with limited resources and competing priorities. Some other Untangle features mentioned by Jeff are that it is easy to set up, run, and maintain. Comparable to SonicWALL and at about 60 percent of their cost, and shave great support.

Sunridge Properties is an Arizona-based hotel development and management business with about 12 users. At Sunridge, staff spends a lot of time on the road checking on the development projects, which requires them to stay connected via e-mails. The company invested in Blackberry, but a constant barrage of spam e-mails kept employees from taking incoming e-mails seriously. Untangle was a perfect choice for them. Setup was simple for IT and it reduced spam by 95 percent. The reduced spam improved responsiveness by the team in the field and gave back time lost while reviewing useless e-mails. The added reporting of blocked threats and general network activity was a nice bonus.

Summer Hill, Ltd. is a home furnishings and fabrics company based in San Francisco with a global reach; they have about 12 users, and one unexperienced IT personal. After many security incidents, the company decided to protect its network using Untangle. Untangle protected the company network with minimum intervention from the IT. Even when they had performance issues with their network, Untangle Support helped to not only find the root of the problem but also to solve it. Summer Hill currently doesn't use the full set of Untangle applications, but they are pleased that they can deploy them at the time of need.

KK Fine Foods is a ready meals manufacturer on the border between England and Wales with 75 users. Untangle came to replace an existing Barracuda 200 spam firewall, which was doing well with identifying the spam, but it needs the administrator's intervention to review the whole quarantine, and releases any legitimate e-mails classified as spam. Untangle provided a better job by allowing each user to manage their quarantine, which saved time and efforts for the IT administrator. In addition to the spam filtering, Untangle provides additional features over the Barracuda 200 spam firewall, such as malware scanning, web filtering, Directory Connector, and Policy Manager.

BGO Architects is a medium-sized architecting company based in Texas with 80 users. BGO Architects doesn't have a dedicated IT team, so 10 to 12 hours a week spent on IT issues was keeping the architects away from their primary responsibilities. Untangle provided a simple way for them to manage the network, reducing the time and efforts required in managing the network, thanks to Untangle's reliability and the reporting feature, which reduces the time required to investigate any incidents and quickly diagnose any network problem. Also, the Web Filter increased the productivity by blocking access to inappropriate sites.

e-Clarity Ltd is a UK-based telecommunication consultancy company that offers IT support solutions, business support services, e-mail hosting, network security, connectivity, systems integration, and IT consulting for companies that range from five to 500 employees from different industries. They are a long-time partner with Untangle. Every customer has their unique network issues; using Untangle and its various modules allowed e-Clarity to tailor solutions specific to the customers' unique situations. Untangle also has many advantages, including low prices, the ability to be installed on recycled hardware, and the ability to select only modules that you want.

Using Untangle in education

The Internet is a revolutionary tool to enhance student learning, but with power comes responsibility. Schools must ensure the safety and productivity of students and staff wherever their online inquiries may take them. Untangle solutions can protect students from online threats, block their access to inappropriate content, and manage their Internet use on school networks, ensuring compliance with IT use policy. Untangle is a cost-effective solution that allows schools to comply with the CIPA compliance. We'll explore some examples of schools that installed Untangle in their networks in this section.

Tehachapi Unified School District is based in Tehachapi, California. This district contains three elementary schools, one middle school, one comprehensive high school, and an alternative education school that includes continuation high school, adult education, and a home-based independent study program. The district has about 4,600 students and 450 staff members.

As the district students were able to override the filters and network policy rules set by the IT team, the district started to search for an easy-to-implement, scalable, and robust solution to replace their bulky, expensive M86 solution. Untangle met those needs at a fraction of the cost of their previous vendor. The district has selected the Untangle u500 appliance, which enabled the IT department to provide teachers and staff with the tools they needed without exposing the network to unnecessary risks. In addition, the Policy Manager and Directory Connector greatly helped the IT department to create different policies for the teachers, staff, students, and mobile devices, and monitored their network usage.

Lake Park Audubon School District is a school district based in Lake Park, Minnesota with about 700 students. When Bob Henderson joined the school district as a Technology Director, he recommended that their failing Lightspeed system's Web Filter be replaced with Untangle. Untangle paid for itself in less than six months as its cost was 40 percent less than the previous solution. Bandwidth Control and Web Cache helped Bob to optimize the network bandwidth usage. In addition, Web Filter helped him block access to inappropriate and proxy sites and ensured that useful learning videos on YouTube can be bypassed. Also, the reports helped him save time in reviewing and managing his network. Bob also provides public Wi-Fi for use during sports and academic events throughout the school year. He relies on Untangle to provide this service without compromising on the performance or safety of his network. He said, "We've had up to 4,000 people and 36,000 sessions running through Untangle. It works wonderfully and doesn't miss a beat".

Mount St. Mary's Academy is a private Catholic school in Grass Valley, California with about 50 users. Untangle is being used to manage and monitor the network traffic. Untangle removed the complexity of security systems and provided time for the IT staff to accomplish other tasks. The IT staff reviews Untangle reports every few weeks against the school policies to see if the policies are attained.

Portland Public Schools District in Portland, MI, comprises four schools, an adult and alternative education center, and two administrative offices. Serving 2,100 students with about six sites and 730 computers, the district has a policy of constantly reassessing what technology options are available, as its systems and software come up for renewal or replacement. David Palme, Director of Technology, said: "School technology budgets are under pressure. However, we aim to not only maintain service levels, but continue to innovate and move forward. Untangle fits that bill". David selected Untangle for the completeness of its security offerings, coupled with the ease with which it can be administered. The district uses Untangle for virus and spam blocking and web filtering. In addition, the Policy Manager and Directory Connector helped David in setting different web policies for staff and students. Reports also helped him to know the network usage. David said, "Untangle gives us everything we need to keep our staff and students safe, and at a cost about half that of competitors".

Western Seminary is a graduate school comprised of three sites that serve approximately 250 users, the main campus, located in Portland, and the two satellite sites, located in Northern California. The aim of Western Seminary was to provide uniform access for the remote sites to the centralized resource on the main campus, such as the student records database. With the annual decreases in IT budgets and increases in the need for network protection, Western Seminary needed an affordable solution that would allow consistency across sites and protect users' online experience. Western Seminary uses Untangle Open VPN to provide the connection between the three sites, and Web Filter to secure users' access to the Internet. Untangle was a great replacement for their existing web filtering solution and at a much lower price.

Barksdale Air Force Base Library and Youth Center needed an inexpensive or free product (due to budget limitations) to help prevent abuse on their limited commercial Internet connection and to meet CIPA requirements. Untangle met their needs, and they installed Untangle on old hardware. Untangle is used to provide web filtering, bandwidth control, virus scanning, and captive portals.

Using Untangle in healthcare

Protecting personal health information is a critical mission for healthcare organizations, and many laws, including HIPAA, were issued to ensure the protection of this information. Untangle helps healthcare facilities to protect their networks with minimal administration overhead and without any need of dedicated IT personnel. Some examples of healthcare facilities that utilized Untangle to protect their networks are explored in this section.

Complete Family Vision Care is an optometry-specialized clinic with three locations, each with more than 10 computers. It was driven by the license exceeding for the existing SonicWALL firewall, and unsatisfied with its reliability, Dr. Havranek, the owner, decided to search for another solution to protect his network and his patients' data. Dr. Havranek was mainly looking for an easy-to-use solution that provides strong network protection, low network downtime, and blocking of malicious websites. So, he decided to deploy three u50 appliances for the three locations as Untangle met all of his requirements and at a price much lower than other competitors.

Orthopedic Associates of Grand Rapids (OGAR) based in Michigan has 24 specialist orthopedic physicians and a total staff of 250 employees spread over three offices. After multiple infections with malware, OGAR decided to add additional layers of security including Untangle. So, they implemented the Untangle server at each site to stop malware, adware, and spam. Untangle helped the IT team to focus on solving the users' issues by removing the administration headache and by reducing the infection rate inside the network. Untangle was easy to learn by the IT staff because of its simple GUI; anyone with basic firewall knowledge could use it. In addition, reporting helped the IT team trace and solve network issues.

Genesis Physicians Group serves 1,700 doctors in the North Texas area. This group acts as an intermediary between its clients and the insurance companies, offering a range of other services including the compilation of patients' outcome data, credential management, and secure e-mails. They have 27 users. Genesis Physicians Group needs to maintain a tight, secure network that ensures privacy and confidentiality. They need to ensure that the physicians' e-mail accounts are free of spam, and the sensitive patients' data is protected from corruption by viruses and exploitation by spyware. Hence, they started to use Untangle as an additional layer of security to address their security issues and to handle network monitoring. Untangle makes the IT job much more smooth as they no longer solve problems caused by malware. In addition, Untangle helps to increase the users' productivity by blocking the game sites during office time. Another great feature about Untangle for them is the Untangle Web Filter flexibility. For example, if the Web Filter blocked a site with drug references, which could be a problem in a medical environment, the site could be easily unblocked from the Web Filter.

Using Untangle in government organizations

The more the government services are offered to the public via the Internet, the greater the efficiency for both parties, and also the more risk for services being compromised. Hence, there is a need to implement a security solution that can help against security threats. In this section, we'll explore some examples that show how Untangle was able to help some government offices to protect their networks and achieve regulatory compliance.

Pickaway County Sheriff's Office has embraced a new technology to keep up to date. It has about 120 nodes. Untangle is used to provide a VPN connection between mobile police units and headquarters. Also, it's used to provide web filtering for both the internal and mobile units. They first implemented Untangle in 2007 as a free package. After that, they started to purchase the premium modules such as the Policy Manager and the Directory Connector. They installed Untangle in transparent bridge mode behind another existing firewall. Within 5 minutes, Untangle was up and running, and started to filter the web traffic.

Virgin Isles **Water & Power Authority (WAPA)** is a public-power utility whose core purpose is to enhance the economic development and the quality of life for people living in the Virgin Islands and the surrounding areas. It has about 350 users across three sites. Forced by budget pressures and the ability of some employees to bypass the web filtering using proxies, WAPA's IT department considered replacing their existing web filtering solution with another more cost-effective, robust solution. After testing Untangle, they decided to purchase the full subscription because of its performance and its ability to prevent people from using proxy sites, which also came in a good price for them.

Using Untangle in nonprofit organizations

Nonprofit organizations face the same problems as that of the for-profit organizations. They need to secure their network but with a lower budget and have less time to deal with IT infrastructure issues. Untangle considers the right solution for the nonprofit organization with it special pricing. It is easy to deploy and manage. In this section, we'll explore some of the nonprofit organizations that leveraged Untangle.

Legal Assistance Foundation (LAF) of Metropolitan Chicago is a nonprofit organization that provides free, high quality, civil legal services to people living in poverty and other vulnerable groups. LAF has about 200 users between employees, students, and volunteers. LAF staff uses their devices to connect to the network from both within and outside the offices. Eric Fong, who is an IT veteran of 11 years, was looking to replace his current expensive solution, which requires special clients' configurations on the users' smartphones and laptops with a next-generation firewall that has the ability to filter websites, block spams and viruses, report incidents, and more. After some online searching, Eric decided to go with Untangle. Untangle enabled Eric to stop spam and malicious software, set up VPNs to securely connect from anywhere, and enforce usage policies. Untangle provided LAF with the most complete next-generation firewall available, and at an unbeatable price. The difference in price was so significant that Untangle had paid for itself in just three months.

First Community Federal Credit Union (FCFCU) is a nonprofit organization that caters to the financial services needs of community residents. FCFCU has about 250 people with 200 computers. FCFCU was dissatisfied with its Websense solution as it was expensive and cumbersome. Furthermore, as a financial institution, FCFCU needs to comply with stringent information security audits throughout the year. Thus, they searched for a security gateway that provides antivirus, web filtering, and reporting features. They decided to turn to Untangle as a way to reduce costs and complexity as well as to meet the gateway requirements recommended by third-party security auditors. Untangle was implemented in three regions as a transparent bridge behind another firewall. Untangle's free package was selected in addition to the Directory Connector, Policy Manager, and Web Filter premium modules. Some Untangle features for FCFCU include the cost of one year of Websense is more than the cost of deploying Untangle in the three regions, and the ability to buy what they only need of the premium modules when they only needs. In addition, the ease of use helped to reduce the time required to learn and manage Untangle. Also, it enabled to investigate incidents more quickly. Finally, the ability of Untangle to complement other products in place is beneficial.

Summary

In this chapter, we reviewed some regulatory compliance techniques with relevance to the IT field, mentioning some of the Untangle features that make it a popular selection for the SMBs. After that, we stated some of the use cases of Untangle in the SMB, education, healthcare, government, and nonprofit fields.

With this chapter, we have completed our journey of Untangle NGFW. We hope that you enjoyed this book and it was a great benefit for you to start your own journey with Untangle NGFW in the real world.

Index

F

Filter rules 88
Firewall application
  about 13, 16, 165
  events, reviewing 167, 168
  Lab-based training 169-171
  reports 168
  settings 167
  technical details 166, 167
First Community Federal Credit Union
  (FCFCU) 332
FTP scanning
  testing 130
FTP traffic settings
  scanning 124
fully qualified domain name (FQDN) 73

G

Gateway Override 72
Get 110
GNU General Public License (GNU GPL) 8
government
  Untangle for 331
Group Policy Object (GPO)
  about 236
  used, for deploying certificate 190
groups, remote clients
  Full Tunnel 280
  Group Name 280
  Push DNS 280
  Push DNS Custom 1 280
  Push DNS Custom 2 281
  Push DNS Domain 281
  Push DNS server 280
GUI
  reviewing 52-54

H

hard disk, Untangle NGFW
  preparing 39
hardware rating summary, Untangle NGFW
  reviewing 38
hardware safe mode, boot option 42

hashing, IKE phase 1 293
hashing, IKE Phase 2 293
healthcare
  Untangle for 330
Heuristic/Signature-based content
  filtering 131
high availability, Untangle NGFW
  configuring 70, 71
  Enable VRRP 71
  VRRP Aliases 71
  VRRP ID 71
  VRRP Priority 71
history, Application Control
  about 204
  reviewing 202, 204
  Sessions 204
  Top Bandwidth Applications 204
  Top Bandwidth Protochains 204
  Top Ten Blocked Applications (by Hits) 204
  Top Ten Blocked Hosts (by Hits) 204
  Top Ten Blocked Protochains (by Hits) 204
  Top Ten Blocked Users (by Hits) 204
  Top Ten Detected Applications
    (by Hits) 204
  Top Ten Detected Hosts (by Hits) 204
  Top Ten Detected Protochains (by Hits) 204
  Top Ten Detected Users (by Hits) 204
  Top Ten Flagged Applications (by Hits) 204
  Top Ten Flagged Hosts (by Hits) 204
  Top Ten Flagged Protochains (by Hits) 204
  Top Ten Flagged Users (by Hits) 204
history, Web Filter
  reviewing 183
hostname, Untangle NGFW
  configuring 73
Hot Spot Shield 209
HTTPS
  and Untangle 186
HTTPS: Certificate Issuer 193
HTTPS: Certificate Subject 192
HTTPS: SNI Host Name 192
HTTPS Inspector
  about 15, 186
  configuring 191-193
  functionality, testing 208
  HTTPS: Certificate Issuer 193

Thank you for buying
Untangle Network Security

About Packt Publishing

Packt, pronounced 'packed', published its first book "*Mastering phpMyAdmin for Effective MySQL Management*" in April 2004 and subsequently continued to specialize in publishing highly focused books on specific technologies and solutions.

Our books and publications share the experiences of your fellow IT professionals in adapting and customizing today's systems, applications, and frameworks. Our solution based books give you the knowledge and power to customize the software and technologies you're using to get the job done. Packt books are more specific and less general than the IT books you have seen in the past. Our unique business model allows us to bring you more focused information, giving you more of what you need to know, and less of what you don't.

Packt is a modern, yet unique publishing company, which focuses on producing quality, cutting-edge books for communities of developers, administrators, and newbies alike. For more information, please visit our website: www.packtpub.com.

About Packt Open Source

In 2010, Packt launched two new brands, Packt Open Source and Packt Enterprise, in order to continue its focus on specialization. This book is part of the Packt Open Source brand, home to books published on software built around Open Source licenses, and offering information to anybody from advanced developers to budding web designers. The Open Source brand also runs Packt's Open Source Royalty Scheme, by which Packt gives a royalty to each Open Source project about whose software a book is sold.

Writing for Packt

We welcome all inquiries from people who are interested in authoring. Book proposals should be sent to author@packtpub.com. If your book idea is still at an early stage and you would like to discuss it first before writing a formal book proposal, contact us; one of our commissioning editors will get in touch with you.

We're not just looking for published authors; if you have strong technical skills but no writing experience, our experienced editors can help you develop a writing career, or simply get some additional reward for your expertise.

Gitolite Essentials

ISBN: 978-1-78328-237-1   Paperback: 120 pages

Leverage powerful branch and user access control with Git for your own private collaborative repositories

1. Learn to manage many repositories and the users accessing these repositories in the Git server.

2. Walks you through the most important ideas and concepts in Gitolite supported by examples and use cases.

3. Master the most powerful tool for fine-grained access control of Git repositories.

Kali Linux – Assuring Security by Penetration Testing

ISBN: 978-1-84951-948-9   Paperback: 454 pages

Master the art of penetration testing with Kali Linux

1. Learn penetration testing techniques with an in-depth coverage of Kali Linux distribution.

2. Explore the insights and importance of testing your corporate network systems before the hackers strike.

3. Understand the practical spectrum of security tools by their exemplary usage, configuration, and benefits.

Please check **www.PacktPub.com** for information on our titles

Packet Tracer Network Simulator

ISBN: 978-1-78217-042-6 Paperback: 134 pages

Simulate an unlimited number of devices on a network using Packet Tracer

1. Configure Cisco devices using practical examples.

2. Simulate networking with multiple branch offices.

3. Create practical networking assessments.

Implementing Samba 4

ISBN: 978-1-78216-658-0 Paperback: 284 pages

Exploit the real power of Samba 4 Server by leveraging the benefits of an Active Directory Domain Controller

1. Understand the different roles that Samba 4 Server can play on the network.

2. Implement Samba 4 as an Active Directory Domain Controller.

3. Step-by-step and practical approach to manage the Samba 4 Active Directory Domain Controller using Microsoft Windows standard tools.

Please check **www.PacktPub.com** for information on our titles